THE COMPLETE IDIOT'S GUIDE TO

Microsoft®

Word 97

SECOND EDITION

Daniel T. Bobola

alpha books
que®

A Division of Macmillan Publishing USA
201 West 103rd Street, Indianapolis, IN 46290

To my parents, who taught me the value of hard work and persistence.

©1998 Que Corporation

International Standard Book Number: 0-7897-1697-6

Library of Congress Catalog Card Number: 98-84857

00 99 98   8   7   6   5   4   3   2   1

Interpretation of the printing code: the rightmost number of the first series of numbers is the year of the book's printing; the rightmost number of the second series of numbers is the number of the book's printing. For example, a printing code of 98-1 shows that the first printing of the book occurred in 1998.

Printed in the United States of America

Although we cannot provide general technical support, we're happy to help you resolve problems you encounter related to our books, disks, or other products. If you need such assistance, please contact Macmillan Tech Support at 317-581-3833 or via e-mail at **support @mcp.com**.

To order other Que or Macmillan Computer Publishing books or products, please call our Customer Service department at 800-428-5331 or visit our online bookstore at **http://www.mcp.com**.

Executive Editor
Angie Wethington

Acquisitions Editor
Stephanie McComb

Development Editor
Lorne Gentry

Managing Editor
Tom Hayes

Technical Editors
Kyle Bryant
C. Herbert Feltner

Production Editors
Kathryn J. Purdum
Lori A. Lyons

Copy Editor
San Dee Phillips

Cover Designers
Dan Armstrong
Barbara Kordesh

Designer
Barbara Kordesh

Illustrator
Judd Winick

Production Team
Maribeth Echard
Cindy Fields
Tricia Flodder
Diana Groth
Linda Knose
Malinda Kuhn
Daniela Raderstorf
Rowena Rappaport
Mary Ellen Stephenson
Christy Wagner

Indexers
Sandra Henselmeier
Robert Long

Contents at a Glance

Contents

6 Proofing Tools (Spelling and Grammar and the Thesaurus)   61

7 If It's Worth Saving, Save It!   77

Introduction

You're certainly not an idiot, but if Word 97 makes you feel like one, then you need a book that can help. You don't need a book that assumes you are, or want to become, a Word geek. You also don't need anyone telling you that Word is one of the most sophisticated and complex word processors in the world, because you've probably already learned that the hard way. You are a busy person working hard in a busy world, and you just want to get your document written, printed, and available for you to use in the future.

Word 97 is the latest version of the world's most popular word processing program. You'll find plenty of new features that will ensure its popularity far into the future, such as improved table-creating tools, easier graphics, superb integration with the Office 97 product suite, and an artificial intelligence help system to show you how to use it all. And, to prepare you for work on the Internet, Word 97 comes with a complete set of Web tools for creating pages on your own Web site.

Why Do You Need This Book?

With so many computer books on the market, why do you need this one? Because it focuses on getting your work done. This book is different because it won't assume that you know anything at all about how to use Word 97. If you need some assistance coming up to speed with Windows in general, a Windows Primer has been included in the back of this book. If you want more information on Windows, you might pick up *The Complete Idiot's Guide to Windows 95*, or *The Complete Idiot's Guide to Windows NT*.

This book doesn't assume you have the time, or the interest, to learn everything there is to know about Word 97. The most common tasks are broken down into easy reading chapters that you can finish in a short period of time. Simply open the book when you have a question or a problem, find the answer, and solve your problem, and then get on with your life.

How Do You Use This Book?

For starters, this isn't a novel you can take to the beach and read from cover to cover. I suppose you could, but people would talk. Rather, it's a book to guide you through tough times while you're at work or home. When you need a quick answer, use the Table of Contents or the Index to find the right section. Each section of the book is self-contained with exactly what you need to know to solve your problem or to answer your question.

You can follow along with any example in the book. If you are supposed to press a particular key on your keyboard, that key will appear in bold, as in:

Press **Enter** to continue.

And buttons or tabs you work with in dialog boxes are bold fonts:

Click **OK** when you're finished in the Save As box.

Sometimes you will be asked to press two keys at the same time. This is called a *key combination*. Key combinations appear in this book with a plus sign between them. The plus means you should hold down the first key while you press the second key listed. Here's an example:

Press **Alt+F** to open the **File** menu.

In this case, you should hold the **Alt** key down and then press the letter **F**, and something will happen on your screen. Then you can let both keys back up; the order doesn't matter. The **Alt** key is popular; it's used with practically all the letters on the keyboard to do one thing or another. These key combinations are explained throughout the book chapters and also on the Tear-out card inside the front cover.

Also included throughout this book are special boxed notes that will help you learn more of the basics, and some of the advanced stuff, too:

Techno Talk

These contain more of the advanced material that you can safely ignore if you don't have the time or the interest.

Check This Out These boxes contain helpful hints, definitions, and shortcuts for clarifying some subjects and getting your work done even faster.

Web Work Here's where you'll meet some of the newest tools in Word 97— *Web authoring tools*, used to create your own Web pages. Look for these boxes to find tips on how to get the most out of your new Web tools.

New 97 Features Experienced users of Word for Windows will benefit from discovering these completely new features in Word 97.

Acknowledgments

Thanks to everyone at Que who made this book possible—Melanie, Katie, and many others who were always there to help, during holidays, birthdays, and in the middle of the night. I still wonder when they sleep. A very special thanks goes to Martha for considering me for this project, and for her guidance and professionalism.

Trademark

All terms mentioned in this book that are known to be trademarks or service marks are listed below. In addition, terms suspected of being trademarks or service marks have been appropriately capitalized. Que Corporation cannot attest to the accuracy of this information. Use of a term in this book should not be regarded as affecting the validity of any trademark or service mark.

Part 1
Creating Your Masterpiece

Great! You paid a couple thousand dollars for a bundle of technological marvel to help you write reports, and the thing takes up more space, time, and energy than your old typewriter ever did. But could that old clunker ever give you as much enjoyment as battling starships, blasting away doomed demons, or wandering through the myst? Certainly not!

And oh yeah, it can also do word processing. And boy, can Word 97 do word processing! You've picked the right product and chosen the right book, so let's get started. Together we can make the basics of creating documents less of a chore so you can get back to the finer things in life. Whatever they may be.

Chapter 1

The Top 10 New Features of Word 97

Word 97 is probably the greatest word processor ever created, but you may need a friend to show you where all the good stuff is hiding. When you don't have time to search the rest of this book, you can check this chapter for the major improvements to Word 97 that will help you create a better document.

1. **Office Assistants Can Help You**

   How would you like a conveniently placed window on your screen where you see an animated version of Einstein watching over your every action, waiting to tell you what he thinks? You wouldn't like it? Me neither, at first. But these Office Assistants, as they are called, grow on you, and serve a purpose beyond the point of mild entertainment. Each will try to guess what you need help with based upon the previous actions you performed. You can also conveniently type your question by just clicking the Assistant, and the Assistant will provide room to type your question, and then answer in the form of relevant Help topics.

Find out more about me in Chapter 4.

If the Genius doesn't appeal to you, choose another from nine different personality types. Maybe you'd rather be watched by a dog or a cat, Mother Nature or William Shakespeare, or just settle for a paper clip. No matter which you choose, they all have the same effectiveness. They provide you with all the knowledge from all the manuals included with Word 97.

2. **Hyperlinking to Hyperspace**

   You can now improve your Word 97 documents by peppering them with simple links to other sources of information like other documents, spreadsheets, graphics, reference material, credits, and so on. All your reader needs to do is to click on the hyperlink to activate it. Poof! The hyperlink takes them directly to the information you have designated. You can hyperlink to information stored almost anywhere, including a file on your hard disk, or one on your company's intranet, or on the Internet, like a page on the World Wide Web! You can even use hyperlinks to jump to multimedia files, such as sound and video clips.

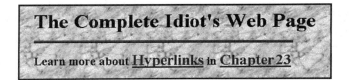

The Complete Idiot's Web Page

Learn more about <u>Hyperlinks</u> in <u>Chapter 23</u>

There are lots of ways to insert hyperlinks. The easiest way may be by using the Hyperlink button. You might prefer the drag-and-drop operation, or maybe use the AutoFormat feature and have them created automatically. You can sort through your options and get all the details by turning to Chapter 23.

3. **Share Your Documents with a Friend**

   Word 97 now comes with an efficient way to share in the creation of your documents. It's now much easier to distribute documents to your colleagues for their feedback and updates. You'll be able to ask for comments and then incorporate those review comments into the same document. You can set revision levels and easily see the changes between levels. For added security, you can set different passwords for separate levels of access to your document. Learn how to share in Chapter 17.

4. **Convenient New Browse Selector**

   Find this new button near the bottom of your vertical scroll bar and click it. You'll find a new menu providing new ways you can choose to browse your document. You can browse by heading, browse by graphic, browse by footnote or comment; you get the idea. There's even Find and Go To to cover all your needs. You can "browse" Chapter 9 for more details on this new feature.

Click any of these for custom browsing of your document.

5. **The New Mouse with the Wheel Support**

   Word 97 provides special support for the Microsoft IntelliMouse® pointing device, which is a new mouse with a rotating wheel that is also a wheel button. You hold the mouse the same way, but your index finger can comfortably spin the wheel up and down. You can also press the wheel down to click it like another button. Using the wheel or wheel button in Word 97 gives you some new and improved navigation functions operated directly from the mouse. You can scroll, pan, AutoScroll, zoom, and DataZoom (for drilling through an outline). Hate the scroll bars? Get yourself one of these new mice and you may never need to use scroll bars again.

Here's the wheel you can spin and click.

The new Microsoft IntelliMouse®.

   Try clicking on what interests you, then turning the wheel to scroll up and down. Better yet, click the new wheel button and then move the mouse around. You'll be AutoScrolling through your document. Try zooming in somewhere on your document by pressing the Ctrl key and rolling the wheel.

6. **Terrific AutoShapes Creator Will Save You Time**

   If you've ever tried the Drawing tool in earlier versions of Word and wished it were more powerful, try it now. You'll find lots more shapes and formatting options, and the new toolbar has been improved. It includes AutoShapes, an inventory of over 125 basic shapes in well-defined categories to get you started. Then you can stretch and pull and color and change them into an infinite number of new shapes.

All the drawing tools you'll need.

Once your drawing is finished you'll have an easier time moving it around with the new Nudge feature. It's just what the doctor ordered for complete control over your artwork. Detail oriented? Try pressing the Ctrl key while nudging and you'll move it in tiny 1-point increments. Chapter 13 will give you the details about these new and powerful graphic features.

7. Combined and Improved Spelling and Grammar Checker

You'll never have to run the spelling or grammar checker again. That's because they can always be running, in the background, waiting to pounce on your misspelled words or grammatical errors and wave the red flag—actually, a wavy red or green line that appears as an underline for any errors. Spelling errors are underlined in red, and grammar errors in green. When you feel like correcting them, just click on an underlined word with the right mouse button and a pop-up menu will provide correct spelling and suggested improvements in your grammar. Just click on the one you want, and it replaces your mistake instantly.

By the way, you can still run the familiar spell checker and grammar checker independently, if you want. You will notice that each is significantly faster, though, because all the errors in your document will have already been looked up. All you have to do is decide on a replacement for each misspelling, and whether or not you agree with the grammar recommendations.

Find out more about the nifty new combination spelling/grammar checker, along with other helpful proofreading tools, in Chapter 6.

8. Two New Views for You to Choose

Word 97 offers two new and different views to help you create and edit documents—the Online Layout and the Document Map.

➤ Online Layout View

This new view is designed to make text easier to read onscreen, instead of showing you exactly how it will look when printed. Try it, and notice that your sentences wrap to stay within the borders of your screen, and all small text is enlarged to 12-point type.

Remember that you can quickly change your view at any time by clicking one of the four View buttons near the bottom of your screen, in the horizontal scroll bar. They've added Online Layout View, perfect for creating and editing documents to be used on a Web site. Word 97 defaults to this new view while creating Web documents, which you'll learn all about in Chapters 23, 24, and 25.

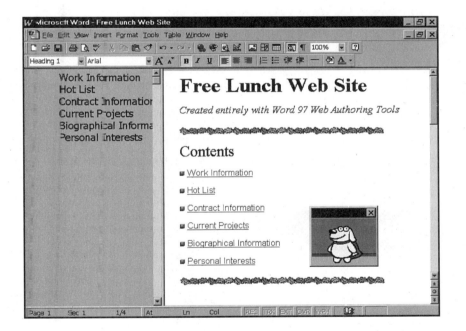

A new view called Document Map, along with Online Layout, helps you browse long documents.

➤ Document Map

This new button on the Standard toolbar turns on or turns off the Document Map, a vertical pane along the left edge of the document window that outlines the document's structure. This view is helpful to quickly browse a long document (or a Web page) and to keep track of your location in it. A variety of new tools such as this are described for you in Chapter 18.

9. **Put Your Favorite Commands on the Toolbars**

   Maybe you're the kind of person that would love to have a unique new button on the toolbar you like best. Maybe you want a button that quickly opens your last five documents, or one that dials your Internet service and checks for your latest e-mail. Or perhaps you just want to change the order of the buttons in your current toolbars. You've got that power in Word 97. Want to go crazy? How about putting menus on your toolbars? Even a popular document or template could sit up there for your convenience. Check out all the Word 97 customization tips in Chapter 21.

10. **Here It Is! The Web Toolbar!**

   The new Word 97 Web Toolbar makes it easy to browse through documents that contain hyperlinks. You can use the Go button on the Web toolbar to open a *Start Page* or a *Search The Web* page (read more about these page types in Chapter 24), and it will be opened in your Web browser. There's a quick Refresh button to keep you current and a Stop button when the Internet is dragging.

   The Web toolbar also lets you add interesting documents you find on the Web to your Favorites folder so you can find them again quickly. The Web toolbar keeps a list of the last 10 documents you jumped to by using either the Web toolbar or a hyperlink.

Take a peek at Chapters 23, 24, and 25 to learn all about the new Internet Web capabilities built into Word 97.

Your toolbar for creating Web documents.

Chapter 2

Installing Word 97

In This Chapter

➤ Word 97 Typical setup for Windows 95, Windows 98, and Windows NT

➤ How to put in what the Typical install leaves out

➤ Rerunning Setup in the future

Installing Microsoft Word 97 is relatively easy—easier than using it, actually. Don't worry about whether you have enough space on your computer for now—Word 97 will let you know during the first stages of installation. So fire up your computer and let's install the world's greatest word processor!

Preparing to Run Word 97 Setup

Microsoft Word 97 comes on disks or on a clean and shiny CD-ROM. Boy, if you bought the CD-ROM version, your life as a Word installer is going to be mighty easy. The disks aren't that bad. You just have to stay awake changing disks until the installation program is finished.

Is My Computer Big Enough for All This?

To install Microsoft Word 97 (or Office 97) on your computer, it must be running Microsoft Windows 95, Windows 98, Windows NT 3.51, or Windows NT 4.0 (or later). Your computer should have a fast microprocessor, at least a 486, but a Pentium is preferred. For memory, you'll need at least 8 MB using Windows 95, and 16 MB using Windows NT. Either way, you'll find 16 MB or more is worth the price to keep you moving faster. Finally, you'll need at least 20 MB of available disk space to run Word 97 bare bones, or close to 70 MB to install all the features of Word 97 (and almost 250 MB to install the complete Office 97 package). Don't panic if you're short on disk space, because you can always choose to run some features directly from the Word or Office CD-ROM.

Running Setup from CD-ROM

Computer turned on? Got the shiny CD-ROM out of the wrapper? Okay, open the CD-ROM drive, pop in the CD, and close the door. Bingo! The installation program starts auto-magically, and you're ready to move ahead and finish the setup.

If for some reason the magic is missing, you can start the installation program on the CD-ROM manually. Double-click the **My Computer** icon on your desktop, double-click your **CD-ROM drive** icon. When you find and double-click the **Setup** icon, the installation process will begin.

Running Setup from Disk

First, you'll have to find the disk labeled "Setup Disk 1" and insert it into your computer disk drive. Now click the **Windows 95/98** or **Windows NT Taskbar** and choose the **Run** command. In the **Run** dialog box, where it says Open, type in **A:SETUP** and then click the **OK** button. In a few seconds you'll see the first installation screen.

Finishing Setup

Click the **Continue** button on the first installation screen, and then enter and confirm your name as well as your company name (optional). You'll want to get it right the first time, however, because Word 97 now includes this as the default summary information for all documents you create.

The next screen suggests the name of a folder that can be used to store all of the Word 97 program files. Click **OK** to choose the default folder location.

Name and Organization Information [?][x]

Enter your full name in the box below. You may also enter the name of your organization. Setup will use this information for subsequent installations of the product.

Name: Daniel T. Bobola

Organization: Bobola Enterprises, Inc.

[OK] [Exit Setup]

Getting things started.

This information will be included in the default summary information for all documents.

Techno Talk blah blah blah blah blah bl b

Prefer a Different Folder?

If you want to store the program files on a different drive letter, or in a different folder, just type over the default path location. For instance, you could type D:\WORD97 to store the program files on your second hard drive, or C:\WORD97 as a new folder on your C drive. The installation program will create a new folder if it doesn't yet exist.

Which Installation Option Is Right for You?

Now you've reached the fork in the road where you can choose the Typical, Custom, or Run from CD-ROM option. Basically, the difference lies in the amount of space they use on your computer. All these options run the same Word 97, but some simply leave out a few bells and whistles. Go ahead and choose the **Typical** installation. It provides the most popular options. If, by chance, you want more, you can always run Setup again and choose the Custom install to pickup whatever you left out the first time. We'll cover this option later in the chapter.

Microsoft Office 97 Setup [?][x]

To choose the installation you want, click one of the following buttons.

Typical
Recommended for most users. Easily installs all Office applications and popular components. (Approx. 120 MB)

Custom
Recommended for expert users. Includes Typical installation and the option to add and remove components. (Max. 150 MB)

Run from CD-ROM
Install Office to run from the CD-ROM. Shared components will be installed on the hard disk. (Approx. 51 MB)

Folder:
C:\MSOffice

[Exit Setup]

You can always start here and add more later.

Click here to add the Web tools or other options.

Saves space, but you'll have to leave the CD-ROM in your drive.

Deciding which installation is best for you.

Really Short on Disk Space?

If you happen to be short on disk space, you can still run Word 97 with full function directly from your CD-ROM drive, although it will be much slower. Choose the last install option **Run from CD-ROM** to add only the barest minimum of program files to your computer hard drive, and leave the rest on the CD-ROM. Remember, however, that anytime you want to run Word 97, you'll need to have the Word 97 CD-ROM in your drive. How will you play music while you type?

How to Put In What the Typical Install Leaves Out

Microsoft would love to see you install the entire contents of Word 97, but the relatively large disk space it consumes on your computer might be needed for other important programs—like games, for instance. All of Word 97 takes up more than 40 megabytes of storage space. The Typical install requires only 28 megabytes, since it leaves out a few things. What are those things? And how can you put them back? You can answer these questions by running the Setup program.

The Custom Setup

The Custom setup is available only the first time you install Word 97. After that, the Setup program provides the same options in the button labeled **Add/Remove**. Custom lets you choose exactly the components you want, nothing more, nothing less. This makes it easy to add only the things you want. Also, if you're low on disk space, you have the opportunity to deny installing something you probably won't need. You can also remove any components that you installed earlier.

The grayed check box means there's more to choose—click the Change Option button.

When this button is active, it means more choices are available for the selected component.

Plenty of room? This quickly chooses all components instantly.

Word 97 à la Carte

It's great to know that Word 97 offers several different components that can be added to your personalized version at any time. You can do this without changing anything you have already installed. Read on for more information about what is offered and just how to access it!

You Can Add These Components Anytime

In several simple steps, you can discover more Word 97 options. Just run **Setup** again and choose the **Add/Remove** option. This option will investigate what you have currently installed for Word 97. It will show you what's installed and what's not. Then simply add or remove check marks in the boxes provided beside the components listed. If any check box has a check on a grayed background, it means more components are available under this category. Click the **Change Option** button to see the individual components for that category. You can select one or more items, or click **Select All** to choose them all quickly. Each time you click into a **Change Option** area, you need to click **OK** to get back out (or **Cancel** if you've changed your mind). Make your choices, then click **Continue** and the Setup program will install or remove each component as requested.

➤ **Web Page Authoring**

If you plan to do any work with Internet documents—whether you create your own World Wide Web site or post documents to an existing one—you'll want to install the Web Page Authoring tools. This includes everything you'll need to create HTML (HyperText Markup Language) documents. Check out Chapters 23, 24, and 25 to see how you can put it to use today!

➤ **Extra Wizards and Templates**

Chapter 20 will teach you that a wizard or a template helps you quickly create perfectly formatted documents. If you like them, you might want to install more. Click the **More Wizards** box if you are interested in either of the two extra wizards. The first is the Newsletter Wizard, which is helpful if you've never prepared a newsletter before. If you plan to follow along in Chapter 19 and create your own newsletter, install this option.

As for the second optional wizard, unless you're a lawyer, you'll be safe to ignore the Legal Pleading Wizard. Lawyers are the only ones who begged and pleaded for this one.

If You Add a Proofing Tool Later   You can choose to install any of the proofing tools during the installation. However, if you decide to install one later, be sure the proofing tools are all stored in the *same* folder you stored the first tool in. This folder will contain the main dictionary, and all proofing tools should be sharing it. The folder is usually located in the C:\Program Files\Common Files\Microsoft Shared\Proof directory.

13

Check This Out...

Unidentified Object The term "object" is used in Word 97 to describe anything you can place in your document that isn't exactly text. This includes many things, such as graphics, equations, scanned pictures, sound clips, and even videos.

➤ **WordArt and Equation Editor**

For adding special text effects and mathematical equations, Word 97 includes two extra applications. WordArt and Equation Editor let you create objects that you insert into your documents. To verify that these applications were installed, open the **Insert** menu and click **Object**. All of your installed applications should be listed under Object Type.

➤ **Converters and Filters**

Your document may look like simple words on a sheet of paper—but while it's stored in your computer, it's written in a whole different language computer language. Different word processors like WordPerfect or Works store their files in a different language from Word 97. Even Word 6.0 and Word for Windows 95 are ever-so-slightly different, so you may need a converter to store a Word 97 document in the earlier formats. So if you have the need to open, edit, or share a document with a colleague using another version or brand of word processor, then you need a Converter. You can choose from a slew of document converters, including all of the most common word processing programs from the past few years.

➤ **Text Converter**

If you happen to have plain text documents created and formatted simply with spaces and tabs, you might benefit from this Text Converter. It helps maintain the general layout of the document while it is converted to Word 97 format.

New Converters Word 97 now includes a helpful Recover Text Converter (it does just that—recovers usable text from any document); a new HTML converter (HyperText Markup Language, the language of the Web); of course, a converter for Word 6.0 or Word for Windows 95 documents; and one for Macintosh documents.

➤ **Graphics Filters**

If you have the need to include graphics created with other applications such as CAD tools or specialized drawing programs, be sure to include the filter from this list. You'll be able to add the drawing or graphic as an object directly into your Word 97 document. And for Web work, you'll want GIF and JPEG filters to add these common graphic types to your document. You'll find most applications represented in this list, and almost all applications are compatible with one or more filter formats in this list.

AutoCad files

Computer Graphics Metafile

CorelDRAW!

Encapsulated PostScript

Enhanced Metafile

GIF (Graphics Interchange Format)

JPEG (Joint Photographic Experts Group)

Kodak CD

Macintosh Picture Import

MicroGrafx

PC Paintbrush (also known as PCX files)

TIFF (Tagged Image Format File)

TrueVision Targa

Windows Bitmap (also known as BMP files)

Windows Metafile

WordPerfect Graphics Import or Export

➤ **Multilanguage Support Features**

Do you have friends located in other countries with whom you'd like to share your documents? Word 97 helps you create, edit, and share documents with people using different localized versions of the same product.

The Least You Need to Know

Great beginning! You've learned that installing Word 97 is not a terribly painful process.

Which installation option is best for me?

Most people get along just fine with the Typical installation option. If you have lots of disk space available, you may prefer additional features found in the Custom installation.

What is left out if I choose the Typical installation?

Two popular options are the Newsletter Wizard and the Web Authoring Tools.

Can I ever add these and other options in the future?

Sure! You can rerun the installation program at any time to add additional features without harming your existing documents.

What if I have almost no disk space left?

No problem. Choose the Run from CD-ROM installation and just leave the Word 97 CD-ROM in your player.

New International Features in Word 97
Several features in Word 97 make it easy to create and edit documents containing any Eastern, Central, or Western European words, phrases, and more. If you plan to share documents with your friends in these countries, install the Multilanguage Support. You'll find it much easier to create and edit documents containing text in more than one language.

Chapter 3

TEN HUUUT!!

Word 97 Basics

In This Chapter

➤ Starting Word

➤ Word 97 toolbars and menus

➤ Typing and printing a simple letter in Word

➤ Changing your mind and editing text

➤ Sampling a wizard to create an attractive memo

Chomping at the bit to get started? This chapter provides a quick review of the basics you'll need in order to navigate your way through the new world of Word 97. Open the gates, and let's begin!

Starting Word 97

You can start Word 97 in either Windows 95/98 or Windows NT by clicking on the **Start** button, selecting **Programs**, and clicking the **Microsoft Word** menu command. The following figure shows which menus to open.

Starting Word 97 in Windows 95 or Windows NT.

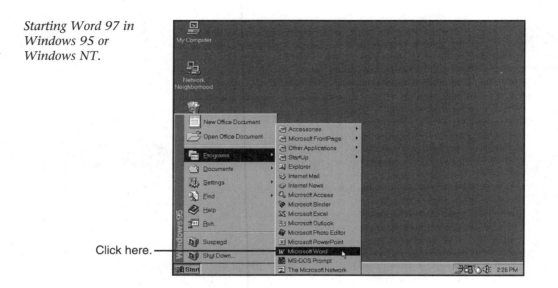

Click here.

The following figure shows what the majority of users see when they open Word 97. Nothing has been created yet. The largest part of the display screen is white with nothing in it. This represents a blank sheet of paper ready for you to type on. You will be using the computer keyboard to type words onto this simulated sheet of paper. That's easy enough to understand. But what are all these gadgets on the screen?

Welcome to Word 97.

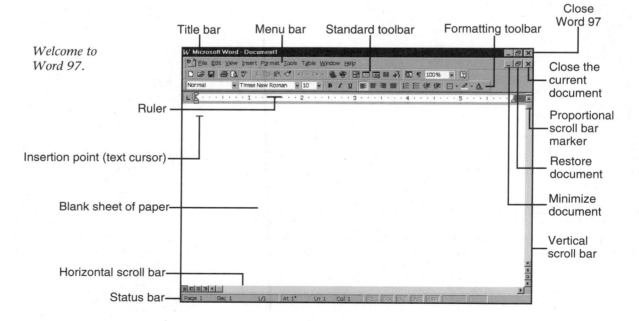

18

Welcome to Word 97

Think of this chapter as your visual index for finding help about the Word screen as you read this book.

Title Bar

The *title bar* is always visible at the top of your screen. Besides identifying Microsoft Word itself in the title bar, Word 97 now places additional information that may be helpful. You now see the name of the registered owner of this copy of Word, and more importantly, the name of the document on which you're currently working.

Menu Bar

Take a look at the row of words near the top of your screen. See the words File, Edit, View, and so on? These words make up the *menu bar*. It's called the menu bar because it holds a bunch of menus. You use a menu when you want Word to do something for you, like print or add footnotes. Of course, you don't see *print* or *add footnotes* because only the names of the main menus are visible. To read the menus, you have to open them. To open a menu, move your mouse on top of the menu item you want and click the left mouse button once.

If you look closely at the View menu, you'll see that some commands are plain, like Full Screen, and do simply what they say. When you click on the Full Screen command, all the toolbars and menu bars disappear, leaving you with much more room for typing your document (and a small button to return to normal). Try it! You can always click the **Close Full Screen** button (or press the **Escape** key) to bring back all of the toolbars, menu bars, and everything else.

Some commands, however, have an icon in front of them, or other symbols attached at the end:

➤ In the new Word 97, many commands now have their associated icon pasted right next to them.

➤ The gray box in front of some commands tells you that this mode (or method of doing something) is currently selected.

➤ The check mark is a standard way of letting you know that an option is "on." For example, the Ruler command is a toggle that can be turned on or off. Select such a command when the check mark is displayed, and you'll turn it "off." When the Ruler command is on, the ruler appears on your screen below the formatting toolbar. When it's off, the ruler is hidden.

➤ An ellipsis (...) at the end of a command will bring up dialog boxes that allow you to choose from many options and settings.

The View menu is displayed.

A gray box means this option has been chosen.

A grayed-out word means you can't use this option now.

A check mark means the option is turned on.

The ellipsis (...) takes you to a dialog box.

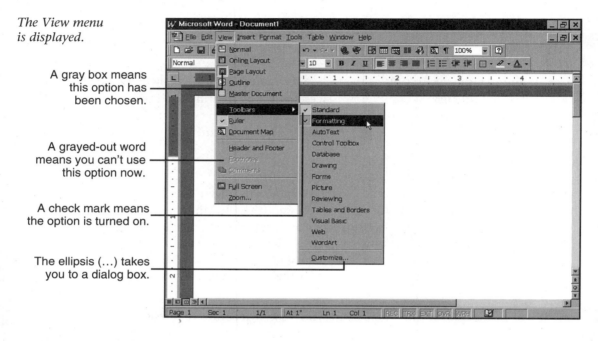

What's on the Menu?

Later in Chapter 21, you'll learn how you can customize these menus. You'll be able to change the order of the menu items, add or remove menu items, and even make up completely new menu items!

The Standard Toolbar

The *standard toolbar* contains icons (or little pictures) of the tasks the average user is most likely to use. That's the average user according to Microsoft, of course. (I'd like to meet the average person that needs to insert Microsoft Excel Worksheets into their Word document so often that they earned their own button on the standard toolbar.) Word 97 now helps you easily change the order of buttons you see, or even add new ones. And this applies to all toolbars, not just the Standard toolbar. Chapter 22 gives you the scoop on customizing your toolbars. But for now, we'll stick with the "standard" toolbars.

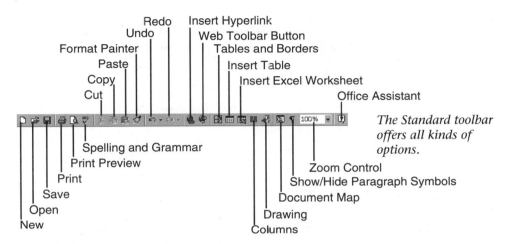

The Standard toolbar offers all kinds of options.

Table 3.1 The Standard Toolbar Buttons

Icon	Button	Description
	New	Creates a new, blank document based on the default template.
	Open	Find and open an existing document.
	Save	Saves current document.
	Print	Prints the current document.
	Print Preview	View the current document as it will appear when printed.
	Spelling and Grammar	Start the proofing tools at the current insertion point. Grammar checking is now included here.
	Cut	Remove the currently selected text or objects.
	Copy	Take a copy of currently selected text or objects to be pasted elsewhere.
	Paste	Insert the previously selected text or object that was cut or copied.
	Format Painter	Click to copy the formatting from one paragraph to another.
	Undo	Please forget what I just did and put it back the way it was.

continues

Table 3.1 Continued

Icon	Button	Description
	Redo	After an Undo, you might want to Redo the same thing.
	Insert Hyperlink	New in Word 97, converts selected text to a hyperlink.
	Web Toolbar	New in Word 97, displays the Web toolbar containing common buttons used in Web page creation.
	Tables and Borders	Displays the toolbar that helps you create and edit tables and table borders.
	Insert Table	Click to display and choose a grid size that creates a table in your document.
	Insert Microsoft Excel Worksheet	And it does exactly that! It inserts the spreadsheet.
	Columns	Displays and creates custom text columns in your document.
	Drawing	Displays the powerful new Drawing toolbar.
	Document Map	New in Word 97, a view for a quick browsing of large documents.
	Show/Hide	Toggles the display of non-printing characters like spaces, tabs, and paragraph symbols.
100%	Zoom Control	Displays a menu of different screen enlargements, to better view your document.
	Office Assistant	Starts the new animated help creatures described in Chapter 4.

The Formatting Toolbar

Here are the buttons you will likely use to spiffy-up the appearance of your words in your document. These buttons help you select fonts, font sizes, make text bold or italic, and perhaps center your words in the middle of the page. Chapter 5 describes using these buttons in more detail. Once again, Microsoft took a stab at what they thought the average user would want on this toolbar.

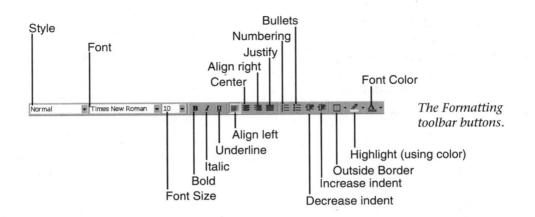

The Formatting toolbar buttons.

The Ruler

This ruler is not your average ruler. If you hold a six-inch ruler up to your screen, you may discover that the two rulers don't match in size, and you may have the urge to return your copy of Word 97 as defective. Resist that urge. Word is fine, and so is the ruler. The Word 97 *ruler* is used to set and display tabs and to indent paragraphs. The ruler is also accurate in size, but the measurement you see is for the *future* printed page, not the page you see on your screen. What you see is usually larger, and that's helpful for your eyes. You can learn more about setting tabs by using the ruler in Chapter 10. If you don't care to see this ruler (most beginners don't need the extra distraction), you can get rid of it by clicking the View menu and removing the check from the Ruler command.

The Scroll Bars

The horizontal and vertical *scroll bars* are used to travel throughout your document. The most helpful of the two available is called the *vertical scroll bar*, but you can recognize it as the thing on the right. The vertical scroll bar in Word represents the length of the document. The top arrow represents the top of the document, and the bottom arrow represents the bottom of the document. The area in between the two arrows represents all of the pages, but the most important part of the scroll bar is that small square. That square represents the current spot you are viewing on the screen. As you move up or down the screen (or page), the square moves, too, showing you where you are in the document.

➤ To scroll your document up one line of text, click the mouse on the up scroll arrow at the top of the scroll bar.

➤ To scroll down one line of text, click the mouse on the down scroll arrow at the bottom of the scroll bar. Riding up and down the vertical scroll bar is the proportional scroll bar marker. It gives you an idea of which part of your document you're looking at (if the marker is near the top of the scroll bar, you are near the top of your document). If it's thin, you have a large document. If it's larger, you have a smaller document (thus named *proportional*). Drag the scroll marker up or down to move quickly through the pages of your document. Click on the marker to see the current page number.

➤ To scroll a page at a time, click either above or below the proportional scroll bar marker in the vertical scroll bar.

Near the bottom of your screen, you'll find the horizontal positioning bar, with arrow buttons on each end and a scroll box (or marker) somewhere in between. You can position your view by clicking on the bar or the arrows in the direction you want to go; this will move the page left or right on your screen.

What's That New Thing in the Scroll Bar?

The Select Browse Object is used to display a pop-up table of the best browsing methods from which you can choose your favorite. You'll find the icon on your vertical scroll bar, and details on how to use it in Chapter 9.

Status Bar

You can find interesting information about your document in the area called the *status bar*. Most helpful is probably the page number. If you have nothing else to do, you can click in different parts of the screen and watch the numbers in the status bar change. These changing numbers are the coordinates of your whereabouts, or text cursor position, on the page. Isn't it useful to know you are 5.8 inches from the top of your printed page, at line 28 and column 13? Microsoft thought so.

What's New on the Screen in Word 97?

New Icon	What It Does for You
	Insert Hyperlink; a Web tool for linking stuff (see Chapter 23).
	Opens the new Web Toolbar (Chapter 24).
	The new Drawing Feature (Chapter 19).
	Document Map; a new view for you (Chapter 18).

New Icon	What It Does for You
[?]	The new Office Assistant to help you (Chapter 4).
[□▾]	A faster Outside Border creator (Chapter 19).
[A▾]	Tool for coloring your words (Chapter 5).
[⏎]	A new browsing tool selector menu (Chapter 9).
[#]	Go to the previous find (Chapter 9).
[⬇]	Go to the next find (Chapter 9).
[≣]	A new view for Web work called Online Layout (Chapter 18).

Don't Like What You See? Change Your View!

You can quickly change your view at any time by clicking one of the four View buttons near the bottom left of your screen, in the horizontal scroll bar. These represent your choice of view, whether it's Normal, Online Layout, Page Layout, or Outline view. You can also open the View menu and choose the view you prefer.

This is for the default Normal view. You won't be bothered by headers, footers, page numbers, and so on; you'll see only the plain text document. It's the fastest of the view choices.

 Word 97 introduces a new view called Online Layout, designed to make text easier to read onscreen, instead of showing you exactly how it will look when printed. Try it, and notice that your sentences wrap to stay within the borders of your screen, and all small text is enlarged to 12-point type. It's ideal for working with Internet Web documents. It provides the look and feel of an active Web page for faster creation and editing.

In Page Layout view, you actually see the representation of a sheet of paper on your screen. That's helpful when you are trying to balance text and graphics on the screen, and also to see what might be stored in your margins (like page numbers or footnotes)

Outline view provides an easier way to manage larger documents, just as an outline helps organize your thoughts. The left column of your screen displays the outline format of the current document, but you need to be applying styles consistently for it to be helpful.

Creating a Quick and Simple Document

Notice that your Word 97 screen is mostly a large, white background. Think of this as a sheet of paper. Look again at the computer keyboard. Think of it as your old typewriter (youngsters can ignore that remark). Just start typing. Everyone can hunt-and-peck out a document, so don't worry if your typing skills aren't the greatest. That's the good thing about Word 97—most of the minor errors that slow down a professional touch-typist will be automatically corrected! Misspellings, grammatical errors, and forgotten capitalization or punctuation can all be corrected for you. Now you can concentrate on getting your thoughts down onto paper (or should I say the screen?). Just start typing.

Just start typing and see what you get.

Start typing, and your text will appear here.

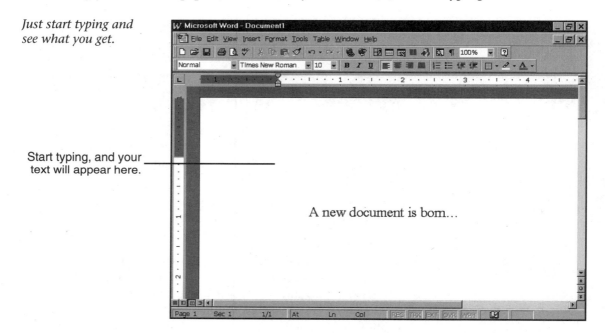

A new document is born...

Enter Text into a Word 97 Document

When you start Word 97, it places your cursor automatically at the top of an empty document window so you're ready to start entering text. To enter text into a document, simply start typing. As you type, your words will appear on the screen, like words from a typewriter. Unlike using a typewriter, however, you should *not* press **Enter** when you reach the edge of the screen. Just keep typing. Word 97 will automatically move your words to the next line as needed. This is called *word wrap*, and it's the most basic feature of any word processor. When you get to the end of a complete paragraph, you press **Enter**. Here are some more hints on entering text in a Word document:

➤ **Press Enter only when you reach the end of a paragraph or to insert a blank line.** If you want to divide an existing paragraph into two, move the cursor to the dividing point (between sentences) and press **Enter**. To put two paragraphs back together, move to the first letter of the second paragraph and press **Backspace**.

➤ **Use the spacebar to insert a single space between words or sentences.** Do *not* use the spacebar to indent or center text on a page. Yes, lots of people like to do it, but it's a bad habit because different fonts assign different sizes to the space. If you mix fonts, things won't line up or center properly. Use tabs to indent and the Center button for centering words and paragraphs.

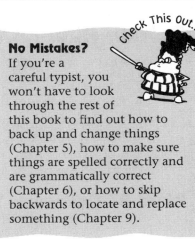

No Mistakes?
If you're a careful typist, you won't have to look through the rest of this book to find out how to back up and change things (Chapter 5), how to make sure things are spelled correctly and are grammatically correct (Chapter 6), or how to skip backwards to locate and replace something (Chapter 9).

➤ **Press Tab (not the spacebar) to indent the first line of a paragraph.** Spaces are not just blank holes on the page; they are real characters. Depending on the fonts you choose for your text, your paragraphs can look uneven if you use the spacebar to align them. Using the Tab key allows Word 97 to line things up for you.

➤ **A dotted line marks the end of a page.** Just ignore the dotted line when you see it. It's there to tell Word for Windows where one page ends and another begins. If you add text above a dotted line, the excess text will flow to the top of the next page automatically. You can also force the end of a page (before it's full) by pressing **Ctrl+Enter**. When you do this, the dots multiply (get more dense) to show that this is a *forced page break*.

Word Wrap

With word wrapping, words are automatically advanced to the next line of a paragraph when they "bump" into the right margin. Likewise, you can insert words into the middle of a paragraph, and the rest of the paragraph will be adjusted downward automatically. If you change the margins, paragraphs will adjust automatically.

Quicker Alternatives to Snazzy Documents

Want to create a professional-looking report for your boss without straining your cranium? Let a wizard show you how.

A wizard is like ordering up some fancy custom stationery whenever you want it. You pick the kind of document you want (like a fax or a memo) and then tell it what you want (general appearance, size, and so on), and the wizard will instantly prepare your Word 97 screen to look exactly as you requested. You just fill in the missing words in order to save yourself from wasting time on the trivial aspects of a document.

Word 97 Document Wizards

To find these wizards, you have to start a new document, but unfortunately you can't simply click the New button on your Standard toolbar. You need to open your **File** menu and click the **New** command (certainly looks like the same icon, doesn't it?). Oh well, it's just one of those quirks of Word. You'll see something similar to this:

You are presented with categories of prepared documents to choose from.

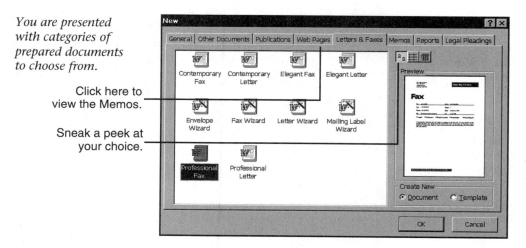

Click here to view the Memos.

Sneak a peek at your choice.

Just above the central display you'll see tab headings like Letters & Faxes, Memos, General, and others. Click on the **Memos** tab.

Memo Me This, Mr. Wizard

Double-click the **Memo Wizard** to get it started. The wizard will come to life, and begin to ask you questions about how you want your memo to appear. You can participate in this banter as much or as little as you feel necessary. You can even skip through the whole thing by doing nothing more than pressing the **Next** button. Press the **Next** button six times and you've completed all of the questions. Then press the **Finish** button at the checkered flag.

This looks like magic, doesn't it? Nice big letters and lines already painted on the page. The parts of the memo are easy to figure out. Someone already stuck the date in for you. They even put your name in the From: line! At least I hope it's your name; it actually inserts the name of the licensed owner of Word 97 automatically. All you have to do is tell the computer who this memo is intended for.

Look at what's written next to the **To:** line. Inside the brackets you will find the suggestion to **Click here and type names**. Try it. Move the mouse arrow until it rests on any word between the brackets. Then click the left mouse button once. The sentence changes in appearance, turning light gray in color, anticipating activity from you. Now type your boss's name—or your dog's name if you're just practicing. They may even be the same, for all I know. The typed name will appear and replace the brackets and sentence. You're ready to move on.

Similarly, you can click on the **CC:** area and type a name for the carbon copy, or click on the **RE:** area and type something regarding what this memo's about.

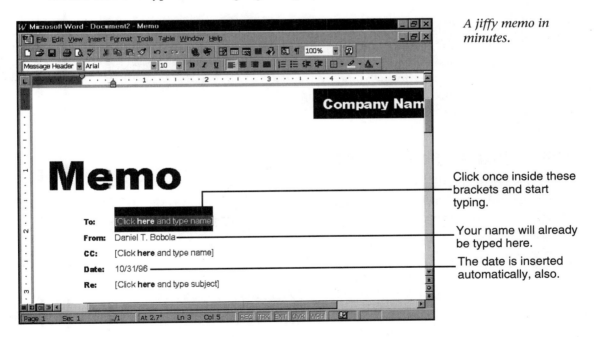

A jiffy memo in minutes.

Click once inside these brackets and start typing.

Your name will already be typed here.

The date is inserted automatically, also.

Now move the mouse arrow down to the part that says **Click here and type your memo text**. This is the main body of the memo. Go ahead and type the memo to your boss. As you did earlier, don't worry about reaching the end of the line. Keep on typing; the computer will take care of moving to the next line as needed, and will also move any special Memo formatting around automatically. When you finish, you'll have a document that's good enough to print.

Oops! Editing Basics

Correcting typing mistakes in Word 97 is easy. Simply press the **Backspace** key to back up and erase text to the left of the insertion point, or press the **Delete** key to erase text to the right of the insertion point.

How do you correct a mistake found in the middle of a paragraph? You simply have to move the insertion point (that skinny blinking cursor) by clicking on the spot where you want it to go. Now you can use the **Delete** key or the **Backspace** key to remove the unwanted text.

You can quickly get rid of entire words by double-clicking on them and pressing the **Delete** key.

Making a Mistake When Cleaning Up Mistakes

If you happen to delete something by mistake and you want to undo the deletion (get the text back), simply press the **Undo** button on the Standard toolbar. In fact, you can keep clicking **Undo** to undo any number of your last actions, in reverse order.

Save That First Document

Before trying anything as daring and daunting as printing your new document, the golden rule is to *always save your work first*. Saving a document is simply making sure that everything you now see on your screen is written down inside your computer, so it's there the next time you want it, which may be weeks, years, or never.

 Click the **Save** button on your Standard toolbar. Word 97 understands that you want to save your new document, but it needs some information from you. Basically, what do you want to call the thing? Since you'll probably have loads of documents soon, you need to name each one so you will recognize it the next time you need it.

Notice that Word 97 has already suggested a name for your document. This name is actually the first few words of your document, and more than half the time this might be good enough. You can either type in a new name now, or leave it as it is. Word 97

automatically saves all your documents to the My Document folder, which is pretty handy. To complete the saving process, click the **Save** button as shown.

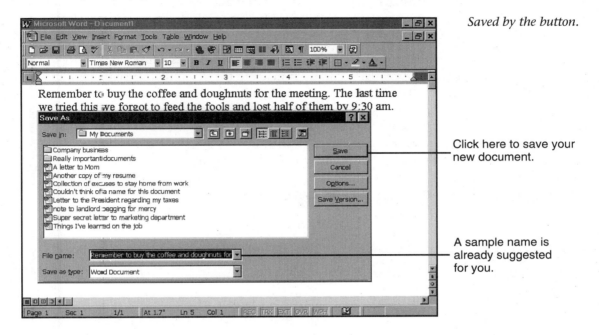

Saved by the button.

Click here to save your new document.

A sample name is already suggested for you.

To learn more about saving things in Word 97, including some helpful options available to you (like changing the folder where you save your documents and automatic timed backups—in case you forget), turn to Chapter 7.

And Printing That First Document

If it's good enough for you, it's good enough to waste paper on. Click the **Print** button on the Standard toolbar. That's it. Seriously, that's it! If you want another copy, press the button again. If you've been blessed with good fortune, this computer is connected to a printer, your report is already finished, and you are happy. You may also want to experience some of the control you can have over your printer. Open the **File** menu and click **Print**, and you'll find the box that allows you to change things like printer settings, paper bin source, number of copies, and so on.

If, on the other hand, nothing happened, you are probably feeling rage, anger, and hatred. That's common when dealing with computers. Call your spouse or significant other and tell them you'll be a few minutes late. Then turn to Chapter 8 to learn more about printing.

Closing Down and Going Home

When you think you've had enough, give your computer a few more seconds of your time. Don't just turn the power off, or you may have an unfortunate surprise waiting the next time you start up (like corrupted documents).

To properly close your documents, open the **File** menu and click **Close** to close the current document. If any changes have been made to the document since you last saved it, Word gives you the chance to save it before closing. Continue closing all other documents you may have currently open. To close Word, open the **File** menu and click **Exit**, or click the Exit button in the title bar. Finally, to close Windows 95 or Windows NT, click the **Start** button on the Task bar, click **Shutdown**, and click the **Yes** button. A message will be displayed when it's safe to turn off the power to your computer.

The Least You Need to Know

You don't have to know much about Word 97 to get some productive work out of it.

How do I start Word 97?

Click the Start button, point to Programs, and click Word 97.

How do I get around in Word 97?

Click the toolbar buttons, open the menus, slide the scroll bars, observe the status bars, and don't be afraid of experimenting.

Can you make it easier to get me started?

Try using one of the built-in wizards such as the Memo Wizard. It takes care of the formatting and placement; you just type your message.

Will my document be here tomorrow?

Only if you save it. Be sure to click the Save button and give your document a name and a home.

Is it hard to print?

Not if you have a printer! Click the Print button and your document will be printed with the default settings. If that's not good enough for you, try peeking at Chapter 8.

Chapter 4

Help!
Using Word 97
Awesome Help

In This Chapter

➤ Getting good help fast

➤ Put your Office Assistant to work

➤ Using the Help Contents, Index, and Find features

➤ Learning with the Assistant Tips

Good help is hard to find, but relax—you've found this chapter. It's dedicated to helping you help yourself with Word 97. Word is an incredibly sophisticated program, so it's no wonder that we sometimes slow down when using a new feature or remembering an old one. Word provides help for absolutely every function and feature inside of Word, through a new gadget called an Office Assistant. They're worth the click to get them started. You may find yourself looking for help just for the fun of watching them get it.

For Starters, Try the Lazy Help

Especially helpful for nonassertive types, Word offers several flavors of help that require no thought on your part. You don't even have to look very hard to find these helpful hints.

Magic Pop-Up Name Tags

Don't knock it—especially those of you who never forget a face, but can't remember a name if your life depended on it. Just look at the Word toolbars. Can you remember which button is which? Sometimes the pictures just don't cut it (A paintbrush? Light bulb? A bent arrow?). Word provides a simple way to remember what the heck any button is used for on any toolbar, and it requires minimal effort. Simply let your mouse arrow float over the button. Don't press any mouse buttons; just wait a moment. Magically, the descriptive name of the button will appear just below the button. In the past, Microsoft has provided a routine method of learning the Word product. Each time you started Word, you could get a quick random tip about some feature, then it would go away until a new one appears the next time you start Word. After a few months you would have been exposed to most of the features in a steady, painless way.

Tip of the Day

Research says if you learn a little bit each day, it's painless and you learn a lot more. That's the thought behind the Tip of the Day in Word 97. Each day, as you start up Word 97, you can be greeted by a single random feature or productivity tip. Read it, then it's off your screen until tomorrow's lesson.

Good news—the Tip of the Day feature is still available in Word 97, but first you have to turn it on. Open the **Tools** menu and click **Options**. Just click to mark the **Show The Tip of the Day At Startup** check box in the **Options** dialog box. Later in this chapter, you will learn how to open this dialog box by clicking on your Office Assistant.

The Office Assistant

You can now have your own little expert assistant give you the grand tour of every feature and function available in Word 97, and only when you need it. At first, it may seem silly to have a dopey dog or ugly cat sitting in the corner of your screen. But these Office Assistants, as they are called, grow on you. Each will try to guess what you need help with based with the previous actions you perform. Or, you can ask your Assistant directly for help whenever you want, just by clicking on the Assistant. You'll have the option to search for specific help on something, or type in a question, and the Assistant will provide relevant Help topics.

Different Assistants are available and each has a slightly different personality; some are more animated and have lots of sound effects (like the paper clip), and some are more quiet and reserved (like Shakespeare). No matter which Assistant you choose, they all have the same effectiveness, which is to help you solve your word processing problems and learn to use Word 97 quickly and painlessly.

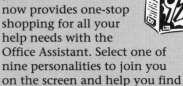

Office Assistant Word 97 now provides one-stop shopping for all your help needs with the Office Assistant. Select one of nine personalities to join you on the screen and help you find the answers when you need them.

Why Should I Try an Assistant?

Microsoft took a big step in the right direction with the Office Assistants. They've given us one place to look for all the help that exists. No more clicking through all the different books (although you can still do that), or searching through the indexed help listing. It's got enough intelligence to stay out of your way and yet give you a subtle hint when it can guide you to a better way of doing something. And help appears at the appropriate time. For instance, you won't be bothered with help in placing a table across multiple pages until your table starts growing across multiple pages.

Here's another example of how the Assistants can help. I've grown so accustomed to the Word dialog boxes that I sometimes hit the **Enter** key right away, accidentally closing a modified document before saving it. With the Office Assistant awake, I now hear this dog yapping on my screen, trying its hardest to protect my document. It's the right amount of silliness to awaken you before making a big mistake.

Choosing Your Own Assistant

 If your Assistant isn't yet on the screen, click the **Office Assistant** button on the Standard toolbar (or press **F1**). You'll always see the same assistant until you decide to change it.

To change your Assistant, right-click anywhere on the **Assistant** and click the **Choose Assistant** command. You'll see the box where you can page through and sample each of them, before deciding to adopt one. If one doesn't work out for you, throw it back and try another. Click the **OK** button to set the current Assistant to be your latest buddy.

You can pick your friends and you can pick your Assistant.

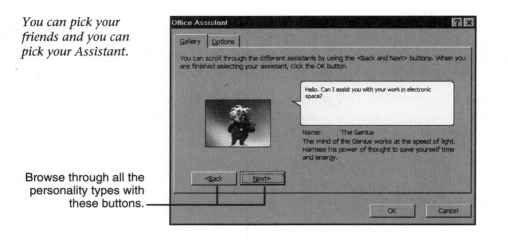

Browse through all the personality types with these buttons.

Don't Forget the Tip

You may find it amusing to have your Assistant on the screen all the time. If you don't make many mistakes, the Assistant won't have much need to help you. In fact, your once-animated Assistant may appear to be bored stiff. But that doesn't mean they're asleep! They keep watching, and if they have a relevant idea for your current activity, a small light bulb icon will appear in the upper-right corner of the Assistant window. To see their idea, click the light bulb.

The lightbulb means your Assistant has a Tip for you.

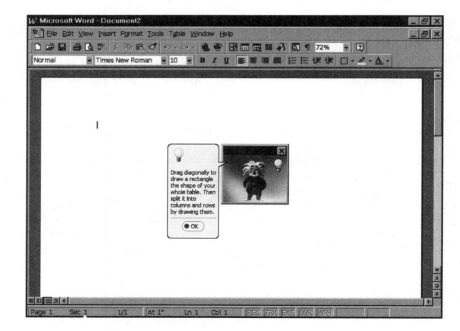

These tips will automatically suggest ways to use Word 97 more quickly and efficiently, like when you're trying to create a big table, or trying to change margins or tabs. The tips are also a great way to get a lot of information about what's going on with some of the new features in Word 97.

If you don't want to wait for the light bulb to appear, you can go see the tips by right clicking your **Assistant**. In the menu that appears, click the **Tips** option. If more than one tip is currently available, you'll be able to browse through them by clicking the **Back** and **Next** buttons.

Asking Your Assistant for Help

The Assistant can't always read your mind, so if you want to ask it a question, go right ahead. Just click it! A balloon of information will appear on your screen. The top half lists help topics related to your current activity, and the bottom half has navigation buttons taking you to the other help functions, like Tips screen and Search. In the middle you see a box where you can type your personal request.

Have some fun. Microsoft packed some real intelligence into this Assistant that actually draws you into the process of asking questions. You can now ask for information using common everyday language, and you'll get the help you need—also in plain English. For example, type **How do I create a Web page?** In response, your Assistant provides a list of possible answers (all about creating a Web page) and you can choose any or all of them to get more help. In this example, one answer you might click to choose is **Tips For Creating Web Pages** to get plenty of good ideas to get started. Be as creative or bold as you dare with the questions you type—it's a great stress-reliever, and it may even help answer your questions.

Customizing Your Assistant

You don't like something about your Assistant? You prefer not to hear the sound effects? You want to be bothered with only the highest priority tips? Then customize your Assistant

Right-click your Assistant to customize.

Word 97 provides a customization menu to tweak how much or how little your friend helps. To open this menu, right-click anywhere on your **Assistant** and click the **Options** command. Here you'll find lots of good choices. Among the better ones:

➤ **Guess Help Topics** This option keeps the Help engine running in the background to anticipate the help you'll need based on your actions.

➤ **Keyboard Shortcuts** You can have the keyboard equivalent of all help tasks for those fingers quicker on the keyboard than the mouse.

➤ **Only Show High Priority Tips** This shows only the tips that relate to time-saving features.

➤ **Show the Tip of the Day at Startup** This is a painless way to slowly and steadily ingest all the features and tips of Word 97.

Ask your Assistant for help.

Click to open any of these help topics.

Type your question using everyday words here.

Browse through some tips by clicking here.

Another shortcut to the Options dialog box.

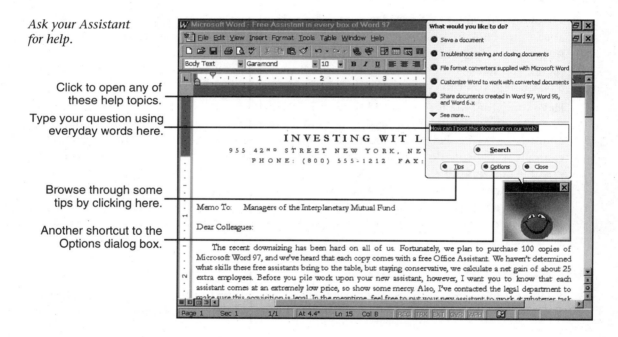

What Happened to the Help Key?

In Word 97, the F1 key now brings up the Office Assistant by default. If you prefer to have the F1 key open the Help Topics (the look-it-up-yourself method), you'll need to change your Assistant Options. Right–click your **Assistant** and choose **Options**. Remove the check from the **Respond to F1** key option, then press the **OK** button. It's back.

You'll want to make sure your Assistant stays out of your way.

Make your Assistant behave by customizing it.

Turn off Assistant sounds here.

This button lets you see the same tips over again.

See a new tip each time you start Word by clicking here.

Dumping Your Assistant

To get rid of your Assistant, just close the window. You can bring it back anytime by clicking the **Office Assistant** button on the Standard toolbar.

If you're dumping your Assistant because you think you've seen all of the animation available, you're probably wrong! Each time you start Word 97, different sets of animation are chosen for the same character, and the variation is quite refreshing for a computer program.

The Help Menu: A Library Stuffed Inside Your Computer

Where are all the paper manuals that used to come inside the boxes of computer software? The information is still in there, but it's not written on paper anymore. All the Word 97 manuals, and there are actually dozens of them, are included as a software program on your program disks or CD. The help gets loaded into your computer during installation and is ready when you beckon for it.

You can find these books by clicking to open the **Help** menu and choosing **Microsoft Word Help**. You'll see a dialog box where you can browse books, look up something in an index, or search for specific combinations of words.

Looking for some good help?

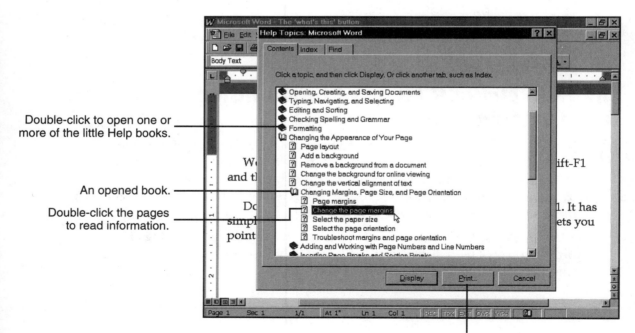

The Little Help Books

Click on the **Help** menu and then select **Contents and Index**. Click on the **Contents** tab to bring it to the front. You'll be treated to a collection of little Help books arranged by category. There are literally thousands of pages of Help available in all these little books. You just have to decide which little book to look in. Let's say you want your text to spread out closer to the edges of the paper. Which book might help? You can give **Changing the Appearance of Your Page** a try. Double-click on the book, and you'll see it open and display more little books and some question marks that represent specific answers.

Double-click to open one or more of the little Help books.

An opened book.

Double-click the pages to read information.

Don't forget that you can print any or all of this.

Browsing the Help Index

To use the Help Index, open the **Help** menu and choose the **Microsoft Word Help Topics** command. Now click the **Index** tab on the **Help Topics** dialog box to bring it to the front. In the **Find** text box under number 1, just type the first few letters of the word you want help with, and the text box below it will fill with the closest matches. Then you can click or use the arrow keys to browse around in the list until you find what you're looking for. Click the **Display** button on selected items to see the same help you found in the little Help books.

Print It! You can also print any of these helpful screens by clicking the **Options** menu in the Help screen and choosing the **Print Topic** command.

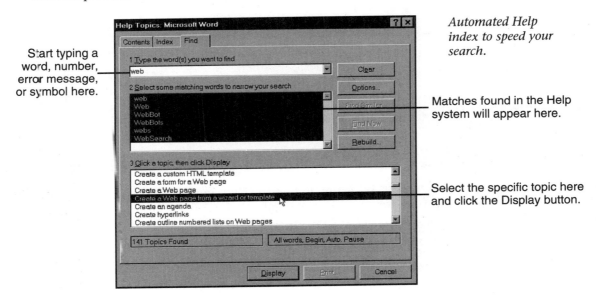

Start typing a word, number, error message, or symbol here.

Automated Help index to speed your search.

Matches found in the Help system will appear here.

Select the specific topic here and click the Display button.

Using the Find Feature of Help

Start to play with the Find feature of Help in Word 97 and see how quickly you can zip through the alphabet. You can search for help by using any combination of words that explain your needs. If a word doesn't show up, it means it's not listed. Try another. Even if you aren't sure of what words to use, you can use similar forms of a word. For example, if you're having problems printing because text is getting chopped off the page, you could try to enter **text cut print** in the Find text box. Word will do its best to figure out what you're asking for and will provide a variety of answers. The correct solution is found and displayed in the following figure. Be creative and test the range of words you can work with.

Finally someone
understands me.

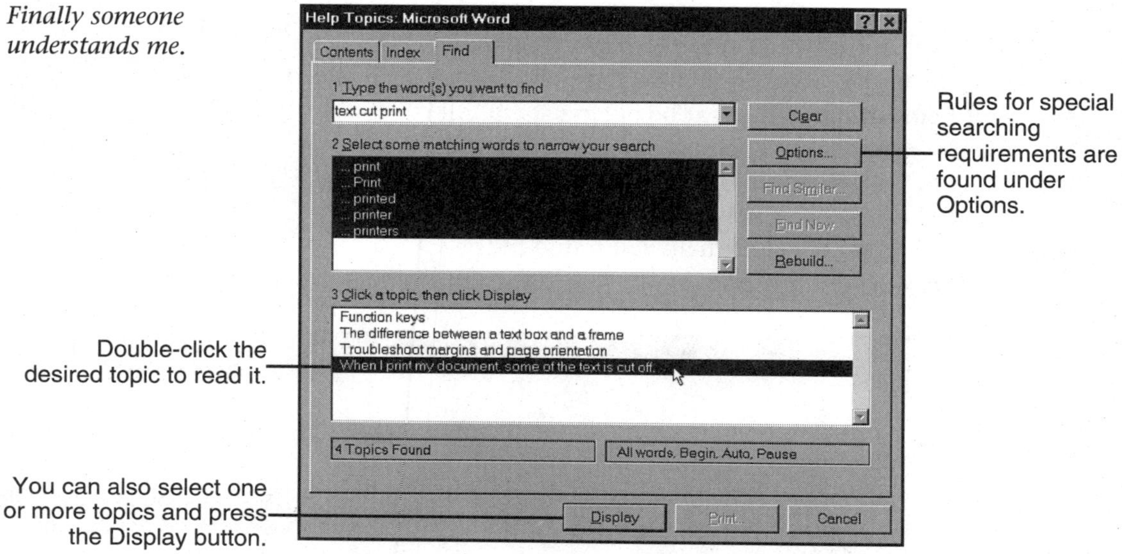

Double-click the
desired topic to read it.

You can also select one
or more topics and press
the Display button.

Rules for special
searching
requirements are
found under
Options.

Click the "What's This?" Command to Point and Learn

You can use the **What's This?** command on the **Help** menu to help you learn just about anything on your Word 97 screens. You can discover what a button on a toolbar really does, what format codes are applied to any text in your document, or learn more details about an option before you choose it.

For example, let's say you don't have a clue as to the purpose of the button sitting next to Paste on the Formatting toolbar. Open the **Help** menu, click **What's This?**, and then go and click on that unknown button. This help feature won't activate that button, but instead provides a descriptive dialog box telling you this is the Format Painter button, and it's used to copy formatting. It even tells you how and when you might want to use this button.

As another example, what if you want the details on some interesting formatting that captures your eye inside a document you've just received? Click the same **What's This?** button and then click directly on the formatting you want to explore. You'll be rewarded with detailed formatting information of every aspect from font to paragraph and page details.

If you change your mind and want to get rid of the **What's This?** pointer and return your normal mouse arrow, click on anything just to unload it, or you can press the **Escape** key. This action returns you safe and sound to normal operation.

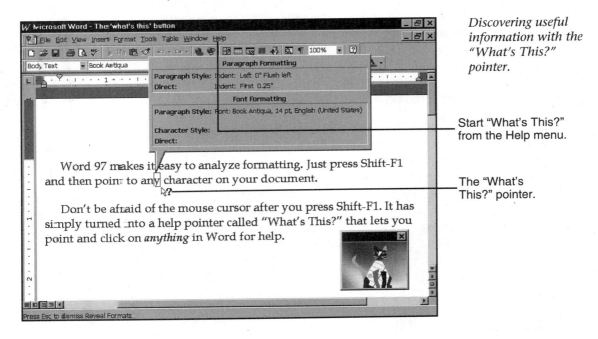

Discovering useful information with the "What's This?" pointer.

Start "What's This?" from the Help menu.

The "What's This?" pointer.

Keyboard Shortcut

Keyboard lovers (and mouse haters) will appreciate being able to select the **What's This?** pointer by holding down the **Shift** key and pressing the **F1** key. This same **Shift+F1** key combination will get rid of the Help pointer if you no longer need it.

Help from the Web

The fourth item on the Help menu is called Microsoft on the Web. It provides a direct link to Microsoft's Web site, containing the very latest information and tips. When you choose one of these options, Word 97 will start your Internet Web browser (assuming you have one) and point it to the right place.

WordPerfect Users Can Join the Bandwagon

If you happen to know WordPerfect but are new to Word, try the **WordPerfect Help** command. It's a great way to put your previous knowledge to productive use. You'll find a great cross-reference guide of the commands you're familiar with, and demos of how this task is accomplished in Word. If you are a WordPerfect user who really hates Word but have to use it, you can always use the combination keys you remember from WordPerfect, and they will function correctly in Word! How the heck did that happen?

About Microsoft Word

The remaining command is the About Microsoft Word command. If you have time to waste, you can read the licensing information for your copy of Word. But, if you click the **System Info** button, the dialog box that appears does provide some helpful, although very technical, information on your computer and programs (if yours doesn't work, you may not have installed it. Use the guidelines in Chapter 2 if you'd like to install this optional feature). You might be asked to peek in here someday to get some information to help solve a problem you're having. Technical support people love this kind of information to help debug a problem. How can you get in touch with Technical Support people for Word 97? Try clicking the **Tech Support** button located directly under **System Info**.... It describes steps you can take to get more help, including telephone numbers and e-mail addresses.

Troubleshooting with Help

What's the best thing to do if something is not working as planned? A good suggestion is to try searching on the word *Troubleshoot*. That's the term that Word 97 uses to explain how to fix something that's broken. When you type the word **troubleshoot** in either the Find or Index tabs, you'll find more than 20 general topics covering everything from bookmarks to tables, and each entry contains up to ten different problems relating to that topic. Active buttons on the help screen reveal the actions to take to resolve the problem, easiest ones first. The help screen stays on top so you can see it. When you finish doing what Help suggests, it will ask you if the problem is fixed. If not, the Help screen will provide the next logical steps to take. This is a mild form of entertainment. It sure beats the alternative of shouting angrily at your machine.

Oops! I Think I Broke It! Troubleshooting has been made easier in Word 97. Just enter the word **troubleshoot** in the Index or Find portions of Word Help Topics, and you'll find dozens of step-by-step procedures to guide you through the problem.

The Least You Need to Know

Getting help in Word 97 does not require a call to 911. It's much easier to use the built-in Help features described in this chapter.

What do I do if I need help fast?

If you're using Word 97, just press the **F1** key. You'll get the complete online help program.

Can I just point to something on my screen and get specific help about it?

Sure. Just press **Shift+F1** (or click the **What's This?** command on the Help menu) to get a help pointer and move it anywhere on the screen to click on the exact detail that may be troubling you.

What's this bouncing paper clip doing on my screen?

That's the new Word 97 Office Assistant, and the paper clip is one of nine different personalities programmed to help you. They sense when you need help and offer suggestions. They provide room to type questions and search for answers.

Do I have any control over this Office Assistant?

Yes, you can change the urgency levels for specific events, and alter the sound effects. Just right-click on your Assistant and choose the **Options** command to locate the settings.

Can you help me troubleshoot my problem?

You said the magic word. Use the **Help** menu command to search for help on anything in Word. For example, **troubleshoot** is a particularly helpful word to search for, in combination with another word describing your problem (such as **troubleshoot printing**).

Chapter 5

Basic Editing and Text Formatting

In This Chapter

➤ Different ways to select text

➤ Review of Cut, Copy, and Paste

➤ Choosing Bold, Italic, and Underline

➤ Selecting a different font

➤ Quick ways to change font size

➤ Copying a good format from one place to another

So now you've got words on the page, and they basically say what you want to say. But there's no pizzazz?! You want more. You've seen it in magazines, posters, and those impersonal form letters in the mail. Wild formatting, huge lettering, and vivid colors fill the page!

Yes, you can certainly cut out assorted fancy letters from newspapers and magazines, and then paste them letter-by-letter onto your sheet of paper, but that's usually done when you want to remain anonymous. How can you get Word 97 to do the kind of stuff you'll be proud of? Sit back and enjoy; we'll break no laws (except perhaps those of good taste) on this subject of character formatting.

What Is Selected Text, and How Do You Select It?

This is a chapter about changing the basic look of your text. If the text is already in your document, you must choose exactly which text you want to change. This is called *Selecting*. You must always *select* text before you can format it, move it, or get excited about it.

Selected text typically doesn't stay selected for a long time. It's simply a middle step necessary for your decision to change something.

You can select text several different ways. No matter how it is done, selected text will always look the same. That's how you know it's currently selected. It usually appears in reverse-video on your screen, meaning if you usually see black letters on a white background, selected text will be white letters on a black background.

One at a Time You can select only one group of words at a time in your document. More than one would be too confusing, so it's just as well.

Selecting Text with Your Mouse

Most people find it's easiest to select text by using the mouse. Open any document containing some text, and move the mouse arrow until it hovers somewhere over some words in your document. Now click the left mouse button, hold it down, and drag your mouse in any direction. Then let go of the mouse button. See what's there? Congratulations! You have just selected text!

This text has been "selected."

Selected text. ———

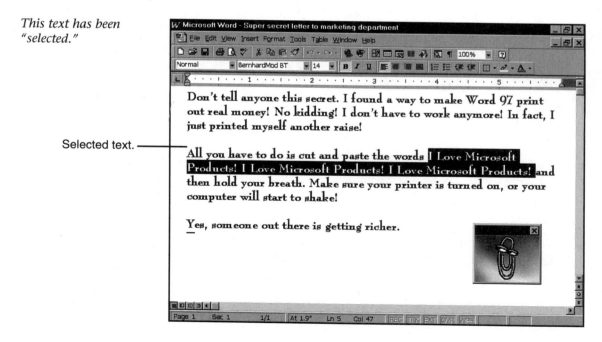

Of course, to be useful, you have to be a good shot with your mouse. Aim well before clicking as you reach the end of your selection, or else you have to start the whole selection process over again. There are other methods to select things, and some will be faster for you, depending on what you're selecting.

The Invisible Selection Bar

You can select an entire line with a single click if you know the trick. Take a closer look at the left border of your text screen. Can't see it, can you? That's because it's invisible, but trust me, it's still there. It's called the *selection bar*, and it always exists as a single thin strip on the left border of your entire document. By clicking in this area, you are selecting everything on this line. Try it, because it's a very common and useful way to select multiple lines or paragraphs of text. Move your mouse pointer to the far left side of an opened document, as shown in the figure. The cursor will change to an arrow, which can be a helpful reminder that you are now inside the selection bar. Click the left mouse button while you're in this area to select an entire line, or click and drag (up and down in the selection bar) to select multiple lines at a time.

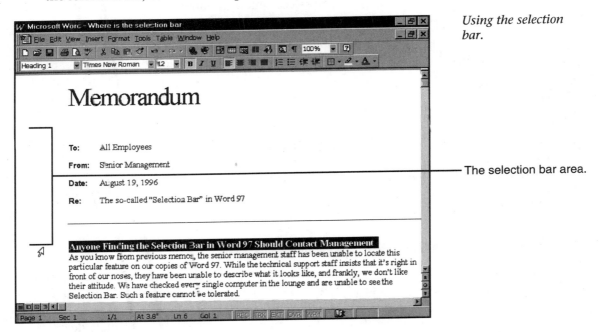

Using the selection bar.

The selection bar area.

Selection Quickies

If you find this method of selecting text a drag, here are some shortcuts you can use when selecting text with the mouse:

To Select This:	Do This:
Word	Double-click on the word
Sentence	Press the **Ctrl** key and click anywhere in the sentence
Paragraph	Triple-click anywhere inside the paragraph
Line	Click in the selection bar next to the line
Multiple Lines	Click and drag in the selection bar next to the lines
Whole document	Open the **Edit** menu and choose the **Select All** command

It's not necessary to have a mouse to do these selection tricks. In fact, sometimes the mouse may be a less convenient way to select. Thank goodness for the keyboard, which provides *hands-on* selecting alternatives for professional typists.

To Select Any Amount of Text Place the insertion point at the start of what you want to select, hold down the **Shift** key, then move the insertion point to the end of the selection. Release the **Shift** key, and your text is selected.

If you prefer to work one finger at a time, move the cursor to where you want to begin the selection, then click the **F8** key. Now use the arrow keys to go to the end—text will be selected automatically. To remove the selection, press **F8** again.

Unselecting Something

If you ever make a mistake and select the wrong text, simply press an arrow key or click anywhere in the document to deselect it.

Deleting Options for Selected Text

Once you've selected your text, you can actually do something with it. The easiest thing to do is get rid of it. Just press the **Delete** key. Bang! It's gone. You can also use the **Backspace** key or the **Cut** button. And don't forget, if you really didn't mean to kill the selected text, you can always click the **Undo** button to undo an inappropriate deletion and give your words a second chance at life. A right-click on selected text also displays the Cut command in the shortcut menu.

Another easy way to delete selected text is to simply start typing the replacement text. The first keyboard letter you press will replace selected text, saving you the time and stress of finding and pressing the Delete key.

Cut, Copy, and Paste

If the term *cut-copy-and-paste* does nothing more than offer daydreams of happy times in kindergarten, you should sit up straight and pay attention! You need to know this before graduating to the fun stuff.

 To cut (or move) selected text, click the **Cut** button on the standard toolbar. Besides deleting, also choose this when you want to *move* selected text.

To copy selected text, click the **Copy** button on the standard toolbar.

 To paste selected text, click the **Paste** button on the standard toolbar.

Copy Your Words to Use Them Again

Sometimes you write stuff that is so good you want to use it again. Once you've selected the part you like, click the **Copy** button on the Standard toolbar. Give it a try.

Hey, big deal; nothing happened, right? Wrong! That **Copy** command just notified millions of little computer nerds living inside your computer. They paid attention and wrote down exactly what you just selected. Your original text is copied into the *clipboard* and will remain there safe and sound.

Now the nerds are waiting for you to tell them exactly where to put the text. Move your cursor (or click) to the area in your document where you want to place the copy. Don't worry if there isn't enough room; any existing things will be pushed around to accommodate your copy.

Now click the **Paste** button. Magically, your selection is copied exactly as it was previously. The trick to copying and pasting is to remember that copying is only the first step. Then you must use the second step called *pasting*.

> **Check This Out...**
>
> **Clipboard** The Windows 97 clipboard is a special storage area hidden inside your computer. Your computer uses the clipboard to store text, numbers, or graphics temporarily as it is moved or copied from one place to another. When you cut or copy something, it gets stuffed *into* the clipboard. When you paste, it comes *from* the clipboard. It's important to remember that the clipboard can hold only one thing at a time, and it's always the *last* thing you've cut or copied.

You Can Keep On Pasting, Keep On Pasting

Maybe your stuff is so good you want it sprinkled everywhere in your document. Do you have to keep going back to select a prior instance and copy it again? Heavens no. Just keep using the **Paste** command and a new copy will continue to appear, wherever your text cursor happens to be. By golly, you can even paste to completely different programs, like WordPerfect or an outgoing e-mail note for the Internet!

Move Your Words with Cut and Paste

If your goal is to move text around, instead of copying text and then deleting the original, save yourself some time and try the **Cut** button. You *cut* the selected text, which gets rid of it from the first place, and then pastes it to a new location directly. This is how confident Windows experts live day-to-day, trusting that the cut text is safe and sound until it's pasted elsewhere. You can do it, too!

Check This Out...

Sentences Start and End Cleanly When you copy or move entire sentences, Word 97 automatically adds or removes extra spaces you may have selected accidentally—as long as the option Smart Cut and Paste is on. To check, open the **Tools** menu and choose **Options**. Click on the **Edit** tab and make sure that **Use Smart Cut and Paste** is selected.

Any time you cut a selection, it's actually copied to the clipboard, which means it's still available to you. That's one of the advantages over the Delete key. If you *delete* a selection, it's gone; but if you *cut* a selection, you still have a chance to use it again somewhere else.

Drag Your Words Around

Try moving selected text another way. After you've selected text, move the mouse over it and the cursor will change to an arrow. Click anywhere inside the selection and hold down the left mouse button for a few moments. The cursor will change appearance slightly (a little box appears at the bottom of the arrow) to let you know it's ready. Now drag the whole thing to a new location. When you reach the new destination, let go of the left mouse button and watch the action. Your selection is moved automatically, and you may have saved some time over using the Cut and Paste buttons.

Check This Out...

Shortcut Menu

Word 97 helps you edit your text quickly with a pop-up menu that appears when you press the right mouse button on selected text. Try it and you'll see the familiar **Cut**, **Copy**, and **Paste** commands at your fingertips.

Please Undo What I Just Did

 Undo has always been an important tool, especially when your computer doesn't listen to you. After you've done something you've regretted (to your document), click the **Undo** button. If it was a few steps back in time, you can click on the little arrow attached to the Undo button and browse through a scrollable list of your last zillion activities. This helps you back up to precisely the point you want. When you undo an action, you also undo all actions above it in the list.

If you accidentally Undo too far, and want something put back the way it was, you can use the Redo button the same way. You'll find both of these buttons on the Standard toolbar.

You can Undo almost anything, including typing, cutting and pasting, formatting, and so on, but not everything. The button label changes to **Can't Undo** if you cannot reverse the last action.

Who's a Character, and What's Formatting?

Character is another computer term. It means a single letter of the alphabet (or a single number or symbol). The word antidisestablishmentarianism is made up of 28 characters.

Character formatting is the process of changing how a character looks. For example, through character formatting you can make a word bold, italic, or underline. You can also change the size of text (its *point size*), making it bigger or smaller. You can also change its style by choosing a different *font*.

Making Your Characters Bold

To initiate bold, click the **Bold** button on the Formatting toolbar. From now on, anything you type will be in bold—that is, of course, until you want to turn it off. It's not hard to do that, either. Simply click the **Bold** button again!

Doing the Italic Thing

Likewise, to initiate an italic appearance, click the **Italic** button on the Formatting toolbar. When finished typing, click **Italic** again to turn it off.

If you get tired of looking at an italicized portion of your document, you can get rid of it by first selecting it, then pressing **Ctrl+I** or the **Italic** button. Just like the Bold commands, this works like a toggle—first on, then off, as many times as you change your mind.

Check This Out...

Apply Formatting Anytime You can just as easily apply Bold, Italic, and Underline to existing text. Simply select the text to be formatted, then click any of these three formatting buttons.

Underlining What's Important

You've got the idea now. Click the **Underline** button on the Formatting toolbar and then start typing underlined text. Click it again to turn it off.

The Bold Underlined Italic Look

Yes, you can mix and match any of these formatting commands. Your text can be bold and italic, underlined and bold, or anything you feel is important. You can even alternate the formatting of individual letters of each word, but you probably don't have the time.

Returning to Normal (or Regular)

You can turn off all character formatting by pressing the **Ctrl+Spacebar** key combination. This also works on selected text containing any combination of character formatting. Simply select the range of text and press **Ctrl+Spacebar**. If you want to get rid of all character formatting, no matter what or where, select the entire document and then press **Ctrl+Shift+Z**. You'll be left with plain, unadulterated text (called *regular*) in the default font and size.

Inserting Symbols to Suit You

Perhaps you want to include one of those unusual words you see in the comics. You know, the weird symbols representing something that shouldn't be in print, like (#!*#!*). Better yet, how about including the symbols that are easy to recognize, like a trademark, or copyright, or fractions?

All these symbols can be found by using the **Symbol** command in the **Insert** menu. It displays hundreds of symbols to choose from. You can double-click the symbol and it will appear in your document at the current insertion point. If the location isn't what you want, you can move it or cut-and-paste it to another location.

Check This Out...

Uppercase and Lowercase Conversions

A neat trick available in Word 97 is called the case rotation. It alternates letters between uppercase and lowercase in a chunk of selected text. The secret key combination is **Shift+F3**. The first rotation capitalizes the first letter in all words in the selection. Press **Shift+F3** again, and all letters will be capitalized. Press it again, and they will all be lowercase again.

You can also delete the symbol, if you don't like it. Just select it and press the **Delete** key. Or, even easier, just press the **Undo** button on the Standard toolbar.

Symbols of our time.

Double-click to select and copy a symbol to the current insertion point.

Fonts and Sizes: How the Other Half Lives

Hope you aren't tired yet, because we've only skimmed the surface of the vast character formatting jungle. Sure, the bold-italic-underline stuff helps, but the letters are still shaped the same way. That's called a *font*. You can change fonts whenever you want, and hundreds of fonts are available globally. When you installed Windows 95 or Windows NT, you also installed many fonts. Installing Word 97 gives you even more to play with. And if that's not enough, you can purchase additional fonts to install and make available to Word 97. Ask your computer salesperson for more information on purchasing and installing additional fonts. What does a different font look like? Here's a sample:

DOES THE COMIC FONT APPEAR HUMOROUS TO YOU?

Wake up your reader with the Impact font.

The Brush Script is casual enough for anyone.

Write Your Own Invitation With Palace Script!

Those first two fonts are included for you in Word 97; the last two I've included as examples of fonts you can purchase to add to your repertoire of tools in Word 97.

Changing Your Font

To change to a different font, click the down arrow in the font box on the formatting toolbar. A list of all fonts available will drop down for you to view. The list is alphabetical, in case you know the name of the font you desire. Browse the list with your mouse or arrow keys and press **Enter** (or click) on the font you want. The font name you picked should now be displayed in the font box. Now start typing. Everything will appear in the new font, and it should print, as well.

You can also change the font of existing text by first selecting it. Then choose a font from the font drop-down list on the formatting toolbar, and the selected text is changed to the new font. If more than one font is used in the selection, they will all be converted to the single new font.

Squander years choosing from among the many built-in fonts!

Your most recent font selections are copied above this line for convenience.

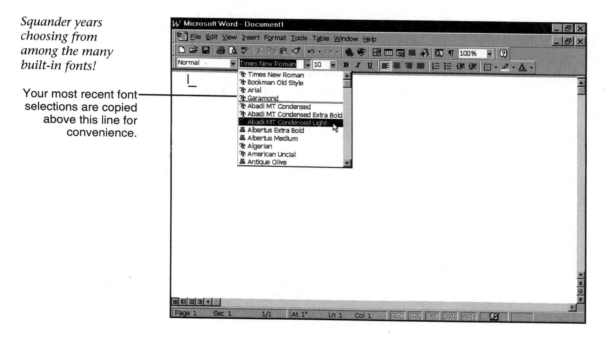

Want More Fonts?

Maybe you are bored with the more than 50 fonts included with Word 97. How can you get more? Rather easily. Thousands are available in stores, mail-order catalogs, or on computer bulletin boards. Some are free, and some cost a great deal of money. You can install the fonts by using the Control Panel in Windows 95 or Windows NT.

Techno Talk

What Is a TT Font?

The TT displayed next to many of the fonts designates them as TrueType fonts, which means they print out exactly as you see them on the screen. Other fonts may have a little printer icon next to them. These are called printer fonts, and they are built into your printer. There is no guarantee that you will see the font correctly on the screen, but it will certainly print in the correct font. The other fonts are merely screen displays, and with these fonts there is no guarantee that you will print what you see. But usually you will.

Only in the last few years has this problem of printing WYSIWYG (pronounced whizzy-wig and stands for What-You-See-Is-What-You-Get) has been solved. Using TrueType fonts is the easiest way to guarantee that your document prints exactly as it appears on your computer screen.

If Size Is Important

You can make your text appear and print larger or smaller by changing the *size* of the current font, just as easily as you made bold or italic, and you have many sizes to choose from. To change the font size, click the **Font Size** box in the Formatting toolbar (scroll through the valid font size numbers). Choose a larger number to make it bigger, and vice versa. If it's a TrueType font, you can also type in sizes outside the displayed range, and your computer will do its darnedest to display it.

Check This Out...

Point Size The correct way to refer to font size is to use the term *point*. The typical document uses a 10– or 12-point font. A point is 1/72 inch. The larger the point size, the larger the letters will appear. Most fonts can be sized from 4 points to 127 points.

The Whole Formatting Enchilada at Your Fingertips

There is yet another way to obtain all of the character formatting tips described in this chapter, and all of them are available in a single dialog box. It's called the Font dialog box, and you can get to it by opening the **Format** menu and then clicking the **Font** command.

One of the best reasons to use this method is the Preview box that displays your choice of formatting *before* you apply it. Take a peek.

Take a Shortcut to Your Fonts! You can also right-click to get the shortcut menu, which has the Font option conveniently located for your benefit. You can use this on selected text or at the beginning of an insertion point for new text.

*The Font dialog box
has it all!*

Click to choose
font, style, and
size from the lists.

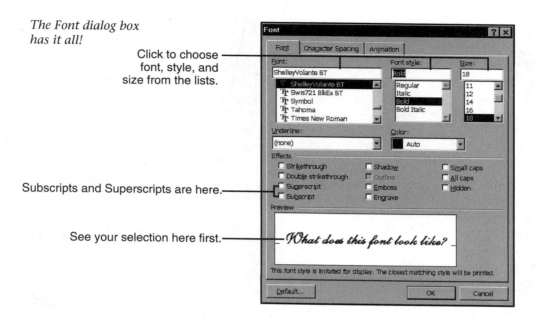

Subscripts and Superscripts are here.

See your selection here first.

Another reason to use this dialog box is to set your default font to whatever combination you like best. Choose the font features you want, then take a look at it in the preview box to make sure it's the way you like it, and then click the **Default** button.

You'll find plenty to wile away the hours while you're inside the Font Dialog box. Check out these features:

Animate Your Words! You can really liven up your text by making the words flash, move, and glisten. Select the text you want to animate, or click the word you want to animate. Open the **Font** dialog box and click the **Animation** tab. Click the effect you want in the Animations box. You can apply only one animation effect at a time. No, these animated effects will not print. When you get bored with the animation, select the text, and then click **None** in the Animations box.

➤ **Give Your Words a Shove Higher or Lower**
Superscript text flies above any normal text, like a reference to a footnote, or the degree symbol or an exponent. *Subscript* text trudges along below normal text. Click the **Superscript** or **Subscript** check box in the Formatting dialog box to change selected text or start the insertion point. If they appear too large, make them smaller by simply changing the Font size in this dialog box. Also, some fonts can't, or won't, appear on your screen as super- or subscript, but they will print out correctly. You have to experiment for yourself (try using Print Preview to see them before printing).

➤ **Character Spacing** Fanatics may want to adjust the spacing between their letters, like a capital T creeping over into little e's private space. It's called Kerning, and if you want to try, click the **Character Spacing** tab in the Font dialog box.

➤ **Animate Your Words**   You can make your word blink, buzz, and baffle your reader. Click the **Animate** tab and choose your weapon from the scrollable list.

Copy Good Formatting from Here to There

Suppose that you just finished choosing the most incredible combination of formatting options available and you want to apply it to existing text somewhere else. Is there a shortcut that can speed things up? You bet, and it's called the Format Painter.

Even if you don't get around to it right away, you can still copy formatting from one place to another later. In your document, find the area of formatting you like and click anywhere inside of it. Then click the **Format Painter** button on the Standard toolbar. Go to the text where you want the formatting to be applied and highlight it. That's it; the formatting will be applied automatically. When you are done, press **Esc**, or click the **Format Painter** again to avoid littering your document with these kinds of changes.

Viewing Format Settings

Word 97 displays text as it will look when it's printed. Fanatics might worry at first that Word doesn't use formatting codes to indicate the formatting details (like WordPerfect). Fret not, I say! To check the formats of a particular character or paragraph, click the **What's This?** command on the **Help** menu. When the mouse arrow changes into a flying question mark, hunt down and click the text you want to check. Word will display the formatting codes for the selected text. To get rid of this information when you are finished, press the **Esc** key.

The Least You Need to Know

Selecting and formatting text is a big deal. This skill deserves to be rewarded. Grab something tasty and ponder the importance of what you've learned.

What's the fastest way to select text?

If you are good with a mouse, just click and drag to select text. If you prefer the keyboard, hold down the **Shift** and use the arrow keys. To get real fancy and select with only one hand, click **F8** first and then use the arrow keys.

Why would anyone want to select text?

To cut, copy, or paste it somewhere else, and Word gives you these three buttons (**Cut**, **Copy**, and **Paste**) on the Standard toolbar. You can also right-click on selected text and see these three commands on the shortcut menu.

Can I do this all using only the mouse?

Yes, after selecting text you can click and drag it to another location.

What else can I do with selected text?

You can quickly change the way it looks by clicking any of the buttons on the Formatting toolbar, including Bold, Italic, and Underline, and that's just for starters. Try clicking and changing the type of Font, or the Font Size, to spice up your document.

How can I make lots of formatting changes at once?

Aim for the Font dialog box. Open the **Format** menu and click **Font**. Choose everything you need, click **OK**, and start typing!

Can I copy just the formatting features from one good area to another?

Sure, but make sure you start by clicking anywhere inside of the "good" stuff. Next, click the **Format Painter** button on the Formatting toolbar. Finally, select the target text and the identical formatting will be applied immediately.

My friend's document contains an interesting font. Can I find out what it's called?

Yes. Word 97 comes with a super-snooper for requests like this. Just open the **Help** menu, click the **What's This?** command, and then click on the unsuspecting text. The details will be revealed!

Chapter 6

Proofing Tools (Spelling and Grammar and the Thesaurus)

In This Chapter

➤ Spell checking your document

➤ AutoText and AutoCorrect miracles

➤ Using the Thesaurus

➤ Getting to know the Grammar Checker

Once in a while, you run into a gadget that makes you feel like you've arrived in the future. Maybe it's your first jet ride, browsing your first Web page, or finding that first gray hair. The new combined Spelling & Grammar Checker in Word 97 does it for me. These tools, along with the improved Thesaurus, will help you find better words and use them correctly.

You won't waste anymore of your precious time running the Spell Checker at the end of a document. It runs continuously while you type, looking up each word and underlining it with a red wavy line if it's not found in the dictionary. It even stores the suggested spelling along with that wavy line, hoping that you will ask to change it.

Those Wavy Red Lines

Unless you're an expert speller, you may notice that several words you typed are underlined with a wavy red line. These words are misspelled, or don't exist in Word's dictionary. Word 97 has installed a little computer troll under your keyboard, watching each word as you type it. The instant you misspell a word, the troll does the wavy underline thing (you actually have to move the insertion point off the word, indicating that you are finished with it, before it is analyzed by the Spell Checker). The red wavy line doesn't print, and no formatting tool can get rid of it, but you can make it go away by correcting the spelling mistake.

How do you find the correct spelling? Try placing the mouse pointer over the word that has a wavy red line under it and click the right mouse button. Word displays a list of suggested spellings. Click the correct spelling from the list displayed.

Spell Checking faster than you can misspell.

A right-mouse click on words provides spelling assistance.

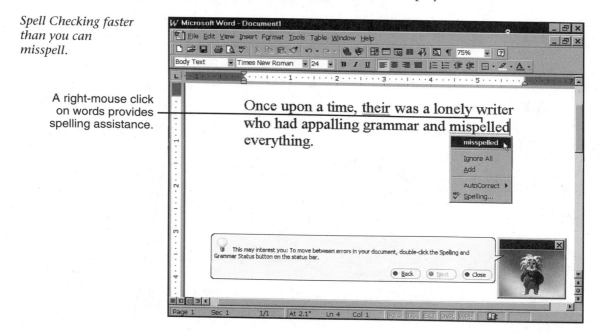

Turning Your Spell Checker On or Off

If you don't have any red wavy lines, you're either a great speller or someone has changed your Spell Checker default settings. By default, spelling is checked automatically as you type, but you can choose to turn this feature off or back on again. To turn on the Spell Checker to check automatically while you type, open the **Tools** menu and select the **Options** command. Click the **Spelling** tab to bring it to the front. To have Word check spelling automatically as you type, select the **Check spelling as you type** check box (or clear the check box to turn automatic spell checking off). If you are allergic to the red wavy lines, you can click to check the **Hide spelling errors in this document** option, and the lines will disappear (this assumes you will be responsible for correcting your spelling errors, like in the old days). Press **OK** to return to your document.

Spelling options available in Word 97.

Make sure this is checked for automatic Spell Checking.

About Word's Spell Checker

When Word 97 checks a document for spelling errors, it looks everywhere, including headers, footers, footnotes, and annotations. Also, if you repeat a word accidentally, or miscapitalize it, Word will let you know with that red wavy underline.

You don't have to fix all of the wavy underlined words as they occur. Some people are paranoid and correct the words immediately, while others (real typists) never even look at the screen while they type. Still others like the red lines and do their best to fill a document with them.

After you finish your document (or reach a convenient stopping point), you can clean up all the misspellings. Those red wavy lines are like flags on a golf course, telling you Word has already found the mistake, compared it with its dictionary, and provided alternatives for you to choose from. All this happened while you continued to type or sipped coffee.

 You can manually start Spell Checking your document by clicking the **Spelling and Grammar** button on the Standard toolbar. If everything is hunky-dory, nothing much will happen, except that you will see a message box telling you that Spell Checker has finished checking your document. If your fingers moved a little faster than your brain, however, you may have a few misspelled words. If so, you will be presented with the Spelling dialog box.

Using the Spelling dialog box.

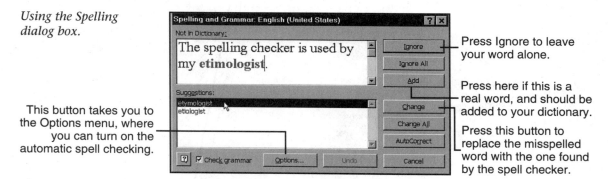

Press Ignore to leave your word alone.

Press here if this is a real word, and should be added to your dictionary.

Press this button to replace the misspelled word with the one found by the spell checker.

This button takes you to the Options menu, where you can turn on the automatic spell checking.

The **Spelling** dialog box displays the misspelled word and suggests alternative spellings. To correct the misspelling, select the correct word and click the **Change** button. If the word isn't in the list, you can type it in the Change To box. Or if the word is okay, you can click the **Ignore** button to skip over the word without making any changes. Word will immediately move to the next misspelled word, and you can continue the process until all misspellings have been corrected (or ignored). A dialog box will appear when the process is finished, telling you that Spell Checker is finished. The following table gives you more information about what the options in the **Spelling** dialog box do.

Check This Out...

Miscellaneous Corrections

There are some interesting miscellaneous items that the Spell Checker will find. For instance, if two identical words are found next to each other, the second instance will be underlined, indicating that one of them should be deleted. But Word also knows that "had had" is often correct and leaves them alone. (How about that?)

Also, if any capital letters occur inside of a single word, the word is underlined for your inspection.

Button Description for the Spelling Dialog Box

Correct the spelling of the word	If you agree with the selected word in the **Suggestions** box, just click on the **Change** button. If you want to, you can type your own correction or select an alternative from the Suggestions list box.
Ignore or Ignore All	Click this button if your word really is a word, such as names, acronyms, and products that often appear in documents. Word will no longer stop if it finds any more of these words existing in your document.
Change or Change All	Press this button if you want to change every word that's spelled a certain way in your document. It acts just like search and replace, and it's helpful if you accidentally misspell or mistype some words often.
Add	There's nothing more annoying than Word always telling you a common word, like your name or street address, is misspelled. To make these words a permanent part of the dictionary in Word, click the **Add** button.
AutoCorrect	This is an incredibly powerful tool that fixes mistakes as you make them. Common typing errors (like typing *teh* for *the* or *adn* for *and*) are changed instantly without wasting your time. If you have your own favorite misspellings, you can add them, along with the correct spelling to this list for instant changing.
Delete the repeated word	If a word is repeated twice and it shouldn't be, click on the **Delete** button. You won't see this button unless Word encounters a repeated word.
Undo a previous correction	You can undo any of your last corrections in your document by clicking on **Undo Last**. This is great in case you click on the **Change** button only to realize that the last word was spelled correctly in the first place.

Wait! That Really Is a Word!

Many words you type are not included in the Word 97 main dictionary, such as your name, address, abbreviations, or acronyms. You can ignore them or decide to add them to the existing dictionary.

ADD Is Now in Your Shortcut Menu When you right-click a misspelling, you'll find Add on the shortcut menu. Choose it to add this word to your dictionary and Word 97 will remember it forever.

To add the word to the computer dictionary, click the **Add** button in the **Spelling** dialog box. You can also click the right mouse button on a misspelled word to add the word to the dictionary (choose the **Add** command from the pop-up menu). From now on, any occurrence of that word will not trigger a red wavy line or the **Spelling** dialog box. Be extra careful adding words to the dictionary so you don't accidentally enter a mistake.

Creating Your Own Dictionary

Wondering where those words are stored when you click the **Add** button? It's a file called the *standard supplemental dictionary*, and it's stored in the Windows-MSAPPS-Proof folder (the file is named CUSTOM.DIC). You can view this file by opening the **Tools** menu, clicking the **Options** command, pressing the **Spelling** tab to bring it to the front, and pressing the **Custom Dictionaries** button. Finally, press the **Edit** button. You'll see an alphabetical list of all words you have added.

Since Word lets you add more dictionaries, you might want to create one yourself. Start with a new document. Type a list of the words that you want to add to the dictionary (acronyms, your name, and so on) and press the **Enter** key after each word. Click the **Save** button, and in the **Save As Type** box, click **Text Only**. In the **File Name** box, type a name for the custom dictionary, such as **My Business Dictionary**. Close the Word file so that it will be available the next time you check spelling. To use this new dictionary, you must click the **Add** button on the **Custom Dictionaries** dialog box, and locate the dictionary document you just created. It will appear just below the CUSTOM.DIC, with a check mark indicating all active dictionaries. Press the **OK** button and then close the **Options** dialog box. It's now working!

Oh yes, you can follow the same procedure to edit either the CUSTOM.DIC or your new dictionaries in case you accidentally add an incorrect spelling of a word. Just click the **Edit** button while you are in the **Custom Dictionary** dialog box. Word turns off the automatic Spell Checker when editing custom dictionaries. Find the entries you wish to remove and delete them. Save and close this dictionary to save your changes.

Skip Certain Text During Proofing

To speed up a spelling and grammar check, you can prevent Word 97 from checking specialized text such as a list of product names or text in another language.

First select the text that you don't want to check. Open the Tools menu, point to Language, and then click Set Language. In the Mark selected text as box, click **No Proofing** at the top of the list.

Check That Web Page All of these proofing tools work just as well on Web pages you create in Word 97. See Chapter 24 for details on creating your own Web pages.

The Magic of AutoCorrect

How many times do you mistype simple words? A common word is *the*, often mistyped as *teh*, or *and*, often typed *adn*. Technically, these aren't spelling errors because you know how to spell them; your fingers just got ahead of your computer. Word helps you by correcting these flaws on-the-fly using a feature called *AutoCorrect*. Plenty of entries have already been added for you (nearly 500 at last count).

To see what entries you already have stored in AutoCorrect, open the **Tools** menu and select the **AutoCorrect** command. Also notice that Word 97 automatically expands many "symbols" into real symbol characters. For instance, typing **(tm)** automatically turns into the trademark symbol.

AutoCorrect forgives common typing errors before you even notice.

You can add exceptions here.

Common mistyped words

These correct words and symbols are inserted automatically.

67

Check This Out...

The Two Caps Feature Is Smart The two initial caps rule is much smarter than previous versions of Word. It no longer mistakenly corrects CDs, PCs, or any other two initial capitals pattern which does not contain vowels. This really reduces the number of false "corrections."

Accidental usage of the caps lock key is automatically corrected with AutoCorrect. For example, when typing *tHIS* with the Caps Lock key depressed, Word will automatically change the typing to *This* and turn off the Caps Lock key.

AutoCorrect also supports an exception list for the "Capitalize First Letter of Sentence" rule. Word doesn't capitalize words that follow abbreviations from the exception list, and Word even watches as you type and automatically adds words to the list if you change an AutoCorrect action.

There's more. You also can add an AutoCorrect entry during a spelling check. When a word you often misspell or mistype is identified, enter the correct spelling in the **Change To** box. To add the misspelled word and its correct spelling to the list of words and phrases that are corrected automatically, click **AutoCorrect**.

AutoText Will Save You Time!

You can use shortcuts to quickly insert frequently used text or graphics in your documents:

➤ If you store text and graphics as AutoText entries, you can retrieve them by clicking a button or pressing **F3**.

➤ If you store them as AutoCorrect entries, Word inserts them automatically as you type, which you learned about in the last section.

➤ AutoComplete Tips (a feature of AutoText) moves you along faster when creating a letter by watching for the most common boilerplate words or phrases. You start to type "To W" and AutoComplete immediately suggests "To Whom It May Concern." When the suggestion appears, you can press ENTER or F3 to accept the suggestion, or just keep typing to reject it.

AutoText is a helpful way to save time typing out repetitive (or just plain long and boring) words. What kind of words? If you're a pharmacist, you might get tired of typing the word for a bladder-controlling drug called pseudophonyhydroxidine. Wouldn't you much rather type PP and have the magic of AutoText expand it automatically to the correct spelling?

Before AutoText can be really useful to you, you first have to load it with the big words (or sentences or paragraphs) you use most often. Either find a document that already contains your big words or phrases, or start a new document and carefully type them in. Don't forget to spell them correctly. Now select the text or graphics you want to store as an AutoText entry. To store paragraph formatting with the entry, include the paragraph mark in the selection. Open the **Edit** menu and choose the **AutoText** command. In the **Name** box, type the shortcut version you prefer, like pp or baffle. An AutoText name can have up to 32 characters, including spaces. Click the **Add** button and this entry will be stored and ready to use.

By default, Word makes the AutoText entry available to all documents. If you want AutoText entries limited to particular documents, you can specify a template in which you want to store the entry by selecting a template name in the **Make AutoText Entry Available To** box. To put the AutoText entries to work, just start typing your document as you would normally. When it's time to add the big word or phrase, just type the shortcut you stored in AutoText (like pp or baffle) right in your document and then press the **F3** key. The shortcut word will be removed and replaced by the actual big word or phrase it represents. You can also print the list of AutoText entries. Open the **File** menu and choose **Print**. In the **Print What** box, choose **AutoText Entries**, then click **OK**.

New AutoText Toolbar You'll find an organized selection listing of common words and phrases used in writing letters in the new AutoText toolbar. Open the View menu, point to toolbars, and choose AutoText. The All Entries button displays the categories and entries, and there's an AutoText button that takes you to the AutoCorrect dialog box.

Using Your Thesaurus

It's right on the tip of your tongue. I can see it. But you can't, which is why you need a Thesaurus. Using big words can help you appear smarter than you are, and it sure helps when doing a crossword puzzle. Improving vocabulary is a sign of higher intelligence in our species, so the next time you choose a word that doesn't exactly convey the meaning you want, try running it through the Thesaurus first.

To use the Thesaurus, just follow these simple steps. First select the word you want to look up, or move the insertion point anywhere inside the word. Then open the **Tools** menu, point to Language, and select the **Thesaurus** command (or press **Shift+F7**). Your word appears in the **Thesaurus** dialog box in the **Looked Up** drop-down list.

You'll find opposite meanings here.

Click to look up another listed word.

This is the Thesaurus dialog box.

Thesaurus: English (United States)

Looked Up:
Happy

Replace with Synonym:
glad

Meanings:
glad (adj.)
fortunate (adj.)
fitting (adj.)
laughing (adj.)
exhilarated (adj.)
Antonyms

glad
blissful
blithe
cheerful
contented
delighted
gay
gladdened
joyful

Replace   Look Up   Previous   Cancel

Use the Thesaurus When You Can't Think of the Right Word

➤ If the word you selected is not found, enter an alternate word and click **Look Up**.

➤ Choose from the synonyms listed in the Replace with Synonym (or Antonym or Related Word) list box.

➤ To change the synonyms listed, choose from general variations of the selected word that appear in the Meanings box. If the Related Words or Antonyms options are listed under Meanings, select either one to display additional choices.

➤ Look up additional meanings for the word displayed in the Replace with Synonym box by clicking **Look Up**.

➤ Decide whether to replace the selected word. Click the **Replace** button to substitute the selected word with the word displayed in the **Replace with Synonym** box, or click **Cancel** to leave it alone.

➤ If one of the words in the left column is close but not exactly what you want, select it and click the **Look Up** button. The word's synonyms appear in the right column.

➤ If the word that you select has no synonyms, the Thesaurus displays an alphabetical list of words. Type a new, similar word or select **Cancel** to get back to your document.

Opposites Attract

Here's a tip for using the Thesaurus. On those rare occasions that you can't think of *any* words that mean what you want, don't give up! Try thinking of the complete opposite meaning. Quite often, the Thesaurus can take the opposite of what you mean and lead you back to what you really mean. (Work with me on this.)

The secret is in the word *antonym*, which we all learned at some point. It means the opposite, and how happy you'll be if it shows up as the last entry in the Meanings box! You guessed it; if you click **Antonyms**, you'll get a list of opposite meaning words. Fancy that. Now you can be completely opposite in what you wanted to say.

But don't stop there! Now click one of those opposite meanings and press the **Look Up** button. Does it have the word antonym listed? That's your ticket. Selecting the *antonym* of an *antonym* of the word you want often discovers the word that works. It's like two wrongs making a right! It's even easier than it sounds. Here are a few examples:

➤ If you can't think up a single positive description of your boss, try *stingy, lazy, cruel,* or *meatloaf,* and then choose **Antonym**.

➤ There seem to be more words describing laziness than whatever the opposite is. Why is that?

➤ Flipping back and forth between opposite meanings helps you enrich your vocabulary by exposing you to many more words than you would otherwise see.

If you don't find a word with antonyms immediately, keep trying. They aren't included as often as you might like them to be, but the words that include them are very delicious. *Delicious?!* Remember the lesson from the Spell Checker—don't use words unless you know their meaning. A real dictionary, and I'm talking about that fat book sitting on your bookshelf, is still the best tool available for helping you use words correctly. It lets you look up a word and see its definition. Neither the Spell Checker, Thesaurus, nor the Grammar Checker (which you are about to learn), can tell you the true meaning, and the proper usage, of any word.

Grammar Checker

If you're a victim of poor grammar, cheer up. You're about to be underlined in a green wavy line. The new automatic grammar checker in Word 97 checks your document for problems of a grammatical nature and suggests ways to improve your writing and to clarify your meaning. Any type of grammar error is identified automatically while you type with a wavy green underline. The process is very similar to spell checking, but those red wavy lines only underlined individual misspelled words. These new green wavy lines won't stop until they've identified the entire string of wording and punctuation that warrants a closer look (and probable correction).

Once you see them, what can you do with them? Just as easily as correcting spelling, you can now correct grammar errors. Just right-click on any portion of the

New Automatic Grammar Checker Grammatical errors are now found automatically while you type. A green wavy line will underline the words or punctuation that doesn't follow the rules of a particular writing style. Right-click on any of these identified grammar errors and you'll be greeted with a shortcut menu containing the most likely corrections. The settings for the grammar checker can be found in the lower half of the Spelling & Grammar tab found in the Options command of the Tools menu.

grammatical error and a shortcut menu will appear offering the most likely corrections. If you don't agree with the choices, or want to investigate further, click the bottom entry in the shortcut menu called **Grammar**, and you'll see the Grammar dialog box.

Check This Out...

Grammatical Find and Replace

Word 97 features new linguistic technology that understands the meaning of words and their different forms. You can now replace the word *buy* with the word *sell*, and you automatically replace all of the *buying* and *bought* with *selling* and *sold* automatically. For more details, see Chapter 9.

This is a view of the Grammar dialog box.

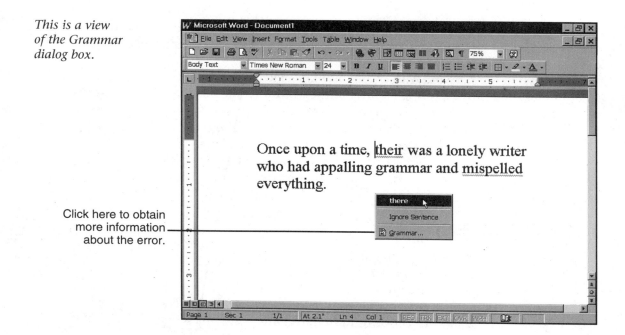

Click here to obtain more information about the error.

Once upon a time, their was a lonely writer who had appalling grammar and mispelled everything.

> there
>
> Ignore Sentence
>
> 📄 Grammar...

Pardon Me, May I Make a Suggestion?

From here, you have these options:

> ➤ Accept a suggestion by selecting one of those listed in the Suggestions box and clicking **Change**.

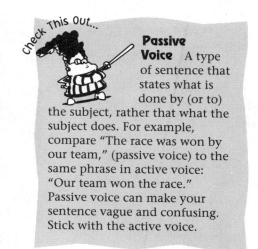

Passive Voice A type of sentence that states what is done by (or to) the subject, rather that what the subject does. For example, compare "The race was won by our team," (passive voice) to the same phrase in active voice: "Our team won the race." Passive voice can make your sentence vague and confusing. Stick with the active voice.

> ➤ Get more information about what's wrong by clicking the **Explain** button. Only certain grammatical errors will have this option available. Otherwise, the description of the grammatical rules that have been broken will appear in the Suggestions box.

> ➤ Make your own correction by clicking inside the document window and changing your text. To check the grammar in the rest of the document, click **Next Sentence**.

> ➤ Bypass the suggestion by clicking the **Ignore** button. You can bypass the entire sentence by clicking the **Next Sentence** button instead. You can tell Word to ignore this "grammatical faux pas" for the rest of the document by clicking **Ignore Rule**.

At the end of the grammar check, Word displays a short summary called *Readability Statistics*. It's like a final opinion, and it is very helpful. If you avoid criticism at all cost, you can choose not to display this information by clearing the **Show Readability Statistics** check box (in the **Grammar** options), but then you probably wouldn't start the Grammar Checker anyway.

There's an important revelation in Readability Statistics that's worth looking at. It's how many sentences use the passive voice. They aren't wrong or bad, but passive sentences can be vague and confusing. Try to keep this number low (like zero).

What's Your Readability?

After Word completes a grammar check, readability statistics are displayed, telling you what kind of people should be able to figure out what the heck you just wrote. Mighty intelligent people wrote formulas to figure this out, and since no one knows which is best, you can choose from all of them:

Flesch Reading Ease	This checks the average number of syllables per word and the average number of words per sentence. Scores range from 0 to 100. The average writing score is about 65. The higher the scores, the greater the number of people who can easily understand your document.
Flesch-Kincaid Grade Level	This also checks average syllables per word and words per sentence, but the scoring indicates a grade-school level. A score of 8.0 means that an eighth grader would understand the document, and that's an average document.
Coleman-Liau Grade Level	This uses word length in characters and sentence length in words to determine a grade level.
Bormuth Grade Level	This also uses word length in characters and sentence length in words to determine a grade level, in case you need another opinion.

Business or Casual?

Maybe you're a bit annoyed that the Grammar Checker doesn't like contractions. That's great for a report to your boss (it also gives you more words and fatter reports), but who cares in a letter to Mom? If you still want to run the Grammar Checker but speed things up a bit, you can change the rules of the review. You can even make up your own set of rules, but for now the quickest solution is to choose between the two most common sets of rules.

Open the **Tools** menu and select the **Options** command. Click the **Spelling & Grammar** tab to bring it to the front. The lower half of the dialog box contains all available grammar options. In the **Writing Style** box, change the default from **Standard** to **Casual** by clicking it (you can also choose more critical styles like Formal or Technical). Don't forget to change back, following the same procedure, if you want a more strict Grammar Checker for future documents.

Use the Grammar Settings.

Click here to modify grammar rules or punctuation requirements.

Click here to change the default rules to Casual.

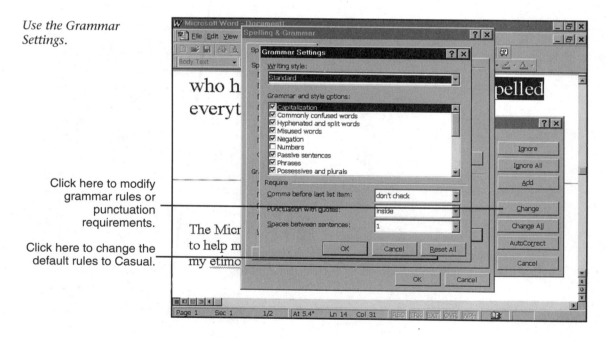

Toning Down the Grammar Checker for Casual Use

If you're interested in digging further into the rules of grammar, click the Settings button located next to the Writing Style choice. This opens the Grammar Settings dialog box. You'll find each rule associated with that particular grammar style, and it's easy to customize by adding or clearing a check from the box of a rule. This means you can choose a general grammar style and also customize it to meet your exact requirements. For instance, you might choose a Formal grammar style, but have it lighten up on your contractions by clearing the check from that specific rule.

Also, this dialog box contains three common punctuation rules at the bottom. These are rules about using a comma with the last item in a list, using punctuation inside or outside of quotes, and the number of spaces between sentences. Different people have very different opinions with these three rules, so Microsoft left it up to you to decide which rules you plan to enforce. The common alternatives are easily selected by clicking the box and choosing from the menu that appears. The defaults are set not to check these rules at all, so if you are interested you must choose an option from the menu.

The Least You Need to Know

Writing a letter or report is hard enough. You focus on content, and Word 97 will take care of the spelling and grammar, even helping you find better words with the Thesaurus.

What are those wavy lines all over my page?

Wavy red lines identify misspelled words. Wavy green lines suggest your grammar is less than ideal. Both Spelling and Grammar Checking are automatic in Word 97 (unless you turn them off).

How do I get rid of them?

Type better. Or, click the right mouse button on any red or green wavy-underlined words to see a shortcut menu with suggestions of improvement directly from the 150,000-word spelling dictionary and grammatical reference inside of Word 97.

I can't misspell some words no matter how hard I try.

Neat, huh? That's the AutoCorrect feature in action. It includes the most common misspellings of tons of words and automatically corrects them the moment you type, without bragging about it. If you sometimes fumble other words, you can just as easily add them to the list.

How do I check just part of a document?

Just select the text you want to check and click the Spelling and Grammar button on the Standard toolbar. You can check a single word, paragraph, or any part of a document.

I use lots of big words. Can Word provide any help?

Certainly! You can create shortcuts for typing long and difficult words or phrases by using AutoText. Add AutoText entries by selecting the big word or phrase, open the **Edit** menu, and choose the **AutoText** command. Give it a conveniently short name and press the

Add button. Now, in any document, just type the short name and press **F3** and it will be replaced with the real thing.

Where did they hide the Thesaurus command?

To look up an alternative for a selected word, press **Shift+F7**. You can also open the **Tools** menu, point to Language, and choose **Thesaurus**.

If It's Worth Saving, Save It!

One good thing about a typewriter is that when you type, you get words on paper, and you're finished. It's not as easy with Word 97 because you have a couple of steps in between the typing and getting the words on paper. The first step should be *saving* your work, and it's the focus of this chapter.

Word Doesn't Remember Unless You Save It

Start a new document in Word and type away. Now stop. Look at the screen and admire your work. Then think about what happens if the power goes out or you turn off your computer at this instant. The screen goes blank, and your creation is blasted to oblivion, with no chance of ever getting it back because you didn't *save* it. What can you do to prevent such a disaster, and where do you start?

Panic is not required if you read this chapter and learn how to save your document (before disaster strikes)! Which of the following options will be the best for saving your work?

➤ Take a Polaroid snapshot of each screen.

➤ Feverishly scribble a copy of what you've just typed.

➤ Attend a memory-enhancement class and practice until you can memorize your entire document.

➤ Hold thermal paper up to your screen and turn the brightness way up.

 ➤ Press the **Save** button on the Standard toolbar (you can also press the **Ctrl+S** key combination).

The final option is correct. Use the Save function in Word. Once you officially save your work, you can always get it back.

File or Document?

Your computer classifies your document as a *file*. The first menu heading is called File, but you should think of it as *document*. *Saving a document* packages everything inside your document into a file, which can be stored on your computer hard disk or floppy disk or both.

How Often Should You Save a Document?

How often should you save a file? It depends on how fast you work and how much trouble it would be to re-create your progress. Here are some rules to live by, as described by famous authors from the late twentieth century:

➤ Save immediately after thinking up brilliant prose or something really funny. Save anytime you think to yourself, "Wow! Did I do that?"

➤ Save before you print in case your printer jams and you turn off your computer before noticing.

➤ Save before you try some tricky functions in Word.

➤ Save right after a tricky function, if you like the results.

➤ Always save existing work before opening a new document.

➤ Always save before closing your document.

Saving a Document for the First Time

The first time you save any document is a little different than any other time you'll ever save it. You have to give your creation a name and a place (folder) it can call home. Save your document now by clicking the **Save** button on the standard toolbar. You will be presented with the **Save As dialog box**.

Saving your document in Word 97.

With this button, you can create a new folder to store your document.

Move up to a previous folder.

Enter any name you'd like.

You can change the document type if you need to.

Your document will be stored in the folder shown in the Save in box. If you want to save your document in another folder, you can search for it using the **Previous Folder** button or by clicking **Folders** in the Display area. You can also create a new folder at this time by clicking the **Create New Folder** button in the Save As dialog box. All new folders are closed when created, so be sure to open it first for saving your new document.

Give That Young Document a Proper Name

To make things easy, Word has already filled in a potential name for your document. Word just happened to grab the first few words of your document. Sometimes that's good enough, and you don't have to do anything more than press **Enter** (or click the **Save** button) to save your document. Or, you can type a better name in the **Filename** box. You can be as creative as you want in naming your file, which certainly helps you to identify it later.

Sharing a Document? Think Twice About the Name You Give It!

Naming limitations may still exist if you, or anyone you share files with, are using any programs that are not Windows 95 or Windows NT compatible, which includes lots of old word processors. For example, if you name your document **Monthly Report for September**, which is perfectly acceptable in Word 97, another word processor may see only **MONTHL~1** as the name. A better name in this case might be **SEPT-REP** or something similar that fits in the eight-character DOS limitation. To find out the DOS equivalent of a document name that is longer than eight characters, right-click your document and choose the **Properties** command from the shortcut menu. It will show you the MS-DOS equivalent filename.

If at first you don't trust your computer or Word 97, or both, you might find it reassuring to prove to yourself that your new document and changes have been saved. Simply open the document once again and look at it. It's easiest to find your document by choosing it from the selection of your last 15 documents. Click the **Start** button on your taskbar, point to **Documents**, and click on the document you just saved (the list appears in alphabetical order). Word 97 starts with this document opened, and it should prove to be exactly what you hoped for.

Renaming Is Easier

You can also easily rename an existing document inside the File Open dialog box by clicking the filename with the right mouse button. Select the **Rename** command and you can type over the old name with a new one. Then press **Enter** to save it.

Saving a Document the Second Time Is Easier, Unless...

 After a document has been saved the first time, it has a name and it knows where it lives. If you make further changes to the document, you simply click the **Save** button on the Standard toolbar and everything is saved! No messy dialog boxes!

But there are times when you *don't* want to save changes to the current document. For example, let's say you've pulled up last week's status report and want to change only the date and call it this week's report. But you also want to save last week's report, in case you need it at the hearing. If you make any changes and click the Save button, you will *lose* your previous report; it is replaced by one with the changes you've just made.

You already know how to accomplish this task. To bring up a previous document, make minor changes, and save them both, you use the **Save As** command found in the **File** menu. Remember to give this modified document a different name, and both will be safe and secure.

Save Them All at Once
Multiple documents opened in Word can be saved all at the same time by clicking the **Save All** command on the **File** menu.

You've Got Options in Saving

There are many document saving options that can make life easier for you. Let's take a look at some of them. From the **Save As** dialog box, click the **Options** button to see the collection of saving options. To select an option, click on it to add or remove the check mark. Here's the scoop on what all these options are for:

Options available to customize document saving in Word.

➤ **Always create backup copy**   If your location is disaster-prone (power failures, hurricanes, floods, and so on), select this option. You'll need it to be able to recover the previous version of your document if your computer crashes after a power failure. This option must be checked *before* your disaster, and you must have saved the document more than once.

➤ **Allow fast saves**   This option saves only the changes to a file instead of the entire file. With this option, saving a file often is a quick and easy process. As a precautionary measure, periodically the entire file is saved, even when this option is in effect. Since computers have become so fast lately, you might want to disable this option, so you get a complete, full save of your entire document each time you save it.

81

➤ **Prompt for document properties**   By selecting this option, you can make the Properties dialog box open automatically each time you perform a Save As, to remind you to add optional information along with your document. For example, you can add keywords that can help you quickly find this document later.

➤ **Prompt to save Normal templates**   This refers to the Normal template file. With this option on, you'll be prompted before changes are saved to the Normal template when you exit Word. You can find out more about templates, and saving them, in Chapter 20.

➤ **Embed True Type fonts**   With this option, the True Type fonts you use are incorporated into the document, so they will display even when the document is opened on a system that doesn't have that particular font. Without this option, the other system is forced to find a likely substitution font, and that can affect the total look you were trying to achieve when you selected the original font in the first place.

➤ **Save data only for forms**   This option saves the data you keyed into a Word form in a format that's compatible with common database programs.

➤ **Save AutoRecover info every: __ minutes**   Use this option to put Word 97 on "automatic." Type the number of minutes you want Word to wait between automatic saves. You can enter any number between 1 and 120, and something around 10 minutes is recommended. It all depends on how much work you're willing to lose. Also notice that you can provide a different folder location to save these files (otherwise the recovered file will exist in the same folder as the original, which might get confusing). You can create a new folder, named something like Recover or Backup to use for this purpose. Then open the **Tools** menu, click **Options**, then click the File Locations tab. Click **AutoRecover Files** and then click the **Modify** button. Find this new folder and then click **OK**. Finally, click **OK** in the Options dialog box to save this choice.

A Word About Fast Saves

Sure, things speed up with fast saves. That's because only the latest changes are saved in a temporary file. When you finish working in the document, clear the **Allow fast saves** check box so that you can save the complete document with a full save. This will remove all the accumulated change files and give you a nice clean Word 97 document. The full save at the end will also decrease the file size of your document.

Update Required for Saving Documents in Word 6.0 or Word 95 Format!

When Word 97 first came out, it had problems saving documents in Word 6.0/95 formats. Such documents were given a non-Word extension and often the formatting and graphics were lost. In June 1997, Microsoft released the Word 6.0/95 Binary Converter for Word 97. It's a good idea to download and install this small program, and you can find it on Microsoft's Web site at: **www.microsoft.com/officefreestuff/word/dlpages. wrd6ex32.htm**. The file will download quickly to a folder you choose, then double-click it to install. After you install this converter, Word 97 will properly save in Word 6.0/95 format when you choose this option in the **Files of Type** box in the **Save As** dialog box.

Protect Your Document with File Sharing Options

Use these options to protect your document against unauthorized changes. You can make your document password protected, which means no one can open or edit the document without knowing the password. These passwords are case-sensitive and can contain up to 15 characters, including letters, numerals, and symbols.

➤ **Password to open**   If you type a Password here, a friend must know the password before they can open and see your document. That's all they'll be able to do, however, because the document will open as read-only. If someone opens your document as read-only and changes it, it must be saved with a different name. Guess what? If you forget or lose the password, you cannot open your document.

➤ **Password to modify**   A password here requires your friend to know it before they are allowed to open your document for editing. If you forget or lose the password, you can only open your document as read-only.

➤ **Read-only recommended**   If you don't want to set a password for your document, but you do want to alert your friends not to change it, choose this option. When the document opens, your friends will see a recommendation to open the document as read-only. If they open the document as read-only and change it, it must be saved with a different name.

Recovering a Document After a Disaster

Stuff happens, what can I say? In the event of some disaster, like a power failure, wait until the disaster has left, then restart Word 97. All documents that were open at the time of the disaster will appear for you. The only changes you may lose would be those made after the last AutoRecover.

You may want to verify that the recovery file contains the information you want before you replace the existing document (at the moment they have the same name), so open the existing document and compare the information. If it looks like you've got the latest and greatest document, go ahead and click the **Save** button. In the **File name** box, type or select the filename of the existing document. Click the **Save** button. When you see a message asking whether you want to replace the existing document, click **Yes**. Make sure you review

Check This Out...

How to Find Recovered Documents If They Don't Open Automatically You can quickly find documents that were automatically recovered by using the **File Open** dialog box. In the **Name** box, type **AutoRecovery** *.* and then click the **Find** Now button.

all documents, if more than one was opened at the time of the disaster. If you choose not to save any of the recovery files, they are deleted when you exit Word 97.

What If It's Mangled and Mutilated?

If your computer locks up when you try to open a particular document, your document may be damaged. Restart your computer and restart Word 97. This time, Word 97 automatically uses a special file converter to recover the text. Hey, at least it's something. If you're lucky, the damaged document will be repaired and appear on your screen. It's best to save it immediately and thank your lucky stars.

If you aren't as fortunate, and a stubborn file refuses to open, you can try something new in Word 97. It's an optional file converter you can use in such an emergency. Use it when you don't care so much for the lost formatting, but want to recover the words (the text) typed into any document. It also works on documents from ancient word processors where file converters no longer exist, and even on files not created with a word processor—like a database or spreadsheet—that still contain some bits and pieces of text you want to recover. Open the **Tools** menu, click **Options**, and then click the **General** tab. Find the option called **Confirm Conversion at Open** and make sure it's checked. Click **OK** to close the Options dialog box. Now you can click the **Open** button and in the Files of Type box, click **Recover Text From Any File**. Now you're ready to open any kind of file whatsoever and drag the text out of it.

Saving a Document to Take Home with You

Feeling brave? Got a disk handy? Give this trick a try and see if you're not bragging about it around the water cooler tomorrow.

Use Word 97 to create and save your document. Place an empty storage disk into your computer drive. Now click the **Open** button to see a dialog box with your document name listed. Right-click the document to see the shortcut menu. Choose the **Send To** command and select **3 1/2 Floppy (A)**, and then sit back and watch the fireworks. Your document will be copied to disk.

Take this disk home with you and reverse the process. You can click to open and edit your work directly from the disk, or you can copy the contents of your disk to a folder on your home computer. Open Word 97 and use the **File Open** dialog box to open your documents. If you need to bring the document back to work the next day, be sure to repeat the steps just described to get your document onto disk.

If Your Home Computer Isn't Running Windows 95 or Windows NT

You can still take documents home and work on them. The only thing to remember is to name your document so it will be recognized using older versions of Windows. You'll also need to save your document in a compatible file format for your home word processor, if it's not Word 97. Yes, that means using the old eight-letter naming scheme. Your document called My Letter To My Boss stored in Word 97 is actually a file named MYLETT~1.DOC, but you would have figured it out soon enough.

Right-click any document to send it to your disk.

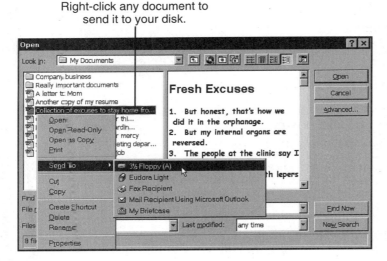

Taking your work home with you.

Closing Your Document and Going Home

It goes without saying, but not without writing, that it's a good habit to save and close your documents before turning off your computer and heading home. This is more important than ever now, because of the way Windows 95 and Windows NT save things (like documents). Your documents are hanging around in memory. When you close Word 97, and then close Windows, you guarantee that all of your documents are written to your hard drive and are now safe and sound. If you simply turn off your computer without closing Windows, there's a chance that a document didn't get written to disk, and is now lost forever.

The proper way to keep your documents safe and sound is to close them. If changes have been made, you will be alerted and granted time to decide on your saving options. Then you can close Word.

Please Remember to Shut Down Your Computer

Wait! There's a new commandment in both Windows 95 and Windows NT. *Thou shalt not turn off thy computer before it has been "Shut down" properly.* So click the **Start** button on your taskbar. Find the **Shut Down** command and click it. Click the **Yes** button, and your computer will do all sorts of computer things for several seconds (like making sure all latest changes are permanently saved and properly closing all files so they don't get damaged). The screen will let you know when it's okay to turn off your computer.

The Least You Need to Know

Prevent despair and anxiety by saving your work often. This chapter provided lots of tips on saving.

 How often should I save a document?

More often than you think. Life is unpredictable. Click the **Save** button on the Standard toolbar. Always save your document before and after any complicated word processing task. It's also a good idea to save your document prior to printing.

I always forget to save. Can Word 97 do it for me?

You're in luck. To set up Word 97 to automatically save your document every few minutes, open the **Tools** menu, select the **Options** command, and choose the Save tab. Place a check in the automatic saving options you prefer.

Can I give my document any name I want?

Yes, you can type long descriptive names, including spaces!

I want to change a document but keep it the same, too.

It sounds like you want to do a **Save As** command. This allows you to open an existing document, make changes, and save it as a new document, keeping the old one intact. You just have to come up with a new name for your new document. The **Save As** command is found on the **File** menu.

What's the fastest way to copy my document to a disk?

The fastest way to copy your saved document to a disk is to right-click on its name in the Open dialog box, then point to **Send To** and chose the **3_ Floppy (A)** command.

How do I keep nosy people out of my documents?

Put a password on them. Without the correct password, the document cannot be opened. To find this option, open the **Tools** menu, select **Options**, and click the **Save** tab.

Okay, I saved my document. How do I get it off the screen?

You can close a document to get it out of your way. Open the **File** menu and click the **Close** command.

Chapter 8

Previewing and Printing a Document

In This Chapter

➤ Fast ways to print your document

➤ Printing just part of the document

➤ Printing several documents or multiple copies at once

➤ Printing envelopes

➤ How previewing saves paper

In a truly paperless society, we humans will overcome our need to convert trees into newspaper and phone books, we'll distribute our communications electronically, and one can only guess what we'll do in the bathroom. But in a paperless society, what will we wrap the dishes with during a move?

That time is still far in the future, so for now you're going to have to print your documents for others to read. That means you still need a printer, some paper, and a connection between your computer and the printer. And you might need some patience. We've come a long way since Gutenberg—but he never had to worry about portrait versus landscape or printer memory overruns.

Printing Basics

It's always a good idea to save a document before you print it. This way there is no chance of losing your latest changes in case you run into printer errors or other problems. Click on the **Save** button on the Standard toolbar. (Check out chapter 7 if you want even more information about all the ways to save documents.)

Printing the active document is easy if you want to print the entire file, and if you want only one copy of it. Later in this chapter, you will learn how to be more selective in what you're printing. But for now, let's start with the basics.

Kill That Print Job! The only trick to deleting a print job before it reaches your printer is *finding* it. After Word has finished preparing your document for the printer, it will temporarily store it in a printer folder. To see the printer folder, double-click on the picture of the printer in your Windows 95 or Windows NT Task bar (it shows up on the opposite end of Start when a print job is pending). When the dialog box opens, you can select your print job by clicking on it and delete it by pressing the **Delete** key.

To print one copy of your entire document, just click on the **Print** button on the Standard toolbar. The active document will start printing according to the print defaults (a "default" describes an option already chosen for you, options like which printer to use, the size of paper, the number of copies printed, and so on. Any of these defaults can be changed at any time).

If you want to print more than one copy (or less than the entire document), you'll need to use the **File Print** command on the menu bar (or press **Ctrl+P**) described next.

The Quickest and Easiest Way to Print a Document!

First, find the document you want to print, and use any tool you want, such as Explorer, Find File, or the Word 97 File Open dialog box, but don't open the document. Just click on it with the right mouse button and choose the **Print** command from the resulting pop-up menu. What could be easier? You didn't even have to open the document.

Printing Only Part of a Document

Society's progress slows to a crawl when someone reprints a 350-page document just because a few words changed on a single page. Do you know anyone like that? Help them save the forests by teaching the technique of single-page printing.

You can learn to print only certain pages in a document if you wish. For example, maybe you only want to print that impressive table on page 297, or maybe you need to reprint corrections on only a single page of a large document (sure saves paper!). Here's what to do:

➤ Open the **File** menu and select the **Print** command. You will see the new and improved **Print** dialog box.

You can print only the current page by choosing **Current Page** in the **Page** dialog box. Make sure you've actually moved to that page, however, or it's likely to print the first page of your document.

Paper Shortage? If the printer runs out of paper during the printing of your document, a dialog box will appear and tell you so. Load more paper into your printer and then press the **Retry** button.

If you want a few pages printed from a large document and they are scattered throughout your document, you can do so as long as you know all of the page numbers you desire. In the **Page range** area of the Print dialog box, click to select the **Pages** option, and your cursor will be placed in the position for entering your page numbers. Type a single page number (such as 7), a page range (for example, 37-42), or a combination of the two separated by commas (for example, 7,18,23-37,95-98,117). When you are finished, press the **OK** button, and your selection will print in the order you've typed them. Once again, it's a great way to save paper and wear and tear on your printer.

You can print only part of a document if you want.

You can enter the specific page numbers to print.

Print more than one copy by changing this number.

Printing Even Less Than a Page (Selected Text)

If you need to print only part of a page, or a graphic, table, or drawing appearing on a page, you can with Word 97. First, find the page containing the text or object you want to have printed and use your mouse to *select* the portion you want to print. Now open the **File** menu and choose the **Print** command.

In the **Print** dialog box you will find a new option called **Selection in the Print Range Area**. Click to select that option and then press the **OK** button, and only the selected text will be printed.

Printing Multiple Copies of Your Document

You can also print multiple copies by changing the number found in the **Number of Copies** box. If you happen to be making several copies of a many-paged document, you will probably want to click the **Collate** option. Collate means the printer will print the entire document, one after another, as many times as you desire. Without the collating option, the printer would print each page that number of times, and then move on to the next page, leaving it up to you to organize, or collate, your document copies.

Techno Talk

Two Ways to Print Multiple Copies

If you have a printer that allows you to select the number of copies to print on some kind of control panel on the printer, you may want to use that option instead of having Word print the extra copies for you. You may find your printer is faster than Word is at this task.

Choosing Your Paper Source

What if your printer has two paper bins, the top for letterhead and the bottom for regular paper; how do you choose your paper source? This setting is stored in the **Page Setup** for each document. Open the **File** menu, choose **Page Setup**, and click the **Paper Source** tab. The choices you see depend on the printer you have installed. Click to choose the source and then click **OK**.

The Paper Source tab on the Page Setup dialog box.

Look Before You Print: Using Print Preview

Before you print your document, you should look at it in either Print Preview mode or Page Layout view. These two viewing modes show you what your document will look like when printed, so you can make sure everything is the way you want it before you print. Use Print Preview for a quick peek of a completed document, or use Page Layout view to create or edit a document while it's displayed exactly as it will print.

To change to Print Preview mode, click the **Print Preview** button in the standard toolbar, or open the **File** menu and select the **Print Preview** command.

Print your document.

View a single page.

View multiple pages.

Toggle to Full Screen view.

Return to Normal view.

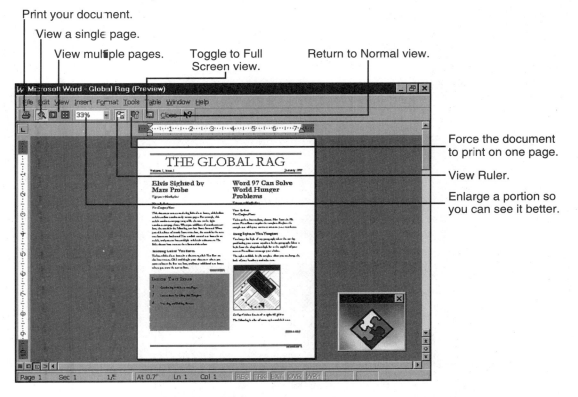

Force the document to print on one page.

View Ruler.

Enlarge a portion so you can see it better.

Preview Before Printing to Avoid Surprises

The purpose of Print Preview mode is to get a good visual feeling for what your document will look like on paper. Don't worry that the text is way too small to read. This is an artistic view. You can quickly find margin problems, pictures that should be moved, or columns that are too crowded. Press the **Multiple Pages** button to get an even more impressive view of a large document, by viewing how articles and graphics are balanced and flowing across pages.

Techno Talk

You Can Adjust Margins in Print Preview If your margins need a slight adjustment, you can make it instantly and see the results before you print. Make sure the Rulers are displayed. To move any margin, point to a margin boundary on the vertical or horizontal ruler. When the pointer changes to a double-headed arrow, drag the margin boundary back and forth a little. You will see the whole margin change on your screen. Drop the margin in the desired new location. Text will automatically flow on the page to accommodate the new space.

You can do lots of interesting things in Print Preview, as you can see by the preceding figure. To print, just click the **Print** button. To edit text, click on the tiny magnifying glass, then click within the document. After you zoom in on the area you clicked, press the **Magnifier** button again—the cursor changes into a regular mouse cursor, ready for editing. Edit until you are tired, then click on the **Magnifying** button again—and the text area again—to return to regular Print Preview.

To return to whatever view you were using before you previewed, click the **Close** button. You can also change to any other view by clicking the appropriate button on the horizontal scroll bar.

Printing Envelopes

Word makes it incredibly easy to prepare an envelope for a letter. The only thing you may find difficult is getting your printer to print the darned thing, so I'll give you some tips in a moment. First, the easy part.

1. From inside your completed letter or document, open the **Tools** menu and select the **Envelopes and Labels** command. When the Envelopes and Labels dialog box appears, type the Delivery Address in the **Delivery Address** box.

Envelopes created and previewed automatically.

Addresses can be filled in automatically.

Envelope preview

Envelopes and Labels	? ×

Envelopes | Labels

Delivery address:

Bill Gates
1400 Pennsylvania Avenue
Washington, DC 20000-0001

Return address: ☐ Omit

Daniel T. Bobola
1997 ActiveX Avenue
Hyperlink, MD 20888-0001

Preview

Feed

When prompted by the printer, insert an envelope in your printer's manual feeder.

Print
Add to Document
Cancel
Options...

Follow this guide to load your envelope into the printer.

2. Next, enter your return address by clicking in the **Return Address** box or by pressing **Tab**. The first time you use this option, Word will ask whether you want to save

the return address. Click on **Yes** or press **Enter** to save it. If you have special envelopes and you don't want to print a return address, then use the **Omit** check box.

To Fill In Addresses Automatically

Word 97 can fill in both delivery and return addresses automatically for your envelopes. Just be sure to apply the style Return Address or Delivery Address where they are used in your document. Word 97 will also assume that the first address in a document is the Delivery Address, if it's the first thing that appears in your document.

3. Before we print our envelope, let's check some of the options. Click on the **Options** button and the Envelope Options dialog box appears.

   ➤ If you want to, you can change the font for both the delivery and the return address. Click on the appropriate options you desire.

   ➤ Check the envelope size. Make sure that the correct size is selected in the **Envelope Size** box. To change sizes, click on the down arrow to open the list box. Select an envelope size by clicking on it. Then click **OK** to return to the Envelopes and Labels dialog box.

Options for specifying fonts and envelope sizes.

Select different envelope sizes here.

Select address fonts here.

Which Way Does the Envelope Go In? If you need to verify the feed options (the method used to insert the envelope in the printer), click on the **Printing Options** tab in the Envelope Options dialog box. Select an appropriate option and click on **OK**.

4. Now you can stick an envelope in your printer, a process called *feeding*. That word was probably coined shortly after a printer *ate* the first print job. Which way does the envelope go in? Follow the pictorial on the **Envelopes and Labels** dialog box. In the lower-right side, there's a box labeled Feed. There's a little picture showing the correct placement of feeding your envelope to your printer. If you still have trouble, refer to your printer manual or a local geek.

5. You can print the envelope now, by clicking the **Print** button, or, or you can print it later (usually when you print the document), by clicking the **Add to Document** button. To print only the envelope for this document, print page 0 (that's right, zero). Word 97 stores the associated envelope for a document on page zero.

Quick Tips for Printing Envelopes

Everyone likes to receive mail in envelopes with clear and distinct addressing, but nobody likes to stick envelopes in a typewriter to create them. They get all curled up, and it's difficult to keep them straight. Your computer printer can help. Most printers today have the capability to print addresses on envelopes, as long as you follow the directions included with your printer and your word processor.

If you have a laser printer:

➤ Unless you are very patient, you'll benefit from having an addition to your printer called an *envelope feeder*. If you don't have one, check your printer manual for instructions on how to feed an envelope through the straightest possible path in your printer, to avoid excessive curling and twisting (maybe there's a side or back panel that opens up).

➤ Check out the little **Feed** icon in the **Envelopes and Labels** dialog box. It shows you how the envelope is supposed to be inserted into your printer—whether it should be centered or against one of the edges.

➤ Most important of all, don't skimp on quality. Buy envelopes that are made for a laser printer. Other envelopes practically melt from the heat, and really gum up the works. And you'll find that the heat from the laser printer will sometimes seal the envelope before you've had time to insert your document.

If you have a dot-matrix printer, you can print an envelope like this:

➤ Line up the left edge of the envelope against the left edge of the paper feed.

➤ Move the tractor feed so the top edge of the envelope is even with the print head. Word will move the envelope up about half an inch before it prints anything, so don't worry that your address will fall off the edge.

Techno Talk

blah blah
blah blah
blah

Bar Coding Your Envelopes May Save Postage Costs

If your printer can print graphics, Word can print two types of codes on an envelope: the POSTNET bar code, which is a machine-readable representation of a U.S. ZIP+4 Code (the standardized geographic delivery route in the U.S.); and the FIM (Facing Identification Mark) code, which identifies the front of a courtesy reply envelope.

To print the POSTNET (Postal Numeric Encoding Technique) bar code, select the **Delivery Point Bar Code** check box in the Envelope Options dialog box. To print a Facing Identification Mark (FIM) in addition to the POSTNET bar code, select the **FIM-A Courtesy Reply Mail** check box. Word cannot print a Facing Identification Mark or POSTNET bar code if you use a daisy-wheel printer. It is expecting a laser printer.

Killing a Print Job (Make It Stop!)

Nobody ever prints a job accidentally, right? I do, and the great new features in Word 97 make it really easy to send too much to the printer. For instance, I often have many documents open at once, in a futile attempt to accomplish more work. Sometimes I forget whether I've pressed the Print button, and press it again. Or sometimes my printer isn't turned on, and I accidentally print the same document four or five times (in frustration) before I realize it. Then I feel really dumb for about two seconds. Then I panic when I realize my printer is about to waste lots of paper printing those extra copies. There are several ways to delete those other undesired print jobs, and this section explains them.

Watch the status bar at the bottom of the Word 97 screen the next time you print a document. For a

Check This Out...

What's a Print Job? The term *print job* refers to the collection of bits and bytes sent to the printer. It's actually more than just the words and formatting of your document. It includes control information unique to the type of printer you own, including details on print options chosen at the time of printing.

short period of time, you will notice a little printer icon with pages flowing out of it. Each page is numbered, matching the document being printed. Word is processing your document in preparation for printing. There's nothing you can really do to stop this process, so let it finish. When your document is finished processing, the printer icon disappears.

If the little printer icon has disappeared, you know that Word has finished processing the document and has sent it to the appropriate print folder in Windows 95. It remains in the print folder until your printer is available to accept it, and then print it. While your print job sits in this folder, you have the opportunity to delete it if you wish.

To find and display your print folder, double-click on the picture of the printer in your Windows 95 Task bar (it shows up on the right side of the Task bar, next to the clock). When the dialog box opens, you will see a list of all documents scheduled to print. Click to select the name of your print job (most of the time, there is only one document in this list anyway, so it's easy). You can delete this print job by pressing the **Delete** key.

If your printer has already started printing the document when you ask to delete it, Word will display a message on your screen. It warns that the job may be in progress. Click the **OK** button because you want to delete the job anyway, regardless whether a few pages have already printed.

What? It's Still Printing?

If your printer has lots of memory (meaning you paid a lot of money for it), you may find the print folder empty, even though you just sent the print job. That's because your printer picked up the entire thing and stored it inside the printer. Still want to stop that print job? Now you have two choices: the right way and the wrong way.

The wrong way is to turn off your laser printer. Sure, it erases that print job from memory, but it also fouls up the printer guts—stuck paper, loose toner, sticky mess—you get the idea. And you have to go inside the printer to clean it up. Once more for emphasis: *Don't ever turn off your printer while it's printing.*

The right way is to find and push the correct button on your printer (but not the power button). The **Reset** button is usually best and has the fastest results. Press it to kill the print job. If you don't have a Reset button or if it doesn't work, you should take the printer offline, and you must find the correct button on your printer to do this. It's usually a button labeled "Online," which it is if the light next to it is turned on. Push the button to see whether the light goes out (or turns a different color). The printer is now offline. Offline means the printer won't accept any more print jobs, and will also stop printing the current job. Soon, but be patient. It may continue to print a few pages, and that's okay. When it finally stops, you know it's safe to turn off your printer to get rid of any lingering evidence of your print job.

Making a Printed Document Match What Appears on the Screen

You may ask yourself someday, "Why does my document print differently than it looks on my screen?" The industry buzzword for the desired phenomenon of printing exactly as it appears is called *WYSIWYG* (pronounced wizzy-wig). It stands for *What You See Is What You Get*, and it's usually what people want. So if your printed document looks different, you aren't getting WYSIWYG, and if this is causing you pain, you might try to fix the situation with the tips offered as follows. Fortunately, Word 97 has almost perfected the technique for printing exactly what you see, but you may have to follow a few steps to confirm it.

Your screen display will most closely match the printed display when magnification is set at 100% in the Zoom dialog box. You can find the **Zoom Control** button on your Standard toolbar. It displays the current magnification, and it's easy to change to another magnification. You might want to change to a higher magnification when viewing small fonts, or change to a lower magnification when designing a page layout or placing large graphics on a page.

To change the magnification, click the **down** arrow attached to the **Zoom Control** button. The drop-down menu will provide a large selection of magnification sizes. Just click on the setting you want and your screen will be adjusted automatically. Notice that one of the magnifications is not a percent, but is called *Page Width*. Choosing this option fits the margins of your page exactly to the size of your screen. It's often the best choice because it provides the largest viewing size without scrolling text off the left or right sides.

If you use *TrueType* fonts, Word 97 uses the same font to display text on the screen and to print (the screen fonts provide a very close approximation of printed characters). That's good because your printer will have to print the same as what you see. You can distinguish TrueType font names listed in the **Font** pull-down box on the Formatting toolbar by the TT symbol next to the name. Where do you get them? TrueType fonts are automatically installed when you set up Windows 95.

The other two types of fonts you may see are called *screen* or *printer fonts*. There's a little picture of a printer next to a printer font. These fonts are used only for onscreen display; the printer uses different fonts to print your document. If a matching font is not available or if your printer driver does not provide screen font information, Windows chooses the screen font that most closely resembles the printer font. That means there's a good chance the printer will not print the same font you see on the Word screen.

The Least You Need to Know

Sometimes getting your document to print can be annoying, but the whole process will go a bit smoother if you remember tips from this chapter.

What happens when I click the Print button on the Standard toolbar?

You will print one copy of all pages of the current document.

What if I want more printing options?

Use the **Print** command on the **File** menu to print selected text or individual pages, choose a different printer or paper bin, or print multiple copies of the document. It's always a good idea to save your document before printing.

Before I waste paper, can I see what it will look like?

Good idea. You can see exactly how your document will look printed. Open the **File** menu and choose **Print Preview**. Click **Close** when you are finished previewing it.

Is it difficult to print an envelope?

The hardest part about printing envelopes is making sure the proper side of the envelope gets printed. The envelope feature of Word 97 will automatically pick up address information from your document, so you won't have to retype it. Open the **Tools** menu and click **Envelopes and Labels**. You'll even find directions on how to properly load your envelope into your printer!

Oops! How do I cancel that print job?

If you want to cancel a print job or change the priority of a print job, use the new Print Manager in Windows 95/98 or Windows NT. Click on the printer icon in the system tray, choose your job, and press the delete key to cancel the job.

Part 2
Fine-Tuning That Masterpiece

Does your document look like something you ripped out of the telephone book? Is it...well...boring? Of course, neither you nor what you typed is boring, so it must be something else. Liven it up! It's called formatting! Start small; experiment with letters or small words, then work up to sentences and paragraphs, and soon you'll be competing with magazine advertisements.

Not feeling too artistic? Let Word 97 take charge while you sit back, sip coffee, and watch automated tools bring your document to life. Now why can't other things in life be this easy?

Chapter 9

Search, Find, and Replace

In This Chapter

➤ Finding words in a document

➤ Using the Select Browse Object

➤ Using Find and Replace to quickly update a document

➤ Fancy ideas using Find and Replace

➤ Changing the past, present, and future forms of a word

➤ Getting rid of things with Find and Delete

Suppose that you've just finished creating a big marketing document minutes before meeting with your new client, only to find out that your client just changed its name from Bud's Cheese Shop to *Cheese Products International*. You can use the Word 97 Find and Replace feature to replace all occurrences of the incorrect name right before your meeting with the Head Cheese. It only takes a matter of seconds. You can also search for a word without replacing it, which can be helpful to locate a particular part of a document. Or you even can search for things to automatically eliminate, like the accidental extra spaces between words or sentences, or tabs that may be hanging around. Since it's almost always easier to attempt to repair a document instead of completely re-creating it, this chapter has been prepared to help you with all the shortcuts related to the Find and Replace features.

Finding Something Inside Your Opened Document

No matter what it might be, if you typed it inside your document, you can find it. You might be looking for a word, a phrase, a name, a number, or a special symbol for any number of reasons. Finding these items can help you return to a particular part of a large document, find out if they exist at all in your document, or find other words that are usually close by.

Select Browse Object
Select Browse Object is used to display a pop-up table of the best browsing methods from which you can choose your favorite. You'll find the icon ⬛ on your vertical scroll bar.

To find a word or a phrase in your document, open the **Edit** menu and select the **Find** command. You will see the Find dialog box. Type the word or phrase you're looking for in the Find What text box. Here are some handy options you can choose from:

If it's there, you can find it.

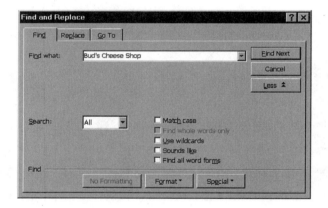

➤ If you want to locate only the word you typed, and not words that include it as a part (for example, you want to find "search" but not "searching"), use the **Find Whole Words Only** check box.

➤ If you want to match upper- or lowercase letters (for example, "Word" but not "word"), then use the **Match Case** check box.

➤ If you want to search backward through the document, open the **Search** list and select the **Up** option.

➤ If you want to search for a word with particular formatting, click on **Format**, select **Font**, **Paragraph**, **Language**, or **Style**, and make the selections you want.

➤ To search for a special mark, such as a page break or a tab, click on **Special**, then select an item from the list.

Shorten Up That Search

Word 97 finds any matching text in your document. It can find things so well, however, that it can drive you crazy. Search normally for the word *me* and you're likely to be bombarded with words like *home*, *tame*, *meander*, and *remedial*. To make Word 97 more precise—to locate only the whole word *me*, for example—select the **Find Whole Word Only** check box in the Find dialog box. When that box is checked, the **Find** command locates only whole words and not letters stored in other words.

When you have selected all the options you want, click on **Find Next**. Word 97 begins the search from the current location in the document, but you can continue the search at the beginning by clicking on the **Yes** button when the message appears.

Word will look for the first occurrence of the selected word. If you want it to continue looking, click the **Find Next** button. To return to your document, click on **Cancel**. To continue your search at a later time (searching for the same text or formatting) or in another document, press the **Shift+F4** key combination.

Finding Special Characters

But what if you want to find something strange, like the next Tab marker located in a document? The Tab is one of many keys that you can't simply type in the Find What text box. The Enter key, which creates the next paragraph, is another. To find these special characters, in the Find and Replace dialog box, click the **Special** button. You will see a pop-up list of various characters that Word 97 can search for but you aren't able to type. Click on the character you want, and it will appear in the Find What box, ready for the search. You will also see a symbol next to it called a *caret* (^) that has to be there, but you can ignore it.

Finding and Replacing Things in Your Document

Believe it or not, the reason most people usually want to find something in a document is to get rid of it, or change it to something else. Word 97 has a special feature to help you with this, and it's called Find and Replace.

Find and Replace has become incredibly powerful. Sure, it will search your entire document for a particular word (or words) and replace it with whatever you want, and maintain whatever format is found. But it's also very flexible and allows creative searching. Imagine being able to search for any occurrence of a particular font (no matter what the words) and replace it with another font. Or find anything in bold or italic and change it to normal text. You can even search to find things to get rid of, and automatically delete them in an instant.

Searching and Replacing Plain Old Text

The text you replace doesn't have to be plain or old, and what you replace it with can be anything you can think of (well, almost anything). You can even search for combinations of letters inside words, like acronyms used in your business that change, and replace them easily.

The process of finding and replacing text looks very similar to just finding text, except you start the process differently. Open the Edit menu and choose the Replace command, or take a shortcut and press **Ctrl+H**. In the Replace dialog box, type the text you want to find in the Find What box and press **Tab** to move to the next box (incidentally, if you already opened the Find dialog box, you can click on the **Replace** button to turn it into the Replace dialog box). In the Replace With box, type the replacement text. Now press the **Find Next** button to search for the next occurrence of what is entered in the Find What box. The dialog box stays with you as the search travels through your document, stopping at each occurrence. Press the **Replace** button to replace the text, or skip it and move to the next occurrence by pressing **Find Next** again.

Replacing what you find automatically.

If you are the bold and decisive type, go ahead and try the **Replace All** button. No holds are barred with this button; it blasts through your document replacing every occurrence before you can scream "OH NO!" Don't panic. Just remember the **Undo** button (or **Ctrl+Z**) which works well at restoring the previous state of your document, and possibly your health.

It's A Good Idea to Always Type Something in the Replace With Box

If you don't type anything in the Replace With box, the **Replace** command systematically deletes all of the Find Whats. It's great to use on imported text files where each line ends with a paragraph symbol. This process can quickly blow them all away (although you might prefer replacing them with a single space key. It's less productive to blow away, for example, all of the words *the* in a document, but you might come across a word that deserves it. You might also try using it to remove all words of a particular size or font, by searching for character formats instead of words.

Replacing Text That Has Been Formatted

You can get particular with the words you search for by selecting the format of the words. For example, you may want to tone down a document by replacing every bold **NO** with normal text. Or you can take normal words and replace them with formatted versions of the same thing, and the formatting is limited only by your imagination. You can also search for words in different fonts and sizes, and replace them with yet another font or size. Here's a simple example to get started.

Replace every bold **No** in your document with a plain No in normal text.

1. Open the **Edit** menu and choose the **Find** command. Type the text you want to find in the Find What text box, and apply any of the formatting to it using any of the character formatting commands on the Formatting toolbar (just press the **Bold** button and type the word **No**).

2. Then press the **Replace** button and type the replacement text in the Replace With box, and indicate the format of the replacement in the same manner (type No without any formatting). You can use any combination of the formatting options for your search or replace.

3. Now press the **Find Next** button to begin your search. The dialog box will remain on the screen as it displays the found words in your document (you usually see enough of the surrounding text to confirm that you really want to replace it; if not, just move the dialog box around the screen by dragging the Title bar of its window).

4. To replace the text, press the **Replace** button. To move to the next occurrence, press the **Find Next** button. Continue this process until you return to the beginning of your document. Click the **Close** (X) button to close the dialog box.

If you don't have any specific words to search for, but still want to replace any words using a type of formatting with another type (like changing any words in 10-point Courier font to 12-point Times New Roman), use the Find Font dialog box. To begin such a search, open the Edit menu and choose the Find command to display the Find dialog box. Click on the **Format** button near the bottom of the dialog box to reveal the many formatting options available for searching. To search for anything related to fonts, choose the Font command from the pop-up menu. This will bring up the Find Font dialog box, which allows you to specify the type of formatting for your search. Just as before, enter what you want to find, and what you want to replace it with. Press the **OK** button to return to the Find dialog box. Then begin your replacing by pressing the **Find Next** button, and pressing the **Replace** button as needed each time the discovered font appears.

Finding fonts, attributes, and other symbols.

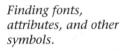

Replacing Formatting Only

Sometimes you don't care about the words, only the formatting. You can search for and replace all occurrences of a specific formatting, regardless of the text. Here's another way to change the formatting of *any and all* words in your document from Bold text to Normal text.

Open the **Edit** menu and choose the **Replace** command. Delete any text in the Find What box and the Replace With box that might be lingering from a previous search or replace. To specify the formats you want to find and replace, you can click the appropriate button on the Formatting toolbar. Press the Bold button, for instance, and the word

Bold will appear just below the text box as the description of what will be searched for. Do the same after pressing the Replace button, and here's the trick—if you want Bold changed to Not Bold, just press the Bold button twice. The description will read Not Bold. Then press the **Find Next** button and you'll be on your way. Each and every entry of bold text will appear in order on your screen, and you have the option of changing them to normal text by pressing **Replace**, or leaving them alone by pressing the **Find Next** button.

Press the Bold button twice to make it non-Bold here.

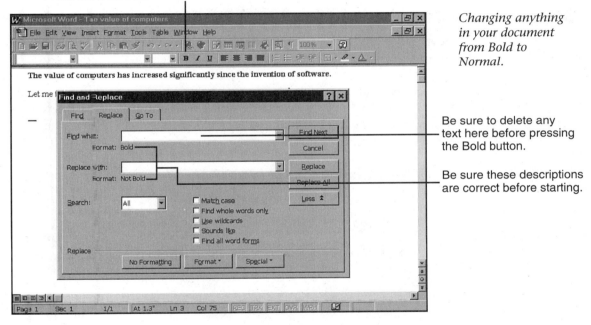

Changing anything in your document from Bold to Normal.

Be sure to delete any text here before pressing the Bold button.

Be sure these descriptions are correct before starting.

Word will even let you totally destroy a document by, say, replacing all normal text with nothing. Just leave the Replace With box completely empty. I can't think of a practical reason to do this, but it serves as a good warning to you. Make sure you know what is in your Replace With box before starting one of these experiments.

Finding and Replacing Graphics, Fields, and Annotations

If you use lots of graphics in your document, you may be happy to know you can find and replace any of them. Who knows, it could be helpful in really large documents. And if you create templates or create annotation comments, you may find it helpful to search on either fields or the inserted annotations.

Stop That Search!

You can press the Esc (Escape) key on your keyboard to cancel any search in progress, especially if it's taking too long or if you've changed your mind.

Open the **Edit** menu and choose the **Find** or **Replace** commands. In the dialog box that appears, click the **Special** button (it's labeled Special). Now click **Graphic**, **Field**, or **Annotation Mark**. If you are replacing something, type what you want to use as a replacement in the Replace With box. This can also be text, graphics, fields, or annotations. Now start your search by pressing the **Find Next**, **Replace**, or **Replace All** buttons.

Special Characters You Can Find and Replace

Word has preloaded almost all of the special characters you are likely to need to search on. If you happen to know the key combination for the special character, you can just type it in the Find What box. Otherwise, press the **Special** button and choose the plain English description of the symbol you want to find. The key combination for the symbol you have chosen will appear in the Find What box, and it won't look like anything you're expecting. You can just ignore these key combinations; Word uses them to find what you're looking for.

No need to memorize special codes anymore.

The symbol code will appear here.

Select from this list of 21 symbols.

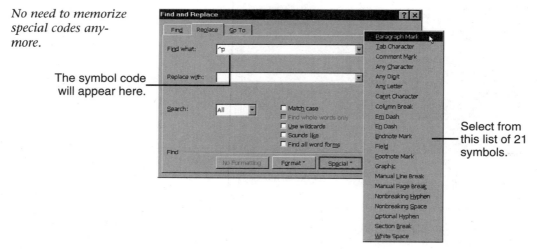

White Space?

That last option on the Special character button may have you wondering what's included in this thing called white space. After all, isn't the background considered white space? Not all of it. White space includes any number and combination of normal and non-breaking spaces, tab characters, and paragraph and section formatting.

So what else is useful to search for and replace? Spaces are a popular item. They end up a lot more than they should at the end of sentences, like twice as much. A single space between sentences is now considered correct, not the two most people prefer to type. Although they may not be causing you harm, you can still get rid of them easily using Find and Replace. Simply open the **Edit** menu and choose the **Replace** command, and type two spaces into the Find What box, and only a single space in the Replace With box. Pretty simple, huh? Since you probably don't want two spaces in a row appearing anywhere in your document, you can press the **Replace All** button to save yourself some time. Every occurrence will be replaced immediately. If you are still a bit chicken, press the **Find Next** button to see them one at a time. Then press the **Replace** button to change them to a single space.

Need another example to get you excited? After importing a text file, you may find five spaces used instead of the appropriate single Tab key. It's a real pain if you are trying to align the document. Taking it from the top, open the **Edit** menu and choose the **Replace** command. In the Find What box, enter five spaces. In the Replace With box, select **Tab character** (^t) from the Special menu. Now press the **Replace All** button, and all those spaces will be turned into tabs, which are much easier to align.

Finding and Replacing All Forms of a Word

What a pain it used to be worrying about all the different forms of a word during a word replace. Famous authors and politicians complained that they couldn't, for example, change all the words *go* with the word *leave*, because they might also have additional steps to find occurrences of *going* or *gone*. These people pushed their weight around Microsoft and got them to include some pretty fancy innards in this version. Accurate replacement of words usually means painstakingly determining the different word forms, or tense, and finding and replacing them. It works, and it's fun. You can also change the entire gist of a letter by replacing words with ones of opposite meaning (called antonyms).

To invoke this new wonder, open the **Edit** menu and choose either **Find** or **Replace**; it works for both functions as well. In the dialog box, click to check the **Find All Word Forms**. Now all your searches will include the past, present, and future with the press of a single button.

Check This Out...

Don't Get Too Crazy with Word Forms
This intelligence of replacing word forms is powerful, but it can't change the underlying structure of your sentence. It won't replace all forms of a verb with a noun, for example, or vice versa, but why would anyone try that anyway?

Getting Fancy with Find

Using advanced criteria, you can specify some pretty complex search patterns. First, from within the Search or Replace dialog boxes, select **Use Pattern Matching** or press **Alt+M**. Then click on **Special** and select one from the list, or enter your search pattern in the Find What text box.

Here's a sample list of patterns and what they can do:

Pattern	What It Searches For	Examples
?	Any single character	s?t finds "sat" and "set."
*	Any string of characters	s*d finds "sad" and "started."
[list]	Any character in the list	w[io]n finds "win" and "won."
[range]	Any character within range	[r-t]ight finds "right," "sight," and "tight."
[!c]	Not character c	m[!a]st finds "mist" and "most," but not "mast."
[!x-z]	Any single character except x, y, or z	t[!a-m]ck finds "tock" and "tuck," but not "tack" or "tick."

Buy, Buying, Bought

Word 97 now features linguistic technology to understand the meaning of words and their different forms. For example, if you want to replace the word *buy* with the word *sell* throughout your document, Word applies some smarts and changes not only *buy* to *sell*, but also *buying* to *selling*, and *bought* to *sold*. Now you can send form letters to your stockbroker.

I Don't Know, but It Sounds Like...

Did you experience the parental spelling paradox as a child? When you asked how a word was spelled, the answer was to "go look it up." It usually resulted in going out to play, because how can you look up a word in a dictionary when you don't know how to spell it in the first place?

This paradox no longer frustrates the youth, or the elderly for that matter, with the **Sounds Like** feature in Find and Replace. You don't have to know the exact spelling of a word to find or replace it, you just have to come close enough for Word to guess it. The better your attempt at spelling, the more accurate your search will be. But you don't even have to be close and Word will still go at it. Have some fun. In either the Find or Replace dialog boxes, click to check the **Sounds Like** check box. Enter your best attempt at spelling in the Find What box, and press **Find Next** to start the hunt for the real word. Don't be so bold as to press the **Replace All** button during one of these unless you are quick with the **Undo** button.

The Least You Need to Know

Finding the important points of this chapter is much easier than replacing them.

Where do I find the utilities for Find and Replace?

To search for words in a document, use the **Find** command on the **Edit** menu. To replace words in a document, use the **Replace** command on the **Edit** menu.

My document uses the words *go*, *going*, and *gone*. Is there an easy way to replace all of them at once?

Yes. And you need only specify the single word *go*. The other two are merely forms of the same word, and Word 97 lets you take a shortcut. Just check the box **Find All Word Forms** in the **Find and Replace** dialog boxes and Word will do the legwork and replace with the grammatically correct form for each occurrence.

Is it possible to get rid of all italics in a document? Or change only a specific font size?

Certainly; you have complete control of finding and replacing formatting options as easy as words. Just click the **Format** button on the **Find and Replace** dialog box and choose the formatting targets.

Can you replace all double tabs with single tabs, leaving everything else alone?

Yes, you'll find the **Special** button on the **Find and Replace** dialog box that lists all the special characters you don't normally see in a document, like tabs, paragraph symbols, page breaks, and so on. You can find and replace these as easily as words.

It's a big document and I'm a lousy speller. I have to find a word but I can't spell it. How can I search for it?

Don't expect miracles, but Word has another trick up its sleeve. Do the best you can, spelling it the way it sounds, and click the **Sounds Like** box in the **Find and Replace** dialog box. Word will take you to everything that comes close, and perhaps you'll find what you need.

Enhancing Your Paragraphs & Pages with Formatting Options

In This Chapter

➤ Aligning paragraphs

➤ Changing a paragraph's indents

➤ Creating bullets and numbered lists

➤ Setting and working with tabs

➤ Centering a page on the paper

➤ When and how to create sections in your document

String a few good sentences together and you've got a report, letter, memo, short story, and so on. Now you'll want to provide your words with the best possible environment, for nurturing growth. Clean and centered on the page, with crisp paragraphs and pleasing spacing. Maybe dignify it with some bulleted lists, or better yet, sophisticated numbered lists. And, of course, add a healthy assortment of properly set tabs. This chapter describes how you can enhance the formatting of paragraphs, pages, and complete documents, so you can be proud of your creation.

Paragraph Basics: First Things First

What is a paragraph? You might not care that the definition of a *paragraph* is "one or more sentences containing a consistent theme," but you should—because using paragraphs helps the flow and clarity of what you write. Paragraphs can be as small as one sentence on a single line or thousands of sentences written across reams and volumes of paper, but most are somewhere in between.

In Word 97, a paragraph is nothing more than a collection of words that ends in a carriage return (a press of the **Enter** key). This includes normal paragraphs as well as single-line paragraphs, such as chapter titles, section headings, and captions for charts and other figures. When you press the **Enter** key, you are marking the end of a paragraph (and the start of a new one).

How Can I See a Paragraph?

At the end of each paragraph, Word inserts a *paragraph mark* that is normally invisible, and for good reason—they can get in your way. However, paragraph marks are important because they contain all of the paragraph formatting commands contained in the paragraph. For example, you can center a paragraph between the margins, change the indentation for the first line, or change the spacing between paragraphs, among other things. All of those details are stored in that symbol. Accidentally delete a paragraph symbol; however, and the formatting of your paragraph may change unexpectedly! The best thing to do if you ever experience this is click the **Undo** button, which returns the original formatting to your paragraph.

Paragraph Format Continues

When you press **Enter** to create a new paragraph, the formatting of that paragraph continues to the next paragraph. Once you make changes to a paragraph (such as changing its margin settings), those changes are effective forever until you change them again.

One of the more peculiar-looking buttons on your Standard toolbar is called **Show/ Hide** Paragraph Symbols. Press it, and you'll see the special formatting codes used by Word to organize your document. These symbols will never appear on your printed document. This show/hide button is also a toggle button, and pressing it again hides the symbols again.

You can use the show/hide button to check on your own word processing habits. Remember the basic rule of not pressing the **Enter** key at the end of each line, unless you want to create a new paragraph? Now you can check yourself by pressing the **Show/Hide** formatting button. You should not see any of these symbols at the end of lines, unless it also happens to be the end of the paragraph. Skipped lines will also show up as a paragraph symbol at the beginning of a new line.

This is called a negative indent   Where the Show/Hide button lives

Displaying the normally hidden paragraph symbol.

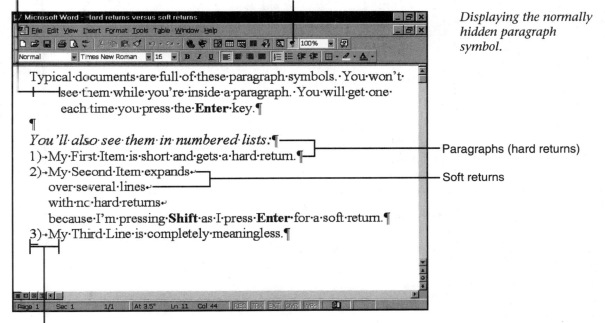

Paragraphs (hard returns)

Soft returns

This is a hanging indent.

Check This Out...

Soft or Hard Return?

If you need to move to the next line without creating a new paragraph (as in a list or an address at the top of a letter), press **Shift+Enter**. This inserts a "soft return" marking the end of a line, as opposed to a "hard return," which marks the end of a paragraph.

Center Lines and Paragraphs on Your Page

To create a paragraph that's centered on the page, meaning equally distant from the left and right margins, press **Enter** to start a new paragraph. Now click the **Center** button on the Formatting toolbar. The insertion point will move to the center of the page. Start typing, and you'll notice that the words spread out from the center of the page. Press **Enter** when you're done, and you will have a completely centered paragraph. You can also center an existing paragraph by either selecting the paragraph or clicking it to get the insertion point anywhere inside the paragraph and pressing the **Center** button.

To change a centered paragraph back to a normal one, aligned with the left margin, place the insertion point anywhere inside the paragraph and press the **Align Left** button on the formatting toolbar. To move from a centered paragraph to a left-aligned paragraph, press **Enter** to start a new paragraph, and then press the **Align Left** button, and things will be back to normal.

Aligning Text Right or Left

Use the Alignment buttons to change where your text lines up. Most documents are prepared with the text *aligned left*, with each line starting at the left margin. It can just as easily be aligned right for things like dates that you want to appear at the top right side of your page.

A Quick Date on the Right

It's common to place the date at the top right as the first step in writing a letter. Word 97 makes this easy. Just click the **Align Right** button, open **Insert** and choose **Date and Time**, and press **Enter**. Then click **Align Left** to get back to familiar territory.

Changing Line and Paragraph Spacing

Someday your boss may ask you to read between the lines, and your vision may not be so good. You can increase the distance between lines in your Word 97 document.

Normally, all lines are single-spaced. However, you can quickly change the line spacing of any paragraph by opening the **Format** menu and choosing **Paragraph**. This opens the Paragraph dialog box, where you'll find the **Line Spacing** box (on the Indents and Spacing tab). Click here to choose from the most common line spacing alternatives, including Single, Double, and something exactly between those two (1.5 lines spacing).

Next, you can adjust the amount of space *between* your paragraphs. For example, maybe you always hit the Enter key twice to leave a blank line between paragraphs. Why not just adjust the space here in this dialog box? The spacing measured in points is displayed in the **Before** or **After** boxes, which you can change. Most people enter a value in only one, usually the After box. That's all you need to keep your paragraphs neatly spaced apart.

Quick Paragraph Formatting

The headquarters for all this formatting is found in the Paragraph format dialog box, and there's a quick and easy way to get it opened. Place the insertion point inside a paragraph and click with the right mouse button. Choose the **Paragraph** command to open the Paragraph dialog box, and you'll have access to all of the features described in this chapter.

Indenting a Paragraph

Regular paragraphs are indented by using the Tab key to indent the first line. That's fine, but sometimes you just have to call attention to an entire paragraph by indenting the whole thing, not just the first line.

To indent an entire paragraph, place the insertion point anywhere in the paragraph and click the **Increase Indent** button on the Formatting toolbar. To return an indented paragraph to the original margin, click the **Decrease Indent** button.

Incidentally, if the first indent wasn't far enough for your tastes, you can go farther. To indent to each next tab stop, just click the **Increase Indent** button again and again until the indented paragraph is placed where you want it.

If you want to indent both right and left sides, use the method called *double-indenting*. Move the insertion point to the beginning of a new paragraph and open the **Format** menu and choose **Paragraph**. In the Paragraph dialog box, choose the **Indents and Spacing** tab to bring it to the front. Now click the **Left** box and enter something like .5 (half inch), or simply play with the up/down arrows and pick a number. Click the **Right** box and enter .5 again. You should keep each side the same, but no one will arrest you if you don't. Click **OK** or press **Enter** and start typing. Your text will be double-indented. I'll tell you more about the Paragraph dialog box later in this chapter.

Making a Hanging Indent

For some reason, certain people like to do exactly the opposite of what you expect. That's what the hanging indent looks like. Instead of the first line starting comfortably inside the paragraph, the hanging indent sticks out (to the left) from the rest of the paragraph. It looks backwards—but it can be put to good use, as you'll read in the next section.

To create a hanging indent, click anywhere in an existing paragraph (or start a new one), open the Paragraph dialog box, and place a negative number in the Left Indention box by clicking the down arrow next to it. You'll see a sample display of text respond to your adjustment, so you'll know when the text hangs "out" the preferred distance from the rest of the paragraph.

Hanging Around Numbered and Bulleted Lists

A special kind of hanging indent is a *numbered* or *bulleted list*. This kind of list is special because a number or symbol (that sometimes looks like a bullet) is placed to the left of all the other lines in the paragraph.

Faster Than Speeding Bullets Now with Word 97, creating numbered or bulleted lists can happen as quickly as you can type! Numbered lists are automatically created when you type a number followed by a blank space and then some text. Bulleted lists are automatically created when you use a symbol like *, o, or > followed by a blank space and text. In either case, when you press **Enter**, you will see the next bullet or number automatically created.

You've seen bulleted lists used throughout these chapters to:

➤ Create snazzy lists like this one.

➤ Highlight what's coming up.

➤ Summarize the important points that were covered.

Numbered lists are especially helpful when you want to explain the specific steps for doing something, such as step 1, step 2, and so on. Ready to number or bullet? Here's what to do.

Click on the **Bullets** button on the **Formatting** toolbar, and then start typing. What you type becomes a bullet on a list. If you press **Enter**, you start a new bullet. You can stop the bullets from appearing by clicking the **Bullets** button again. Similarly, when you click the **Numbering** bullet, each time you press **Enter**, the number is increased by one. You can interrupt a numbered list by clicking the right mouse button and selecting **Skip Numbering** from the shortcut menu. To resume numbering later in your document, click the **Numbering** button on the Formatting toolbar.

Doesn't Look Like a Bullet?

If you want to create different bullets or numbering, use the Bullets and Numbering command on the Format menu. You can change the type and size of bullets, the numbering system (letters, Roman numerals, or decimal numbers), and the amount of space between the number or bullet and the rest of the paragraph.

Using Tabs

What are *tab stops*? They're a way of moving, or indenting text consistently in a paragraph. Press the **Tab** key, and you move in one tab stop. Normal tab stops are set every half inch. Word 97 also includes a few different types of tabs you may want to try, including a centering tab marker to align the decimal points in a column of numbers.

If you want to change the distance between tab stops, or change the type of tab marker you want to use, do something weird first. Place the insertion point *to the left of where you will be adding the desired tab stop* (this prevents existing text, and you, from getting confused when the change occurs). Now take a look at the ruler near the top of your page. (If you don't see your ruler, or aren't sure, open the View Menu and choose the Ruler command so a check mark appears next to it.) At the far left of the ruler is a box with a strange symbol inside; it looks like an L unless you've already clicked the button. This button toggles through the available tab markers, and when you click the button, the type of tab changes. Select the type of tab you want to apply to the paragraph, then click in the Ruler where you want the tab marker to appear. A little marker will appear, indicating a tab stop location. You can change the tab stop location by dragging it with your mouse to the left or right. You can get rid of tab stops by dragging them off the ruler.

Tab Markers

Word 97 uses four different types of tabs which can be viewed on the Ruler.

Use the Right Tab to quickly right-justify text.

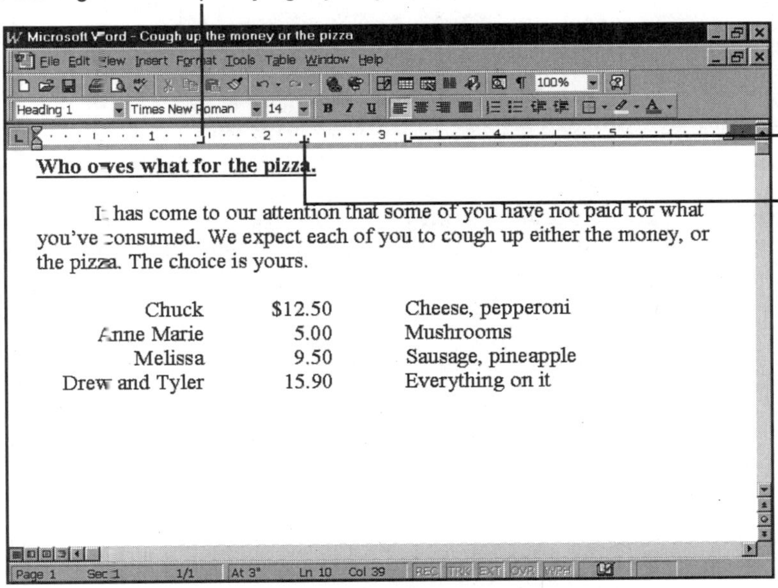

Tab symbols you may see on your ruler.

The Standard Left Tab.

The Decimal Tab is an easy way to align numbers.

➤ **Left Tab**   The most common tab is the left tab, which operates just like a type-writer.

 ➤ **Right Tab**   The right tab causes text to line up right-justified at that tab stop. This can help create interesting titles, which are, of course, single-line paragraphs.

 ➤ **Center Tab**   This is great for one-word columns of text. The center tab lines all the words up in the center, left-justified.

 ➤ **Decimal Tab**   Place this tab where you want to align numbers by their decimal point. The number is right-justified before you press the period key and then left-justified on the decimal.

Using Leader Tabs

Sometimes tabs can be used to provide interesting effects in your document. For instance, have you ever wondered how they get that line of dots that extend out to the page number in a table of contents? Me neither. But it just so happens that you can use something called a *leader tab* to get the job done.

No dots (the default) X

Little dots X

Dashes- X

Underlining _____X

To create these leader tabs, start by positioning the insertion point on the line where you want to start them. Set a tab stop as described previously, then choose the **Tabs** command from the **Format** menu. You will see the Tabs dialog box.

Now click to select the style of leader you prefer and then press the **OK** button.

Now start typing. Type the text to appear in front of the tab stop. Press the **Tab** key. Bingo! The leader will appear, and all you are left with is to decide what to type at the other end. Press the **Enter** key to end each line containing a leader tab.

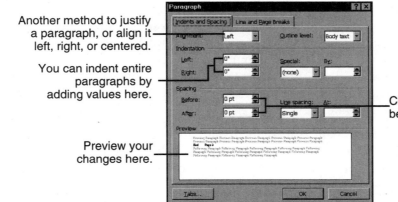

Word running your tab for you.

Type the distance for your leader here.

Pick your leader type.

The Paragraph Dialog Box

Yes, the paragraph is so important that it has its own dialog box inside of Word 97. All of the features and procedures described in this chapter (and a whole bunch more!) can also be performed from this dialog box. You can find it by selecting the **Format** menu and then choosing the **Paragraph** command. You can also click the right mouse button to see the formatting shortcut menu, and choose the **Paragraph** command.

Another method to justify a paragraph, or align it left, right, or centered.

You can indent entire paragraphs by adding values here.

Preview your changes here.

The most common paragraph formatting features are found on the Indents and Spacing Tab.

Change the spacing between paragraphs here.

You've already learned how to make all these changes in this chapter. This dialog box simply provides one place where you can do all this at once. The remaining paragraph formatting functions can be found by clicking the Line and Page Breaks tab to bring it to the front.

Here, you will find less-known features like the Widow/Orphan option, which prevents single lines of a paragraph from appearing at the bottom or top of a page. To prevent a page break between paragraphs, check this box. You can also access all the Tab and Tab Leader options by clicking the **Tabs** button at the bottom of the dialog box.

Less-known, but still interesting, paragraph formatting options.

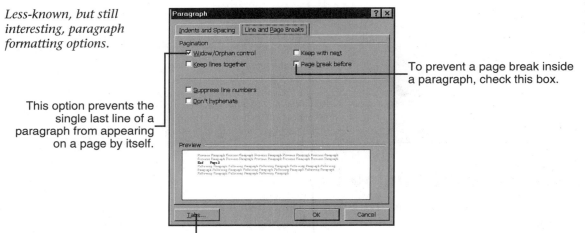

To prevent a page break inside a paragraph, check this box.

This option prevents the single last line of a paragraph from appearing on a page by itself.

You can find all the Tab options here.

Break Up Your Document into Sections

A *section* is a part of a document that has different formatting settings from the main document. These settings might include margins, paper size, headers, footers, columns, and page numbering. A section can be of any length: several pages, several paragraphs, or even a single line (such as a major heading). You can include as many sections as you wish in a document. In Word 97, a *section break* is used to divide two different sections in your document. There are a lot of good reasons why you might want to include sections in your document. Here are a few ideas:

➤ To create multiple chapters in a long report. Each chapter would have its own chapter titles (called headers), and you'll find it even easier to have Word generate a table of contents or an index for the whole document.

➤ For legal documents that require line numbering in some sections but not in others.

➤ To create a company newsletter with various formats. You could create a section just for the front-page heading so that it reaches from margin to margin on a single line. Underneath, you could change to a three-newspaper column format for the text of the newsletter.

➤ For business reports printed in portrait orientation (for example, 8 1/2-by-11 inches) with a chart that's printed in landscape orientation (11-by-8 1/2 inches).

➤ In a small manual, where each section has its own page numbers. The table of contents section could use Roman numerals (I, ii, and so on) for page numbers. Each section after the Table of Contents could start with page 1. Since the title page wouldn't need a page number, you could suppress page numbering on just that page.

➤ To include text in two different languages (for example, a human resources memorandum). The document could be divided into paired sections—one section for English and another for Spanish.

Before you create your first section break in a document, do yourself a favor. Set the most common document formatting options first. For example, if you want most pages to have two newspaper columns, go ahead and set them up *before* you start dividing up your document into sections. Otherwise, you'd be left to duplicate the common options within each section, and you have better things to do with your time.

When you're ready to start dividing up your document into sections, place the insertion point at the desired continental divide, open the **Insert** menu, and choose the **Break** command.

Choosing a break in your document.

Under **Section Breaks**, choose from these available options:

Next Page   The section starts at the top of the next page.

Continuous   The section starts right after the previous section, even if it's in the middle of the page.

Odd Page   The section starts on the next odd-numbered page. That's typically the next right-hand page.

Even Page   Yes, the section starts on the next even-numbered page, which is typically the next left-hand page.

When you have made your selection, press the **OK** button to close the Section dialog box, and you're done!

So Now That I Have a Section, What Do I Do with It?

These are some of the changes you can make that affect just a section of a document, instead of the whole document:

Margins   You learned how to change the margins of a document from the Print Preview window earlier in this chapter. If you decide to create different sections in your document, you can change the margins within each section separately. You'll learn to do this later in this chapter.

Paper Size and Page Orientation   You can choose from lots of paper sizes (such as 8 1/2-by-11 inches and 11-by-14 inches), and even change the paper size by section (but that could cause printing delays if a paper tray is empty or not supported by your printer). Certain sections may look better with a different orientation (landscape versus portrait). I'll tell you more about page orientation later in this chapter.

Headers and Footers   A *header* is stuff that's printed at the top of the page, like a chapter title or date, and a *footer* is stuff (like page numbers, filename, and so on) printed at the bottom. You'll learn how to create these in Chapter 11, but you get the idea that these are ideal candidates for section use in a document.

Page Numbers   These are usually included as part of a header or footer. You can change the page numbering system from the default of 1, 2, 3 to something else, such as I, ii, iii or A, B, C. You can change the page numbering system within a document by creating sections and using different numbering schemes for each section.

Newspaper-style Columns   You can create columns in your document that appear like those you find in a newspaper or a magazine. If you ever want to vary the number of columns inside of the same document, you are required to set up a new section. You will learn how to set up columns of text in Chapter 18.

Check This Out...

What Are Those Double Lines I See?   In normal view, sections are marked by a double line. Section marks are like paragraph marks; they contain the formatting for that section. So if you delete them, that section will revert to the formatting of the section before it. It's best to learn to ignore these lines; they won't print, and deleting them causes you to lose your formatting for your section.

Deleting a Section Break

To delete a section break, just select the section break symbol with your mouse, and then press the **Delete** key. Be careful! When you delete a section break, you also delete the section formatting for the text above it. That text above becomes part of the following section, so it picks up the formatting of the text below it. If you really didn't want to do this, click the **Undo** button on the Standard toolbar.

Copying the Formatting Between Sections

When a document has more than one section, you can copy section formatting by copying the section break. When you paste the section break into a new location, the text above the section break automatically picks up the formatting of the new section break.

Formatting in the Last Section

You may notice that the last section of your document has no section break. That's because the section formatting for the last section in a document is contained in the final paragraph mark of the document. To copy the formatting of the last section to any other section in your document, just replace any existing paragraph mark with the last paragraph mark by using the **Copy** and **Paste** commands on the **Edit** menu.

Centering Your Page on the Paper

If your document doesn't fill up a single page, you will have some empty space near the bottom. If that bothers you, why not center what text you have, with equal spacing from the top and bottom edges of the page? Even inside a large document, you may want the effect of having some important text centered from top-to-bottom in the middle of a page by itself. Word 97 provides an easy way to do this.

Easy stuff first: Here's an example of a single page document, with just a few sentences or paragraphs wanting to be centered, between top and bottom, on the printed page. Open the **File** menu and choose the **Page Setup** command. When you see the Page Setup dialog box, click the tab that says **Layout** to bring it to the front. Near the bottom of this box you will see the

Confused? If you thought this section described how to center a line between the left and right margins, flip back to Chapter 5.

label **Vertical Alignment**. That's it! Click it to pull down the choices, and in this case, choose **Center**. Press the **OK** button, and Word will center your text on the page.

Formatting your document with the Page Setup dialog box.

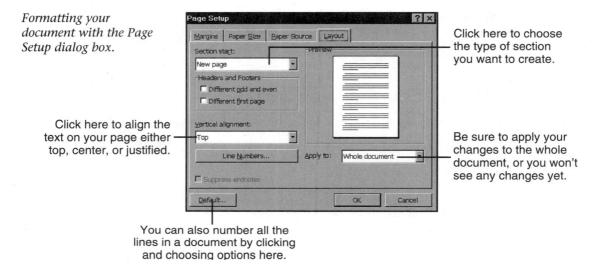

Click here to choose the type of section you want to create.

Click here to align the text on your page either top, center, or justified.

Be sure to apply your changes to the whole document, or you won't see any changes yet.

You can also number all the lines in a document by clicking and choosing options here.

Centering a Page Inside a Large Document

Centering one page inside a large document is a little bit different than centering a single-paged document. You see, the page settings are things that affect all pages in a document. So if you jump to the middle and try to center one page using the Page Setup command, you'll change the alignment of your entire document. Here's the correct way:

Find the page containing the text you want to center. Insert a page break at the top of the page and choose Next Page as the type of break. Add a page break before and after the actual text you want to center. Now you've safely isolated that page, and you can center it quickly with the Page Setup command.

If you have existing text you want to center, and it happens to appear in the middle of your document, you can take a shortcut. Simply select the text you want to have centered, open the Page Setup dialog box from the **File** menu, and choose **Center** in the **Vertical Alignment** text box. Word 97 will automatically insert section breaks before and after the selected text, to isolate the centered formatting.

Setting the Page Size

Although you probably plan to print on standard, 8 1/2-by-11 inch paper, Word for Windows 95 will allow you to change the paper size to anything you want. Start by

126

placing the insertion point at the beginning of the document or the top of the page. Open the **File** menu and choose the **Page Setup** command. Click on the **Paper Size** tab to bring it to the front. When you click on the **Paper Size** drop-down list, you will see the paper sizes offered by Word. Make your selection and prepare to click the **OK** button.

Wait! There's the **Apply To** box again. You must decide if you are changing paper for your entire document or if you really want a mixed-bag of different paper sizes making up this single document (probably not). Since that's unlikely, don't wait; just click the **OK** button to change the size for the entire document.

Deciding Between Landscape and Portrait Mode

If you think of pictures hanging on a wall, you will get the idea. Portraits (pictures of people) are usually taller than they are wide. Scenery or landscape shots are usually wider than they are tall. Documents are easier to hold and read in portrait mode. Spreadsheets are easier to follow in *landscape* mode. Presentations are usually created in landscape for the same reason. Landscape is also called sideways printing.

To change your document to landscape mode, open the **File** menu and press the **Page Setup** command. Click the **Paper Size** tab to bring it to the front. Choose either **Portrait** or **Landscape** and watch the Sample document rotate in the Orientation area to demonstrate the effects of your selection. Press the **OK** button, and the change will be applied to your document.

Copy the Formatting of a Paragraph

In Chapter 5, you learned that you can quickly copy character formatting by using the **Format Painter** button. You can use this same button to copy the formatting of one paragraph to another, which can save you lots of formatting time. Start by selecting the entire paragraph that is formatted to perfection. Now click the **Format Painter** button located on the Standard toolbar. Finally, locate the paragraph you want to have the same formatting and click anywhere inside of it. The paragraph formatting is applied instantly. You can repeat these steps as often as you like throughout your document, or even apply the formatting to paragraphs in other documents.

Sit Back and Watch Word 97 Do the AutoFormat

If you are feeling daring and no bungee cords are at hand, give AutoFormatting a try. No, not on a real document, but just a scratch document (scratch means you can live without it). Type up a few sentences in a new document to test out this feature. It's supposed to help you by taking care of everything—lock, stock, and barrel. Unfortunately, it rarely works. But don't take my word for it; screw up a document yourself. Here's how:

1. Type some words and sentences on a page.

2. Open the **Format** menu and choose the **AutoFormat** command.

3. Click the **Options** button to have a gander at what interesting things might happen.

4. Click the **OK** button to run it.

5. Don't like what you see? Click **Reject Changes**, and everything will return to normal so you can do this process manually.

Am I being unfair to this feature? Probably, because if you happen to create a scratch document the way Microsoft intended, AutoFormat will do a good job. But if you pay that much attention to the way you enter text, you might as well spend the time learning how to control the formatting yourself. Give it a try yourself. It might help improve the readability of files you get off the Internet, especially the longer text files and e-mail.

The Least You Need to Know

Now you can have your paragraph and format it, too. This chapter reviewed helpful tips and reminders about formatting.

When does a sentence become a paragraph?

In Word 97, when you press the **Enter** key. A paragraph symbol is created, and all formatting for the paragraph is stored with that symbol.

What's the easiest way to change the paragraph formatting?

The Formatting toolbar contains buttons like Align Left, Align Center, Increase Indent, Bullets, and Numbering. Just click to apply them to any paragraph.

How can I tweak the spacing on a single paragraph in my document?

You can change the spacing before, after, and within paragraphs with the **Paragraph** command on the **Format** menu.

Can I copy just the formatting from one good paragraph to another?

Yes, but make sure you start by clicking anywhere inside of the "good" stuff. Next, click the **Format Painter** button on the Formatting toolbar. Finally, select the target text and the identical formatting will be applied immediately.

Why can't I apply more than one type of page formatting in my document?

You can, but understand that page formatting is separated by section breaks. Create a section break with the **Break** command on the **Insert** menu. You can now apply new page formatting after this section break.

What's That in the Margins?

You may not be satisfied with the constraints of a normal page of text in Word 97. If you are interested in journeying beyond the normal confines of a typical document, this chapter gives you the know-how to create elements that appear in the margins, the famous headers and footers. In fact, we'll even adjust those margins for you.

Natural Extensions to Your Pages

If you open a textbook or a novel and look closely at the pages, you will notice there is a lot more information than just the words on the page. You will find *page numbers* at the top or bottom of each page, either in the corner or centered. Usually you find information at the top of each page. By convention, the top of the left page of an open book contains information such as the *book title* or *section name*, whereas the top of the right page includes the name of the current *chapter* or the *title* of the article. These bits of helpful information are referred to as *headers* if they are located at the top of the page, and *footers* if at the bottom.

If you attempted to add these professional touches to your own documents by staying within the margins, you would quickly notice a substantial loss of writing real estate. Luckily, you can add all of these features to your documents in space that otherwise wouldn't be used—the margins.

Margin Review

Word 97 automatically sets your margins at one inch from the top and bottom, and 1.25 inches from the right and left sides. If you aren't happy with these default settings, you can change them.

Adjusting Margins Using Page Setup

Laser Printers Can't Print Here

Remember not to set your margins less than 0.5 inch on the left or right side if you plan to print using a laser printer. All laser printers are designed to ignore any text within a half-inch of the paper edge.

Look Good with Three-Holed Paper

If you plan to print using three-holed paper, set the left margin to 2 inches. This setting will allow comfortable viewing of your text even if the pages are placed in a tight three-ring binder.

You can either change the margins on your entire document, or just on selected text. Open the **File** menu and choose the **Page Setup** command. In the Page Setup dialog box, click on the **Margins** tab if it isn't in front. The actual margin settings are listed near the top left of this box, and you can change them easily by typing over the value (you can leave off the inch symbol) or by clicking the increase/decrease arrow buttons for any item.

Don't forget to look in the Preview box. The sample document demonstrates the effect of your changes immediately. This is a live picture of a sample document that changes as you choose different margin values.

Now look at the Apply To drop-down list near the bottom of the Page Setup dialog box. Now it's big decision time. If you happen to be in the middle of your document and you are changing your margins, you must decide if you want them changed starting at this point, or changed throughout your entire document. Choose either **Whole Document** or **This Point Forward**.

Click the **OK** button, and your new margins will be applied to your document. Automatic formatting will occur to adjust any existing text, columns, or pictures.

Click to increase or decrease margins...

Or type a number (to indicate distance) directly here.

Changing your margins in the Page Setup box.

Adding a Header or Footer

You can make your document more interesting by creating your own headers and footers, and placing whatever information helps to clarify your document to your reader.

To make your document even more interesting, you can use a unique header or footer on the *first page only* of the document or each section, or omit a header or footer on the first page of the document or section. And for anyone creating a document with printing on both sides of individual pages, to be fastened or bound like a book, you can use different headers and footers on odd and even pages or for each section in a document.

> **Check This Out...**
>
> **Headers and Footers**
> A *header* is information that can be printed in the top margin of a page, either on every page, every odd page, every even page, or just the first page. Typical information included in a header includes book titles, chapter headings, and sometimes page numbers. A *footer* contains information such as page numbers and footnotes and is printed at the bottom of the page, in the bottom margin.

Putting Useful Things in Headers and Footers

Large documents really benefit from constructive use of headers and footers. An open document lying on your desktop can be instantly identified with the title or subject of discussion, and the page number provides a relative location within the document.

But don't waste toner; always put *useful* things in your header or footer! Include good information like the date, document name, page number, title, and other information that helps identify your document or where you happen to be within the document. And understand that certain conventions apply to where you place information. For instance, if your document will be bound, you will have right- and left-hand pages. Book titles usually appear on the left-hand page header, while chapter or section title are on the right-hand page header. Although Word doesn't provide a way to automatically insert book titles and section headings into headers, they aren't that hard to create. What does Word provide? Handy and helpful information like the date or time, the author, or the name of the document. These examples are simple enough to learn, so let's get started.

To create a header or footer, open the **View** menu and choose the **Header and Footer** command. You'll see the Header and Footer toolbar. If needed, click inside the header area to establish the insertion point, and begin typing the desired text. Press the **Tab** key one time to center this text, and twice to right-align it. You can add character formatting, such as bold or italic, by clicking on the appropriate buttons on the Formatting toolbar. If you'd rather be in the footer box, click the **Switch Between Header and Footer** button.

Just in case you tried—you cannot edit text and graphics in the main document while the header or footer areas are visible.

To change the text style or font, use the buttons on the Formatting toolbar

Page number, date, and time are also helpful

Creating a Header or Footer inside your margins.

Tab between entries

Filename and Path are often helpful

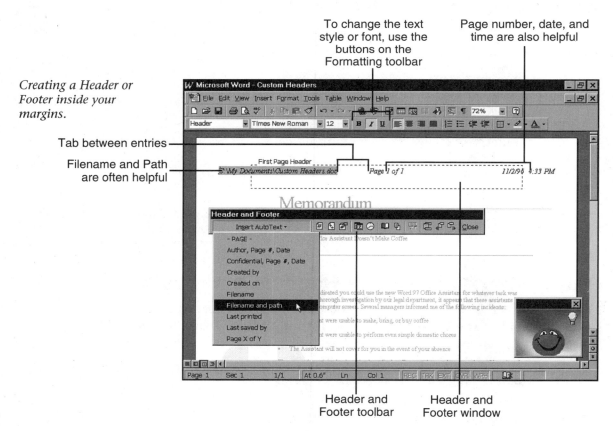

Header and Footer toolbar

Header and Footer window

In the Header and Footer toolbar, there are several buttons for creating the header and footer information you want. Here's a rundown on what they do:

Insert AutoText   Choose from the most common items for your header and footer, like filename, author, date last printed, and so on.

Page Number   Inserts the current page number of your document. Provides a single number—the total number of pages in your document.

Page Number *of* **Insert Number of Pages** (although it's easier to use "**Page X of Y**" found in Insert AutoText).

Format Page Number   Change the font to match your page text (helpful, since the default is Times New Roman).

Date   Inserts today's date into your header/footer.

Time   Provides a current time stamp.

Page Setup   Brings up the Page Setup dialog box.

Show/Hide Document   Helps you concentrate on the header/footer by hiding your document temporarily (until you press it again).

Same as Previous   Copy the previous one to this location. Useful to match up even and odd pages.

Switch Between Header/Footer   This moves you quickly between the two.

Show Previous   Take a look at the previous page header/footer.

Show Next   If you're in the middle of a document, take a peek at the header/footer on the next page.

Close   Returns you to your document, saving the header/footer changes.

You can type whatever you want to have appear, such as a title or heading, or you can choose from a whole list of the most commonly requested header/footer items provided by Word 97. The list provided by Word 97 is found by clicking the **Insert AutoText** button on the Headers and Footers toolbar. Some of these header and footer things are pretty smart, because they can display information that can change, like the date or time, or things unique to the document, like the title or author. The instant you place these in your document, they change to become the name or value of what they represent. The three most common—Page Numbers, Date, and Time—are included right on the Headers and Footers toolbar. Just place the insertion point at the location in the header or footer where you want them, and press one of these three buttons. You can mix or match any combination of them in the same header or footer.

Finally! Things You Really Need in a Header/Footer

Word 97 now provides an easy way to add the most commonly requested items in a header or footer. What are they? How about the Author, Filename and Path, Page X of Y, the word "Confidential," the time Last Printed, the person Last Saved By, and a few more.

How easy is it? Just view the Headers and Footers toolbar and click the AutoText button on this newly designed toolbar. Just pick what you want from this list! You can place as many as you like in either header or footer.

Formatting Those Page Numbers Is Easier

Because there's now a Format Page Number button on the Headers and Footers Toolbar, just click this button and you'll have the correct selection of your page number, waiting for you to choose a different font, size, color, and so on.

Using Different Headers/Footers on the First Page

You can use a unique header or footer that appears only on the first page of the document, like a special title. You can also get rid of a header or footer on the first page of the document or section. Word also provides the capability to put a header or footer only on odd or even pages, and you can also limit your headers and footers to appearing in only a particular section of your document.

By clicking on the **Page Setup** button on the Header and Footer toolbar, you can select special options such as Different First Page (for a header that's different on the title page, for example) and Different Odd and Even Pages (for headers that are different for the left- and right-hand pages). If you want, you can also change the placement of the header or footer in relation to the edge of the page.

Check this box to alternate headers or footers by page.

Check this box to remove headers/footers from first page.

Customizing Headers/ Footers in the Page Setup dialog box.

Want Only Page Numbers? There's an Easier Way

You don't have to create headers and footers just to add the page number to every page in your document. Instead, you can open the **Insert** menu and select the **Page Number** command. Under Position, select either **Top of Page** or **Bottom of Page**, and also choose alignment. Click **OK**, and you've got page numbers!

Viewing Headers and Footers

So where are they, you ask? You certainly created them, and you may swear to this fact, but they disappeared from view when you pressed the **Close** button. Don't panic, unless you have doctor's orders—then it's okay. The headers and footers are really there, trust me. Of course, you could print your document to see them, but in the interest of saving paper, you can also view the headers and footers if your document is in the Page Layout view. Open the **View** menu and choose the **Page Layout** command. Your normal editing view will be replaced with a more accurate rendering of what your pages really look like. The headers and footers in the margins are printed in a slightly lighter color on your screen so you don't confuse what they are.

Editing Headers and Footers

To edit a header or footer that you've already created, go to the page containing the header or footer you want to edit. Open the **View** menu and select the **Header and Footer** command. You will see the Header and Footer toolbar. You may have to press the **Switch Between Header and Footer** button if the other one is displayed first.

Now make any changes you want by typing over what's there (or use your normal editing technique), and press the **Close** button when you are finished.

You can also take a shortcut to the Header and Footer toolbar if you happen to be in Page Layout view. You'll notice the header or footer you've created are exposed in the margins. Double-click in this area and it will activate the header/footer toolbar for quick editing of your header or footer.

The Least You Need to Know

Things can hide in the margins of our documents. Headers and footers are natural extensions to our documents, and there's no reason to avoid them—especially now that you've learned lots more about it.

So what are headers and footers?

A header or footer refers to helpful bits of text or graphics placed somewhere in the margins of your document. They typically appear in the same place on each page. The best example is a page number; you don't notice it or think of it as being part of your document until it is printed.

What kinds of things can I put in a header or footer?

Besides basic text you can include dates, filenames, pages numbers, titles, and even small graphics.

What's the best way to view headers and footers?

Editing and viewing a header or footer is easiest when you are in the **Page Layout** view. Simply double-click any header or footer and the editing box will be activated.

It looks like my footer is being squished. What can be done?

You can change margins to give your headers and footers more breathing room. Open the **File** menu and click the **Page Setup** command. Here you can adjust the margins and view the results at the same time.

Decorating Your Document with Graphics

A picture may be worth a thousand words, as long as it's legal and no one gets hurt. Think of how much typing you'll save! Even if your picture isn't worth a thousand words, illustrating your document with pictures or graphics can make your pages more appealing and help convey meaning much faster to your readers—assuming you pick the right graphic and put it in the right place. You pick the graphic and the location. The time is now, and here's how you do it.

Graphic A *graphic* refers to a picture used in a document. Computer graphics are pictures stored electronically, as files, on hard drives, disks, or CD-ROMs. Graphics come from lots of sources, including software packages, friends, electronic bulletin boards, and the Internet.

Adding Pictures to a Document

We need to come to terms with our terms. Everyone knows what a picture is, and a picture by any other name looks as sweet. Shakespeare would have told Microsoft that the word *graphic* is an adjective, but in the modern computer world, it is also the term used for anything resembling a picture.

You have a lot of freedom working with graphics. The freedom starts by finding or creating any possible graphic you can think of, and you have lots of sources and tools to help you. Next you get to choose how and where you place the graphic in your document. Finally, you have the ability to adjust and manipulate the graphic in unlimited ways.

Where Can You Find a Good Graphic?

If you aren't an artist, you will have to hunt for graphics to use. Lucky for us that we live in the digital age, where computer graphics abound, so the hunt for existing graphics is relatively easy—especially compared with creating a graphic from scratch. Most computer programs, like Word 97, come packaged with lots of graphics ready for your use. You are free to use the graphics that come with Word 97 without worrying about who owns them. The pictures that come with Word 97 are called *Clip Art.* Clip Art describes the format of simple graphics that are stored electronically. You can browse through all the Word 97 Clip Art and choose a graphic to insert into your document from the Clip Art Gallery. You'll learn how to do this a little later in this chapter.

Who Owns a Graphic?

Speaking of artists, it must be pointed out that most graphics (drawings as well as pictures taken by camera) are considered art, created and owned by an artist, and should be treated as such. Many graphic images (especially popular images) are copyrighted material in many countries. That means you can't simply copy them or scan them and then use them as your own in your own document; you are required to obtain permission from the author or owner of the graphic, and even reference the source in your document.

Also, you can't just take a picture of someone and use it without their permission. It's a privacy issue, and a legal one as well. To avoid such problems, look for graphics that are considered *in the public domain*, which essentially means they are free to copy and distribute as you like. The graphics that come with Word 97 are free for you to use in any way you like.

If you are an artist, you can create your own graphics with the new Drawing tool featured in Word 97 (see Chapter 18), or you can use even more sophisticated drawing programs available for purchase at your local computer store or mail order catalog. You create and view the graphic on a computer screen, and print it on a computer printer. The software program allows you to save the graphic as a computer file that can be stored on a disk. Once you've stored the graphic as a file, it can be imported into your document in Word 97. You can also draw your graphic on a piece of paper, using a pen or pencil, and then scan it using a scanner. A scanner converts a picture on paper into an electronic file (graphic) on a computer disk.

You can purchase graphic images at a store, by looking for software packages containing graphics categorized by subject. You can find ready-to-use computer graphics in topics ranging from Aquatic Animals to Zealous People Climbing to the Top, and the price ranges from cheap to you-want-how-much???

If you don't want to pay for graphics, you can find a wide assortment of public domain graphics on computer bulletin boards and many locations on the Internet. Look for directories, categories, folders, or other storage locations with names like pictures, graphics, bitmaps, PIX, GIF, PCX, JPEG, and TIF. Be forewarned that lots of graphics contain mature themes, with content that may shock and offend you. Sometimes you can't tell the nature of the graphic by the name or location until you download and view it. Still, you can find lots of quality graphics free for the asking if you are patient enough to look for them.

All of these graphics have file formats associated with them, and the most common have extensions like PCX, BMP, GIF, TIF, JPG, and WMF. Who cares? You should, if you want to use the graphic in your document. Make sure the graphic is in one of these common forms that you can work with, or you won't even be able to get started. If you see a nice graphic created on someone else's computer and you have permission to copy it, you must ask for it in a file format you can use. You ask for a graphic by asking for the format you want, something like: "Could you please save it in PCX or Bitmap format for me?"

Graphic Formats Word 97 Can Use

You can insert many popular graphic file formats into your document. Word 97 provides these graphic converters, called filters, to allow your graphic to become a part of your Word document. Some graphics, like bitmap images, don't even need a filter. If you didn't install the filter you need when you installed Word on your computer, you can run the Setup program, choose Add/Remove Programs, and add the filter (see Chapter 2 on Installing Word 97 for more details on running Setup).

➤ AutoCAD Format 2-D (.DXF)

➤ Computer Graphics Metafile (.CGM)

- ➤ CorelDRAW! 3.0 (.CDR) file

- ➤ Encapsulated PostScript (.EPS) file

- ➤ Enhanced Windows Metafile (.EMF)

- ➤ Graphics Interchange Format (.GIF)

- ➤ HP Graphics Language (HPGL) file

- ➤ JPEG File Interchange Format (.JPG or .JPEG)

- ➤ Kodak Photo CD (.PCD) file

- ➤ Macintosh PICT (.PCT) file

- ➤ Micrografx Designer/Draw (.DRW) file

- ➤ PC Paintbrush (.PCX) file

- ➤ Portable Network Graphics (.PNG) file

- ➤ Tagged Image File Format (.TIF)

- ➤ Targa (.TGA) file

- ➤ Windows Bitmap (.BMP, .RLE, .DIB)

- ➤ Windows Metafile (.WMF)

- ➤ WordPerfect Graphics (.WPG) file

Adding a Graphic to Your Document

You now know where to find graphics and what kind of graphics Word 97 can use, the next big question is how to insert graphics into your document.

Word 97 provides a vastly improved method to place a graphic in your document. You simply locate the graphic you want to use, then click the **Insert** button. Nothing could be easier! Especially if you compare this method to previous versions of Word and other word processors that required the use of *frames* to "hold" a graphic in your document. Based on where you find your clip, here are the ways to insert it into your Word 97 document:

- ➤ **From the Clip Art Gallery** If you want to use the Clip Art that comes with Word 97, open the **Insert** menu, point to **Picture**, and choose **Clip Art**. You'll find the Clip Art Gallery dialog box where you can choose from hundreds of graphic clip art images. Find the clip you want and click to select it. Then click the **Insert** button to insert the graphic at the insertion point in your document.

➤ **From Another Software Program**   If you want to insert a graphic from somewhere else, such as one of the supported graphic formats of another software program, just open the **Insert** menu, point to **Picture**, and choose **From File**. You'll find the Insert Picture dialog box, where you can apply your treasure hunting skills to find the proper folder and file. Then click the **Insert** button to insert the graphic at the insertion point in your document.

➤ **Draw Your Own**   You can also draw your own pictures by using tools on the new Drawing toolbar. Interested? Turn to Chapter 18, where the Drawing toolbar and tools are covered in detail. You can create special text effects by using new WordArt tool on the Drawing toolbar, and you have added features, such as 3-D effects and textured fills.

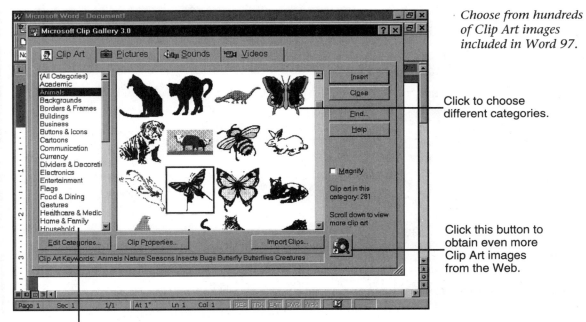

Choose from hundreds of Clip Art images included in Word 97.

Click to choose different categories.

Click this button to obtain even more Clip Art images from the Web.

Click to select a graphic, then click Insert.

No More Frames to Worry About!

If you've used Word in the past, you know how frustrating it was to forget to use a frame when pasting clip art. You will no longer have to worry about such a minor detail! Word 97 doesn't even mention the word frame when reviewing clip art graphics. Just find your graphic and insert it into your document. You'll have complete control over the size and position with nothing more than a click and a drag.

In fact, since inserting graphics is now this simple, you may try to reach new levels of artistic expression. How about placing graphics directly into special parts of your document, like a table, or a header, footer, or footnote? Basically, Word 97 will let you stick a graphic just about anywhere your heart desires. Whether or not you or the audience of your document will be able to recognize and interpret it is based on the size, quality, and location of the graphic you choose. Once you have the graphic in your document, you can improve it. When you select a picture, the Picture toolbar appears with tools you can use to crop the picture, add a border to it, and adjust its brightness and contrast.

Instant Graphic.

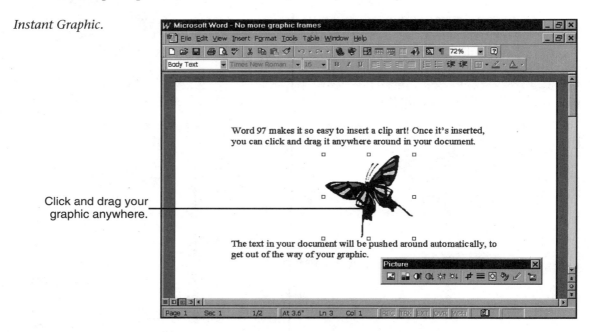

Click and drag your graphic anywhere.

Make Life Easy with the Picture Toolbar

Each time you click on a graphic, the Picture toolbar will appear. This is a handy friend indeed, because it's got everything you need to adjust and tune your graphic to perfection. Spend a minute or two and see what power is packed into this new toolbar.

 You can add new graphics right here by clicking the **Insert Picture** button

 To convert your color image to black and white, or shades of gray, click the **Image Control** button.

142

Just like the knob on your video display, you can click the **Contrast** buttons and adjust the contrast inside a graphic. Use it to reduce or enhance the visual details of your graphic. Use the **More** or **Less** buttons to find the balance you require.

And just like the other knob on your video display, you can click the **Bright-ness** buttons and adjust the visual impact of your graphic relative to the rest of your document. You get a **More** and **Less** button once again.

 To cut away unnecessary parts of your graphic, use the **Crop** button. After clicking the **Crop** button, position the pointer over the graphic handle nearest the offending portion, and drag the handle until you see only what you want. You crop from the outside to the inside, and you can choose any or all of the sides to crop.

To quickly place a line border around your graphic, click the **Line Style** button. Choose the thickness of border you prefer, and instantly your graphic will be framed with a border. To change the border thickness, click **Line Style** again and choose a different thickness.

You'll find more details about text wrapping later in the Chapter, and this button is the quickest way to use it. Click the **Text Wrapping** button to choose among the different ways that text can flow around your particular graphic.

Here's the jack-of-all-trades button for graphics. The **Format Picture** button brings up the Format Picture dialog box, which contains all the color, brightness, contrast, and cropping tools, along with size, position, text wrapping and line bordering adjustments.

 This is the **Set Transparent Color** button, but it's not used on graphics you insert. It's used for pictures you draw freehand, using the tools on the Drawing Toolbar, which you'll learn more about in Chapter 18.

After monkeying around with your graphic, you may decide you liked it best at the beginning. To remove all of the adjustments of the previous buttons, click the **Reset Picture** button. The graphic will appear as it was when first inserted.

More About the Clip Art Gallery

Your Clip Gallery includes a wide variety of clip art images—literally hundreds—including household objects, maps, people, buildings, and scenic backgrounds. The contents are displayed in alphabetical order based on the name given to the graphic. You can scroll up and down the list of pictures and preview them yourself. If you want to find something in particular, the Clip Gallery includes a handy **Find** feature to help you locate just the right images for your document. When you've found a picture you want to put in your document, select it and click **Insert**.

Clip Gallery Is Now Tied to the Web!

You'll see a new icon in the lower right corner of your Clip Gallery dialog box. It's called the **Connect to Web for Additional Clips**, and if you're into clip art, this is the nirvana button. If you have access to the World Wide Web, you'll connect to a special Web page that lets you choose from a vast array of clip art, and the ones you choose will be automatically added to your own Clip Gallery.

Lots more Clip Art on the Web!

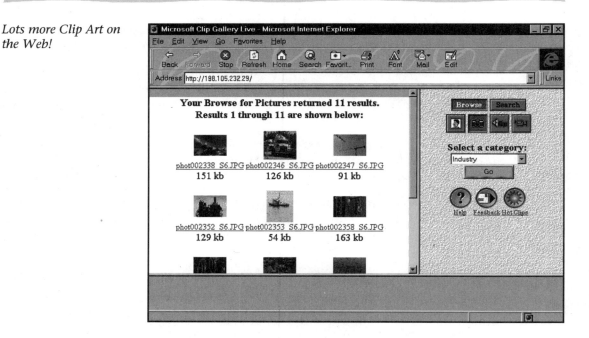

Improved Microsoft Clip Gallery!

The Clip Gallery has been improved in Word 97. There are hundreds of different art clips to choose from. They are categorized and can be easily browsed. You can search and find exactly what you need with the Gallery **Find** button. You can edit the categories, and add (import) additional clip art into your gallery. There's even a **Magnify** button to let you see more of the details before inserting the art into your document. Finally, to save disk space, the entire collection can be run from the Word 97 CD-ROM.

Break Up That Graphic

Most clip art is in *metafile* format. One benefit of this format is that you can convert clip art to a drawing object, and then edit it. Try it yourself by selecting it, and then click **Ungroup** on the **Draw** menu. You can then modify it just as you can any other object you draw. For example, you might insert a clip art image of a building, ungroup it, edit the shape to make it appear closer to your own, and even save the modified image as a new clip art image.

You can also draw your own pictures by using tools on the Drawing toolbar. For more information about drawing, turn to Chapter 18.

Flow Text Around Your Graphic for a More Professional Result

Did you notice the empty space around your picture in the last example? Not exactly what you expected? We can do better. The problem with simple pasting is that a graphic takes up all the space to the left and right of it. Nothing flows gracefully around it.

You can make text flow gracefully around your graphic by using the new Wrapping tools in Word 97. Once you choose the wrapping style for a given graphic, you can move the graphic around, and text will flow naturally around it.

First right-click the graphic you want text to flow around. Choose **Format Picture** on the shortcut menu that appears. In the **Format Object** dialog box, click the **Wrapping** tab to bring its contents to the front. The top row displays the five different text wrapping styles, and the default is Top & Bottom, which is why lines of text in our first example stopped abruptly above and below wherever we placed the graphic. Try choosing **Tight**. It works well for most odd-shaped clip art. The other options include flowing text *inside* your graphic, and allowing text to flow on top of your graphic.

The Wrap to options in the second row give you additional ways to wrap text around a graphic. This set of options is particularly useful when you must wrap text around a large graphic, which makes the text difficult to follow from one side of the graphic to the other.

Right-click your graphic and choose Format Object to get this new menu.

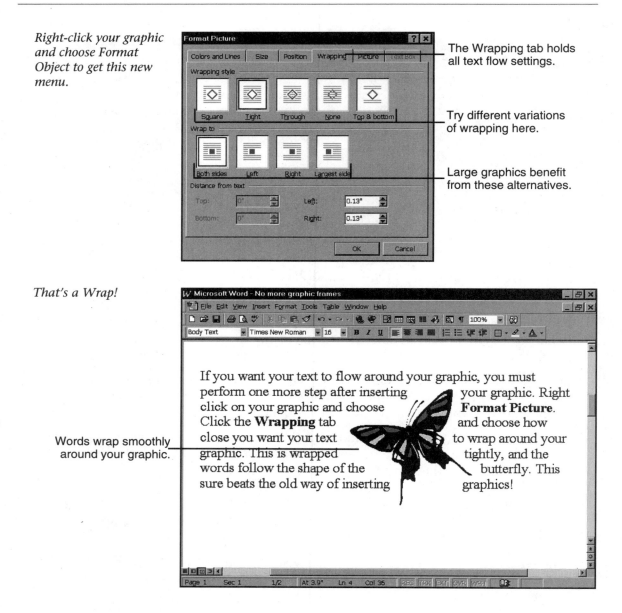

The Wrapping tab holds all text flow settings.

Try different variations of wrapping here.

Large graphics benefit from these alternatives.

That's a Wrap!

Words wrap smoothly around your graphic.

Deleting a Graphic

To get rid of any graphic, just click on it to select it. Now press the **Delete** key. It's gone without a trace.

Editing Graphic Images Inside Your Document

Now that the original graphic has become a part of your document, is there anything more we can do with graphics, once they're inside of our document? Only squishing, stretching, elongating, enlarging, shrinking, and moving it all around. And when you select a picture, the Picture toolbar appears with tools you can use to crop the picture, add a border to it, and adjust its brightness and contrast.

If that's not enough, you can also delete them.

Move 'em and Size 'em in Here

You can also resize and move graphics in the Format Picture dialog box. Find it by clicking the Format Picture button on the Picture toolbar, or else open the Format menu and choose Picture. Click the Size tab and you can change the values for the height and width of your graphic. Click the Position tab if you want to use actual distances for the horizontal and vertical placement of your graphic.

Moving Graphics Around

Once you've got a graphic placed in your document, it can be moved anywhere inside your document. To move a graphic, you must start by selecting it. Click the graphic once to select it. Using the left mouse button, you can now drag the graphic around your document. Don't worry about the underlying text on the page—it will be moved automatically and flow around the new graphic location.

Word 97 won't let you split a graphic between two pages, so anything extending beyond the bottom margin will be pushed to the next page. The same goes for the sides—Word won't allow a graphic to spill over the edge of your paper. You should consider that helpful.

Making a Graphic Bigger or Smaller

You can change the size of any graphic placed in your document. Simply select the graphic by clicking it once. A selected graphic will reveal its object *handles*, which are the eight little black boxes on the sides and corners of the box surrounding your graphic. Once you've located these handles, you can grab on to them and size the graphic. Click and drag a corner handle inside and out and watch as it resizes automatically. The top and bottom handles make it easy to make a graphic taller or shorter, while the side handles make it skinnier or fatter. Corners do both at the same time.

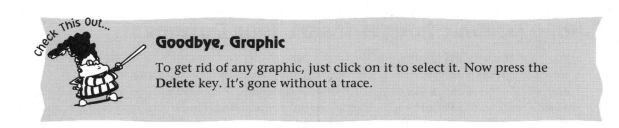

Goodbye, Graphic

To get rid of any graphic, just click on it to select it. Now press the
Delete key. It's gone without a trace.

Improving Image Quality

If your graphic is too light or dark, is the wrong color, needs better contrast, or should be
cropped (did we miss anything?), you'll be thankful for the **Format Object** dialog box or
the **Picture** tab, to be exact. Right-click your graphic object and choose **Format Object** on
the shortcut menu. Click the **Picture** tab and you'll find slider bars for all of these adjustments. You also have the ability to crop your picture by setting the measurements in the
crop boxes at the top. If you don't like any of your changes, you can click the **Reset**
button on this dialog box to restore the graphic as it was.

Adjust any graphic to
your liking.

Click the Picture tab.

Brighten a dark graphic.

Change the contrast
to bring out detail.

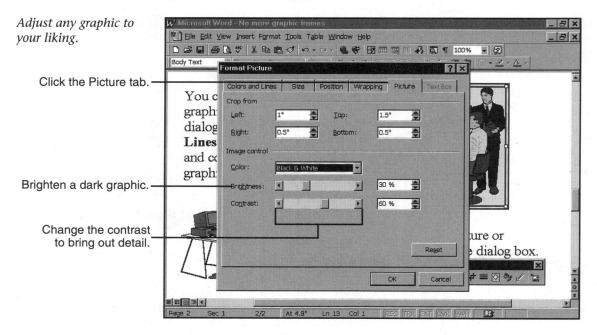

Putting a Border Around Your Picture

Some graphics look better with a border. If the graphic did not come with a border, you can create one. Borders can be placed around any graphic, whether or not it has been placed inside a frame (although Word 97 doesn't require frames, it still supports them, in case you happen to be working with documents saved in earlier file formats). First select your graphic by clicking once on it, so Word will get the idea of what you want a border around. You can certainly open the **Format** menu and choose the **Borders and Shading** command which brings up the Format Picture dialog box, but why not try the shortcut mouse commands for a change? Click once on your graphic to select it. With the mouse arrow on top of the graphic, click the right mouse button. A pop-up menu will appear that's called the *Shortcut menu*, because it's one-stop shopping for all of your formatting and editing needs. Choose the **Format Picture** command with either mouse button, and you'll arrive at the same Format Picture dialog box in a snap.

Once inside, make sure the **Colors and Lines** tab is in front by clicking on it. Choose the thickness of the border by clicking in the Line Color text box and choosing either a color, or one of the Patterned Lines displayed when you click this option. You can also provide a background color or texture to your graphic by clicking in the Fill Color text box. Choose a fill color from the palette, or click More Colors for a wider variety. To experiment with different textures and effects, click the Fill Effects and try the options on any of the Gradient, Texture, Pattern, or Picture tabs.

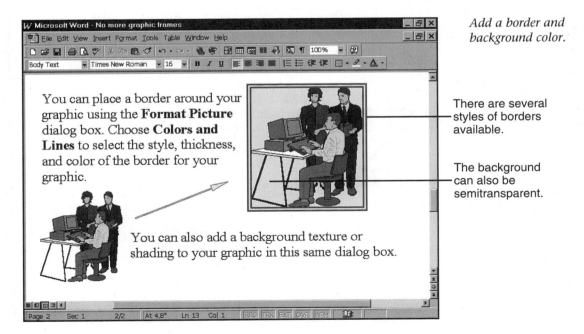

Add a border and background color.

There are several styles of borders available.

The background can also be semitransparent.

To add or remove a shadow from any graphic in your document, open the View menu, point to Toolbars, and choose the Drawing Toolbar. Click to choose your graphic, then click the Shadow button on the Drawing Toolbar. Click the shadow type you prefer from the selection provided, and the effect will be applied to your graphic. To change the length of the shadow, click the Shadow Settings and choose one of the four Nudge Shadow buttons and watch your shadow grow or shrink to your command.

Adding a Callout to a Detail in Your Graphic

A callout is that text-in-a-balloon stuff you see in the Sunday comics. Callouts can be helpful in clarifying details in your pictures or graphics, and are easy to apply because they just sort of lie on top of your graphic. You can edit and shape the callout using tools on the new Drawing toolbar. Let's put a callout on our graphic.

Open the **View** menu, point to Toolbars and choose the Drawing toolbar. Once you've got it open and near your graphic, click the **AutoShapes** button and point to Callouts. Choose the style and shape of the callout you prefer, and it will appear as a floating object on your document. You can immediately start typing text into it, but it's better to drag it into position first, and then resize it larger by dragging the Callout handles. This is better because the default callout size usually only holds a few letters of typed text, and the rest is hidden until the callout is resized to display them. Now click inside the Callout and type anything you want. To start a new line, press Enter. You can also format this callout text using any of the formatting features in Word. When you are finished, click outside of the callout area.

The Drawing Toolbar now provides callout options.

You can drag any toolbar wherever you wish.

You'll learn more about these other tools in Chapter 18.

Callouts can be applied to graphics, text, or anything.

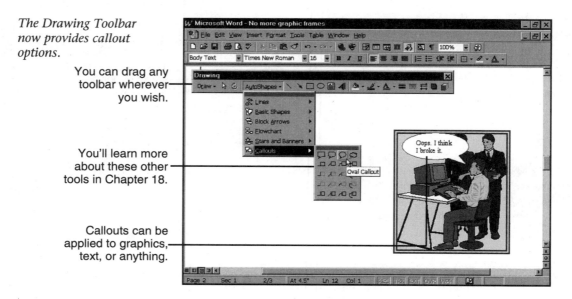

Adding Captions to Things

You may need to do some explaining on certain pictures imported into your document. You can do this by adding descriptive titles to objects like a graphic, table, figure, equation, or others. These descriptive titles are called *captions*, and Word 97 provides an easy new way to apply them. You can automatically add a caption to an object when you insert it. Or you can manually add a caption to an item in a document that already exists.

Placing a Caption on an Existing Object

If you have a graphic, table, or other object you want to add a caption to, first select the object. Once an object is selected, you can open the **Insert** menu and choose the **Caption** command. The Caption dialog box allows you to select from existing caption names (like Figure or Table), but you can also create your own by typing in the New Caption box.

You can also select the position of the caption by clicking and choosing from the list of options presented in the Position pull-down box. You can choose from above or below your object.

Use captions to clarify which graphic you discuss in your text.

You can choose different labels or positions for your caption.

Click here to add captions automatically each time you insert an item.

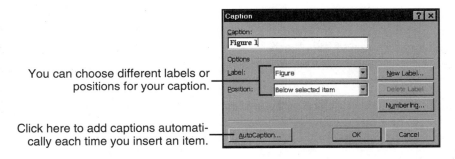

Adding Captions Automatically

If you plan to add several graphics to a document, and want a caption for each, make it easy on yourself by turning on AutoCaptions. If you set this up while placing your first graphic, you'll save tedious steps for the rest—the captions will be placed automatically. You can automatically add a caption to a table, figure, equation, slide, video, spreadsheet, sound recording, and just about anything else you can think of.

Open the **Insert** menu and select the **Caption** command. In the Caption dialog box, click the **AutoCaption** box. Select the options you want to be captioned automatically when you insert them in a document. Captions will now be inserted automatically when you add the type of item selected in the AutoCaption dialog box. Better yet, they will be consecutively numbered to your specifications if you prefer, so you won't have to remember the last number you have used.

Linking and Embedding

It's time to congratulate yourself. You've learned more than you may realize. Sure, you know how to insert a graphic into your document, but did you realize you have been *embedding* them? Embedding is a fancy way to say that you've included all the required tools to edit that inserted object. But don't take my word for it, see for yourself. Double-click on any of your inserted pictures included in Word 97 and watch what happens. The application used to create and edit these pictures, Microsoft Paint, opens up inside of Word, allowing you to directly edit your graphic. This is the advantage of embedding objects; you embed everything necessary to edit that object later.

Now it's time to learn even more. Suppose that graphic you are inserting belongs to someone else—they are continuing to update it, perhaps storing the latest version on a network. If you simply embed the graphic, you will only have the latest version as of the date you embedded it. To get a later version, you would have to delete the currently embedded object and replace it with the more updated version existing elsewhere. But there's a better way to do this, which you will learn now, and it's called *linking*.

Linking Up

Linking simply means you make a connection between a graphic (or any object) in your document and the original source of the object. That way, if the original object is ever updated or changed, even if the owner forgets to tell you, your document can have the latest update appear automatically.

To create a link to the selected picture rather than embedding it, you open the Insert menu, point to Picture, and choose **From File**. Now select the **Link To File** check box in the Insert Picture dialog box. The picture will appear just as it did before. The only difference is that each time you open this document, Word will automatically update the picture with the linked source, and you will see the latest updated version of the picture. Of course, this requires that the linked source be available when you open this document (no problem if it's linked to another location on your computer's drive, but could potentially be a problem if linked to another location on your network, or the Internet).

Finally, this whole discussion applies to much more than simply pictures and graphics. Object Linking and Embedding, also known as OLE, applies to spreadsheets, presentations, drawing and painting programs, and even other documents, or portions of documents, included inside of your document, or inside of any other OLE-compliant application. Your Word document could be included as an object linked or embedded in a Paint picture, or Excel worksheet, for example.

So What's Embedding?

The alternative to simple pasting of a graphic or linking to an existing graphic is called embedding. The difference between linking and embedding is where the actual object is stored. When you import a graphic and link it to its original application, the graphic is not stored as part of the document. Instead, a link (or connection, if you prefer) is maintained between your document and the program that created the graphic. Because the graphic is not actually part of your document, when you open that other program and make changes to the graphic, those changes are not reflected within your document until you update it. The link helps your document find the changed graphic and update the linked version of it.

With embedding, on the other hand, a graphic is stored as part of the Word 97 document. Just as in linking, however, there is a special connection between the document and the program that created the graphic. But this time the connection takes a different form. When you want to make changes to an embedded graphic, you don't go to the program that created it, but to your document. Double-click on the graphic, and you'll see the original program used to create the graphic right inside your Word document, where you can work within its program window to make your changes. Finish making your changes, exit the graphics program, and you're returned to your document where the graphic already reflects your changes. Unlike a linked object, an embedded object is updated immediately as soon as changes are made. That's because you're not making changes to an object that's stored somewhere else, but to the one that's stored within your document.

To embed an existing graphic into your document, start with the graphics program. Open and select the graphic, then open the **Edit** menu. Choose the **Copy** command. Now switch to Word 97 and place the insertion point where you want the graphic to appear. Open the **Edit** menu and choose the **Paste Special** command. In the Paste Special dialog box, make sure that the Data Type has correctly identified your graphic (OLE includes lots of things, but usually it's a **Picture** or **Bitmap**, and often it's actually the name of the other program used to create the graphic). If everything is in order, click on the **Paste** button and press **OK**. Your graphic should appear, and is now officially embedded into your document. Remember that all you have to do to make changes to your graphic is to double-click the graphic, and the graphics package will open automatically.

OLE Applications

Windows applications that support object linking and embedding (OLE) can exchange information between objects. Use *linking* to automatically update the information in an object when the source information changes. Use *embedding* to insert an object from one application into another. Both applications must support object linking and embedding.

153

The Least You Need to Know

Anyone can place quality graphics into their documents because Word 97 already comes packaged with a great selection of Clip Art.

What's the fastest way to stick a graphic into my document?

You can quickly place a picture (a graphic) into your document by opening the **Insert** menu, pointing to the **Picture** command, and choosing **Clip Art**. Find the graphic you want, click **OK**, and the graphic will be included in your document.

I'm bored with the Clip Art on my computer. Is there any more?

Boatloads. If you ever need more than the hundreds of Clip Art images that come with Word 97, click the **Connect To Web For Additional Clips** and say hello to zillions of them.

My graphic is too big for my document. How can I squish it?

All graphics can be shaped and resized by selecting them (click on it) to reveal their handles, and then clicking and dragging any of the handles in the direction needed for the desired size.

I've got lots of graphics and need a simple caption to appear under each. What's the best way to do it?

Open the **Insert** menu and choose **Caption**. Click the **AutoCaption** button and select the style and words you prefer. Now insert the captions in your document. They will maintain a consistent format and be consecutively numbered automatically.

I want a balloon with text inside of my graphic, just like in the comics. What should I do?

You need a callout (that's what it's called). Locate your **Drawing** toolbar, click the **AutoShapes** button, and point to **Callouts**. Choose the style and shape and it appears on your document. Drag it into place and then click to type inside.

Chapter 13

Make Your Documents Sing & Dance (Adding Multimedia Features)

In This Chapter

➤ Spicing up your document with voice clips and sound recordings

➤ Adding video clips to your document

➤ Editing sound and video clips inside your document

➤ Animating text and other effects

Think your document is too boring to send to your audience? Want to knock their socks off by adding real sounds and video recordings? It's no longer considered rocket science to add these multimedia effects to your document, especially since Word 97 provides all the help. Blast off today with sounds and videos by following along in this chapter.

Tell Me Again, What's Multimedia?

The term Multimedia has evolved to become the description for any or all of the objects that make you take notice in a document. It might be a sound effect, a voice, animated objects, or video segments. This was once a big-time technical event that you could sell tickets to, but with powerful and affordable computers it has become an everyday event. There's no reason you can't add some to your own documents.

Give Me Some Examples!

Here are some examples of multimedia paving the way to riches and glory in today's world, and you can be a part of it:

➤ Add sound effects like applause or breaking glass to an instructional document to help guide the reader to a conclusion.

➤ Supplement a training document with short video segments that demostrate the key ideas.

➤ Include speeches or conversation so the reader (listener) can hear the inflection and other nuances that provide additional meaning.

➤ Leave voice messages in everyday announcement documents like cafeteria menus or daily bulletins.

➤ Dictate a letter to your secretary without typing a word.

➤ Speak your mind and record it as part of your status reports to your boss.

Check This Out...

Multimedia Effects Are Great for Web Pages!

Stored videos, speeches, and other recordings are great for your Web documents. You can add them as described in Chapter 23.

What Do I Need to Get Started?

If you've purchased your computer in the last year or so, it most likely contains everything you need to get started in multimedia. That is,

A **sound card**   This enables you to play back recorded sounds in your documents. Sound cards also include the capability to record sounds, but first you'll need a microphone with the correct connector to plug into your sound card. A sound card by itself produces enough sound to be heard using headphones, which can plug directly into the sound card. If you want to hear the sound without wearing headphones, you'll need speakers.

Speakers   But not that little one that beeps inside your computer. Speech and music sounds require real speakers, usually connected outside of your computer case, but sometimes they are integrated into the case (often in laptops) or even on the sides of your computer display. Nothing fancy is needed, and a good small pair (two provide stereo sound) won't cost much more than dinner for one in the city (less than $30). Speakers plug right into your sound card, and also require electrical power in the form of batteries or an AC-adapter that plugs into a wall outlet.

A capable **video card**   Multimedia includes graphics animation and video, and the video can slow down your computer if it's not prepared to handle it. The way to speed things up is to get a fast video card with lots of video memory.

A **microphone**   If you want to record your own voice, you'll need a microphone. Most sound cards come with a microphone that gets the job done, but you can spend lots more money if you want.

A **CD-ROM player**   A multimedia computer can play your music CDs in the background while you work on other things. Most software, clip art, and computer games are now purchased on CD-ROM, so this investment is almost a necessity.

If you don't have any of this, all the components are readily available at your local computer store or dealer. If you are handy with a screwdriver, you can probably install all of them yourself. Or, your computer store can install them for you at a reasonably small fee.

Upgrading Your PC?

If you discover that your PC is just not up to snuff, and you need a little help figuring out what it takes to bring it up to a Multimedia machine, check out Que's *The Complete Idiot's Guide to PCs*, 4th Edition, by Joe Kraynak.

Want to watch real video or animations on your computer screen? You'll need a media player program. By a stroke of incredible luck, you have purchased Microsoft Word 97, which includes the incredible Media Player that gets the job done nicely. You'll learn more about the Media Player program later in this chapter.

Want to record your own video? You'll need either a digital camera that connects to your computer, or an adapter for a common VCR camera that connects it to your computer. These can get a little more expensive, into the hundreds of dollars, but the prices are coming down every day.

Adding Sound Clips or Video Clips That Already Exist

If you don't have a microphone to record your speech, it doesn't mean your documents have to be silent. You can add sounds that have been prerecorded. It's becoming more common to find sound files in places all over the Internet, but you don't have to look that far. The Word 97 (and Office 97) CD-ROM comes with lots of categorized pre-recorded sound bites that you can use in your documents.

To practice inserting a sound into your document, place the Word 97 or Office 97 CD into your CD-ROM drive in your computer, and open or create a document you want to contain sounds. The sound clips are stored on the CD and can be accessed from inside of Word 97.

Sample sound clips (and video clips also) are available from the Microsoft Clip Gallery. The easiest way to get there is to open the **Insert** menu, point to **Picture**, and choose the **Clip Art** command. Another perfectly acceptable way to get there is to open the **Insert** menu, choose the **Object** command, then find and select the **Microsoft Clip Gallery** in the **Object Type** selection box. The Clip Gallery dialog box will open and the CD-ROM will be accessed automatically to display additional clip art pictures, sounds, and video clips.

The Clip Gallery also provides sounds and videos.

Find sounds (and store your own) here.

Click to select any video or sound.

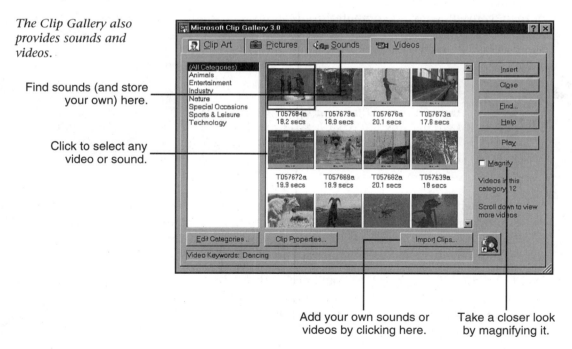

Add your own sounds or videos by clicking here.

Take a closer look by magnifying it.

See the tabs for Clip Art, Pictures, Sounds, and Videos? Word 97 considers sound clips and video clips to be just another object you can add to your document, like a graphic. Click the **Sounds** tab to bring it to the front, and make sure All Categories is selected in the list of categories on the left. You'll see several sample sound clips, each with a descriptive name and a time duration. Once you find a sample sound clip you want to include in your document, click to select it, and then click the **Insert** button. The sound clip gets inserted into your document at the cursor position.

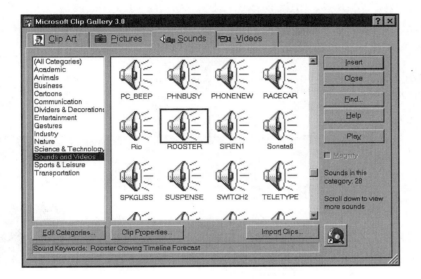

The Gallery is loaded with pre-recorded sounds bursting to get into your document.

A second way to insert sounds into your Word document is through the Object dialog box. Use this method if you've been given a sound clip file from a friend, or you've just downloaded one from the Internet, for example. After placing the insertion point in your document at the desired location for the sound, open the **Insert** menu and choose **Object**. In the Object dialog box choose **Media Clip** from the Object type list. Now locate the sound file you want to add and click the Insert button.

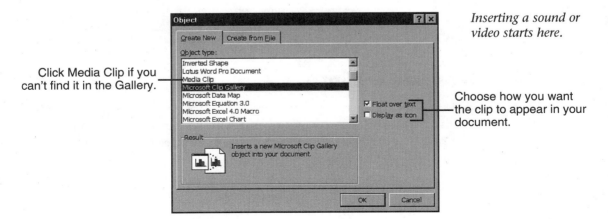

Inserting a sound or video starts here.

Click Media Clip if you can't find it in the Gallery.

Choose how you want the clip to appear in your document.

159

You can use this Media Clip object whenever you want to insert sound, video, voice recording, and other multimedia effects.

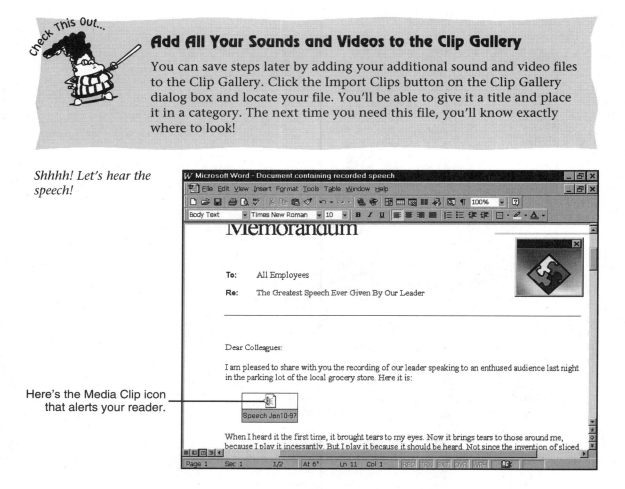

Check This Out...

Add All Your Sounds and Videos to the Clip Gallery

You can save steps later by adding your additional sound and video files to the Clip Gallery. Click the Import Clips button on the Clip Gallery dialog box and locate your file. You'll be able to give it a title and place it in a category. The next time you need this file, you'll know exactly where to look!

Shhhh! Let's hear the speech!

Here's the Media Clip icon that alerts your reader.

Let's Hear Those Sound Clips

Once the sound is inserted in your document, it will appear as a small media icon. To play the sound, just double-click the icon. The sound will start automatically. When it's finished, you can hear it again by clicking the Play button, or else double-clicking the icon again.

```
W Microsoft Word - Document containing recorded speech            _  🗗  ✕
🗐 File  Window                                                     _  🗗  ✕
```

Memorandum

To: All Employees

Re: The Greatest Speech Ever Given By Our Leader

_____

Dear Colleagues:

I am pleased to share with you the recording of our leader speaking to an enthused audience last night in the parking lot of the local grocery store. Here it is:

When I heard it the first time, it brought tears to my eyes. Now it brings tears to those around me, because I play it incessantly. But I play it because it should be heard. Not since the invention of sliced bread has an event so touched the lives of those we love so dearly.

```
Double-click to Play Media Clip
```

Double-clicking automatically plays the recorded sound.

Inserting Voice Comments When Revising a Document

You can attach voice recordings as a part of revising a Word 97 document. To listen to your voice comments (these were called annotations in earlier versions of Word), your audience must have a sound card installed on their computer. To record comments, you must also have a microphone.

This might sound confusing at first, but Word 97 offers two different and distinct methods to record voice comments in a document. The previous part of this chapter showed you how to add sounds using the Clip Gallery and the Media Object. Here we discuss the second alternative called the Comment, which is inserted in a similar way. When would you use a Comment over a Sound Clip? Comments are usually used by multiple people during a document revision, because it provides an additional window on the screen to help identify and organize the comments of the reviewers. To insert a voice comment, open the **Insert** menu and click **Comment**. The bottom of the screen will split into the Comments pane, where your voice comment can be recorded. Click the **Insert Sound Object** button and record your voice comment. If Word displays a message asking whether you want to update the sound object, click **Yes**. After recording the comment, click the **Close** button.

To test your recorded comment, right-click the **Sound** icon in the Comments pane and choose Play from the shortcut menu. If you don't like it, you can click the **Cut** button or press the **Delete** key to remove this comment, then record another. Once the comment meets your approval, you can save your document and the sound will remain as part of the document. To close the Comment pane, click the **Close** button.

Record your voice comment inside a document.

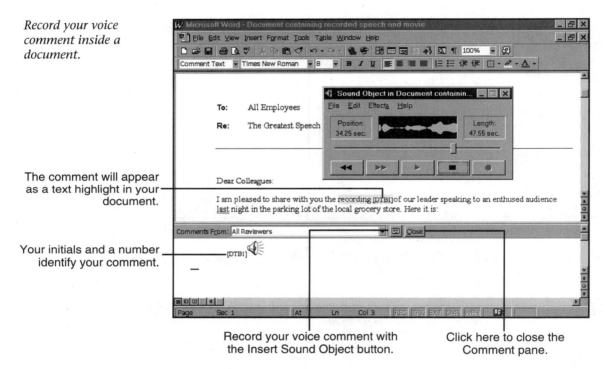

The comment will appear as a text highlight in your document.

Your initials and a number identify your comment.

Record your voice comment with the Insert Sound Object button.

Click here to close the Comment pane.

Listening to Comments in Your Document

When a friend opens your document and wants to listen to your comment, they simply double-click the sound icon and the Media Player will appear. Click the **Play** button in the Media Player and the comment will be played back. Click the **Close** button (the upper right corner of the window) to close the Media Player when you are finished listening to the comment.

Launch Options for Multimedia

As a listener of comments, you can choose when a media clip will play. This happens only when you double-click it, as soon as the document is opened, or as a customized event (bring up Media Player, but wait for me to click the Play button). You can choose one of these settings in your Media Player. Open the **Tools** menu and click **Animations Settings Object**. Place a check in the option you prefer.

Adding Video to Your Documents

If you can figure out how to place sound in your documents, you'll have no problem placing video, because it's done the same way. Word 97 considers both sound and video to be equivalent—they're both Media Clips. So we follow the same steps for adding video clips as we did for adding sound clips.

For inserting prerecorded video clips that come with your Word 97 (or Office 97) CD-ROM, place the CD-ROM in your computer, open the **Insert** menu, point to **Picture**, and choose **Clip Art**. In the Clip Gallery, click the **Video** tab to bring the samples to the front. Click to select the video clip of your choice, then click the **Insert** button. The video clip will be inserted in your document. To play back the video clip, double-click it with your mouse. To close the clip, click anywhere else inside your document.

To insert a recorded video clip from another source, follow these steps. Open the **Insert** menu and choose **Object**. In the Insert Object dialog box, choose the **Microsoft Media Clip**. This will place a small media clip icon in your document. Now open the **Insert Clip** menu and choose between **ActiveMovie**, **Video for Windows**, or other supported formats that may exist on your computer. Locate the actual video file and click the **Open** button. The icon will change to a view of the first frame of your video.

All the controls for playing your video are now on the screen. You can play, rewind, fast-forward, and so on. Once you click outside of the video and on your document in the background, the video controls will disappear until they are needed again. To play the video again, just double-click the media icon.

Choosing the Type of Video Clip to Insert.

Most videos from Microsoft will be either ActiveMovie or Video for Windows.

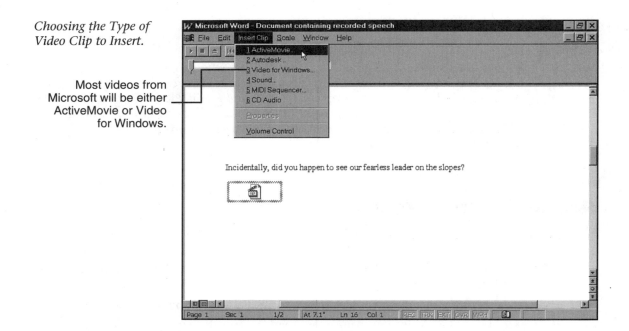

More on the Media Player for Multimedia

The easiest tool to use with multimedia is the Media Player, and it's included in Word 97. The Media Player application allows you to embed video clips, animation clips, MIDI (Musical Instrument Digital Interface) sequences, and sound clips in your Word 97 document.

To open and learn more about your Media Player, click the Windows 95 or Windows NT Start button, point to Programs, then point to Accessories, next to Multimedia, and finally choose the Media Player icon. Whew! Want an easier way to open it? Just find a supported multimedia file and double-click. The Media Player will open automatically in preparation of playing the file.

With the Media Player open, notice the **Device** menu. Click to open it and you'll find the list of all categories of supported multimedia files, including videos, sound, and audio CDs. By choosing each device, you will get a file open dialog box that views only those files of the proper type for that device (choose Sound and you'll see only sound files, and so on). When the Media Player is opened by double-clicking a multimedia file, the proper device is automatically chosen for you.

The other very important command on this **Device** menu is the **Volume Control**. Choose it to adjust the volume and balance (between the right and left of your stereo speakers) for each of your multimedia devices.

The Media Player includes all the buttons you typically see on a tape recorder or VCR. You can play, stop, pause, rewind, and fast forward to arrive at any point inside your sound or video clip. Here are some tips on using the buttons in the Media Player:

➤ **Rewind or Fastforward.** To rewind the recorded sound or video, drag the slider to the left (rewind) or right (fast forward). You can also click one of the following buttons to rewind to a specific spot:

 Rewinds to the previous selection mark or to the beginning.

 Rewinds in small increments.

 Fast forwards to the next selection mark or to the end.

 Fast forwards in small increments.

➤ **Rewind automatically.** To have your multimedia file rewind automatically when it's finished playing, open the Edit menu and click Options. Click to choose either Auto Rewind or Auto Repeat.

➤ **Change the Scales on Your Media Player.** Depending on the type of file you are playing, you can choose a scale that represents time in seconds, frames in the video or animation file, or tracks on the CD. With the multimedia file opened, click to open the Scale menu. Now choose the type of scale you want to display.

Check This Out...

Play It Back Quick!

A fast way to play back most multimedia files is to use the right mouse button. Simply right-click on the media icon and choose the appropriate command from the shortcut menu that appears.

Finding your way around the Media Player controls.

Play

Stop

Pause

Drag the slider to the left to rewind, to the right to fast forward.

To play just a portion, click these at the starting and ending point in the selection, and then click Play.

Another way to play—right-click and use the shortcut menu.

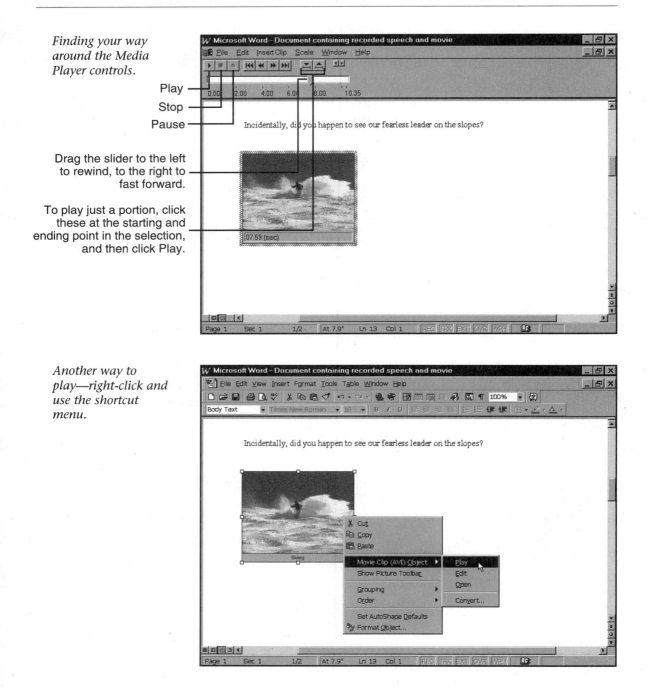

When to Link a Large Multimedia File Instead

Since multimedia files (like sound, but especially video) are so large, they are often stored with others like themselves in a shared area on a central server (perhaps a file server at your business, but it could be a folder on your computer). Instead of inserting these large files into your document, making your document very huge, you can point to them instead. You do this by linking a multimedia file to your document. An added benefit to linking multimedia files to your document is if anyone updates the original multimedia file, your document points to the update automatically. All you need to do is double-click on the multimedia icon to get the updated version.

To try linking for yourself, open the **File** menu, click **Open**, and then find and double-click the multimedia file you want to link. On the **Edit** menu, click **Options**, and then specify the options you want. On the **Edit** menu, click **Copy Object**. Open the Word 97 document you want to link the file to, and then click where you want it to appear. On the **Edit** menu, click **Paste Special**. Click the format you want to use, and then click **Paste Link**. It sounds like a lot of steps, but you'll benefit by having a document that's much smaller in size (since the media file is stored separately), and if the media file ever changes, your document will be updated automatically.

> **Link Sound Files to Your Document**
> When a sound (or video) file is linked, the new document is updated automatically if the information in the original recording changes. If you want to edit the linked recording, double-click it. The toolbars and menus from the program that was used to create the information appear.

The Least You Need to Know

Your documents may benefit from a prudent use of multimedia effects such as sound and video. This chapter reviewed the methods used to place multimedia in your documents, such as:

➤ Look in the Clip Gallery that came with Word 97. You'll find lots of prerecorded sound and video files.

➤ Quick voice comments can be included in a document by opening the **Insert** menu and choosing **Comment**. Then click the **Insert Sound Object** button and record your message.

➤ Record your own audio clips by inserting a Media Clip icon in your document. Then open the icon and select a format, then record your file.

➤ Editing sound and video clips inside your document is easy when you use the Media Controls.

Chapter 14

Your Table Is Being Prepared

In This Chapter

> ➤ Creating a table to organize your information

> ➤ Making your table look nicer with borders and shading

> ➤ Moving around inside a table

> ➤ Making changes to an existing table

> ➤ Putting a caption on a table

> ➤ Getting rid of tables you hate

The word *table* possibly comes from the Latin word *Tab-Bleh*, which loosely translates to "Using only the Tab key to create a table makes it look like Bleh!" You don't want your tables to look like bleh, and neither do I, so this chapter was written especially for the subject.

Microsoft Word 97 provides several Table features that build good tables with a minimum of effort. Using a table is a good way to line up information neatly. And just because it's a table doesn't mean it has to be a box with gridlines separating your words or figures, either. Tables can be subtle, even invisible, and still have the power to control the placement of your information.

Setting the Table

Sooner or later you are going to have information in your document that you'd like to appear organized. You should consider putting the information in a table. What exactly is a *table*? If you say a box with rows and columns, that's right, and in Word, the box is not even needed.

Tables present information in rows and columns. They're great for organizing information in your faxes, letters, memos, and reports. You can use tables to show lists of data, personnel rosters, financial information, scripts, and procedural steps. A reader usually finds it easier to locate and understand detailed information when it is presented in a table. You will discover that you can place just about anything in a table, including pictures, and then format the content of the table using all of the features you learned in the past few chapters.

Check This Out...

What Is a Table?

A *table* is a collection of rows and columns, just like a simple spreadsheet. Each row and column inside a table is made up of units called *cells*. A single cell is where a row and a column intersect. A cell is where you type a table entry. The smallest table consists of a single cell (not very useful), while the largest can contain thousands of cells, spanning as many pages as is necessary. Entire documents can be created inside a table.

A common résumé is one of the best examples of a document that's easier to create and edit using a table rather than tabs or margins. You might not think it at first, until you generalize that tables are nothing more than text lined up neatly in columns. A résumé has dates or companies lined up on the left, and experiences described to the right. A perfect match for a table. Tables are also an easy way to align paragraphs side-by-side. What about table lines, you ask? Well, tables don't always require lines or borders, which aren't always needed or wanted. Let's *table* any further discussion until we review the basics.

Creating a Table Years Ago—Using the Tab Key

There is nothing wrong with the Tab key. By golly, it's one of the few keys on the keyboard that you know exactly what happens when you press it. A nice indent—or many indents, if you press it many times—that always lines up evenly within a paragraph. Yes, they should make a movie about the good old reliable Tab key someday.

Well, okay, that's stretching it. But I bet you have used the Tab key in the past to create simple (or complicated) tables. There's nothing wrong with that at all. In fact, a very small table with two columns and short words can still be created easily using nothing but the Tab key. But, if your table requirements include any of the following, you may find that tabs just don't make the grade when it comes to controlling the appearance of your tables:

➤ The need to hold more than a column or two of information

➤ The desire to line up paragraphs side-by-side

➤ The desire to use the length of tables that will extend beyond a single page

➤ The desire to apply special formats to individual rows or columns

➤ The desire to add gridlines and borders to show off your table

Any or all of these requirements point you to using the Word's Table feature, which can be as easy or sophisticated as you want to make it.

The Cool Way to Create a Table

By far the easiest way to create a perfect table in Word 97 is using the Table feature and the mouse. You can also use the keyboard, (covered later) but you have to think more when using the keyboard. The mouse way is a no-brainer. The basic concept is that you fill in a table after you create it. So let's create one.

You must first open or create a document, and it should be the one where the future table will exist. Now decide where you want the table to exist in your document, and place the insertion point there. Did I mention it's always a good habit to save a document before going on vacation or trying a stunt like this? Now click the **Insert Table** button on the Standard toolbar.

The table grid will drop down, presenting the most popular table sizes. Picture in your mind the size of the table you want, then use your mouse to select it. Drag the mouse down and to the right to highlight the size of table you desire. As you drag the mouse pointer, the grid expands to create rows and columns like a miniature table. The resulting table size will be displayed at the bottom of this grid. When you release the mouse button, your table will be created precisely the way you sized it. An empty table is instantly created in your document, waiting to be filled with your wisdom. How's that for simplicity?

The easy way to create a table using the Table button.

This is the Table button.

Drag to shade a table the size you want.

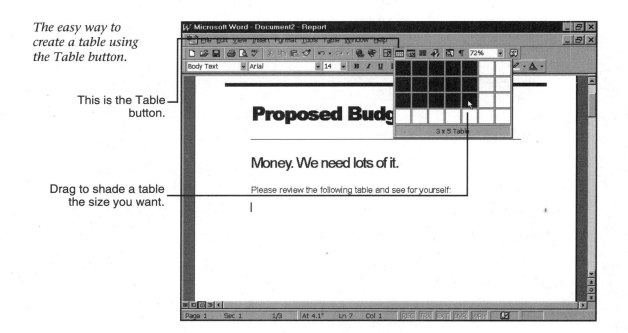

Still Another Method of Preparing Your Table

If your mouse died, you can still create a table using the keyboard. Word actually offers more options this way, but there are more steps to follow. Once again, make sure you have the document you want opened and saved. Place the insertion point where you want the table to be created. Now open the **Table** menu and select the **Insert Table** command. The Insert Table dialog box will appear.

Enter the number of columns in the first box. Press the **Tab** key to move to the second box (or click it with the mouse button). Enter the number of rows in the second box. You don't have to be exact at this point because you can easily change the shape after the table is created. Leave Column Width set to Auto to let Word manage them (if you type more, the column will automatically get bigger). Of course, you can set your Column Width now if you know the size you need. Now click the **OK** button to create your table.

There you go—a table built to your specifications. But it's empty, and empty tables serve little purpose in a document (unless you are creating graph paper), so now it's time to fill it in.

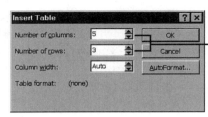

Word's table manners improve with this dialog box.

Type in any number of rows or columns to get started.

Gridlines Prevent Gridlock

If you have trouble coloring between the lines, you will be thankful for table *gridlines*. Word displays dotted gridlines in a table so that you can see which cell you are working in. When a cell is selected, the area inside the bordering gridlines is highlighted. But if gridlines gets annoying, they can be turned off at any time. You can switch between displaying and hiding table gridlines by opening the **Table** menu and clicking the **Gridlines** command, which will toggle between on and off. Gridlines cannot be printed. If you want to print lines between cells, you have to add borders to the table, which is covered later in this chapter.

Drawing Your Tables by Hand

Now you can use a new drawing feature of Word 97 to draw tables similar to the way you use a pencil to draw a table. Just substitute the mouse for the pencil. Ready to try? Click the **Tables And Borders** button on the Standard toolbar and you will see the Tables And Borders toolbar.

By default, the **Draw Table** button is already selected when you open the **Tables And Borders** toolbar. Notice that the mouse pointer now appears as the icon of a small pencil on the drawing space of your document. If you don't see the pencil, be sure to click the **Draw Table** button on the Tables and Borders toolbar.

To start drawing, just click and drag with the left mouse button. The fastest way to draw a table is to create the outside border first, then the lines inside. To draw the outside border, click where you want the top left corner to start, then drag to the desired bottom right corner. No matter how nervous you are, a perfect rectangle will be drawn to your general requirements.

Now draw the row and column lines. Don't worry if the lines aren't even; Word 97 has tools to straighten them out later. The drawing tool helps by drawing only straight lines. Start by dragging inside your table where you would normally sketch a row or column to appear. Connecting each line to the edge of your table happens automatically as you approach the edge with your drag.

 If you make a drawing mistake, you can erase it with the **Eraser** button. Erase the same way you draw, by clicking and dragging the left mouse button over the mistake. You can erase entire lines this way, or just parts of lines. The eraser works only on lines you draw with the **Draw Table**, so don't try using to edit footnotes in your document.

 Maybe you've had a rough day and your row lines aren't evenly distributed. To spread them out perfectly, select the rows and then click the **Distribute Rows Evenly** button. They'll be perfect in no time.

 Likewise, you can select your columns and click **Distribute Columns Evenly**, to balance the width and line them up perfectly.

If you lose your creative spirit, you can always click the **Table AutoFormat** button on this Tables and Borders toolbar, and choose a predesigned table to suit your needs.

That's all you need to create a great table, with the feeling of accomplishment that you drew it all yourself. You'll find that sometimes this is the only way to draw complex tables that have combined row headings in multiple areas, or mixed-width columns.

You may be curious about the other buttons on the Tables and Borders toolbar, and we'll get to them soon enough. This served as your introduction to the basic table creation tools and skills required with Word 97.

Converting Existing Text to Tables

If you've already got text in your document, and you'd like to see it entered into a table, why not try a new feature of Word 97? It's called **Convert Text To Table**, and it works quite well on text or numbers that are already aligned in your document using tabs or commas. This might include a list of names or numbers in your document, or it could be the result of an import of information from a spreadsheet or database, which are often delimited (separated) by a tab or comma.

Give this a try by selecting the entire range of text you want to include, then open the **Tools** menu and choose the **Convert Text To Table** command. You'll see the Convert Text to Table dialog box that allows you to enter specific values for options about your table, but it's worth a try to choose the **AutoFormat** button. **AutoFormat** will attempt to create the most appropriate shape of table based on the selected text. If the result doesn't satisfy you, click the **Undo** button and try again. This time try setting the available row, column, and format options yourself, and click the OK button to see the result.

You can also perform the reverse of this command. The reverse is taking a table in your document and converting it to plain text. This might be something you try when you want to break down a large table into smaller pieces. Select the table, then open the **Table** menu and choose the **Convert Table to Text** command. All table lines, borders, shading, and special effects will be removed, and you will be left with the collection of text or numbers that once appeared in the table cells.

Filling In Your Table with Useful Stuff

Once a table has been created, it's a straightforward process to fill it in. If your insertion point isn't already in the first table cell, you can get it there by clicking anywhere inside the cell. Once inside, just start typing. The cell will automatically adjust to accommodate what you type. You can type in words, numbers, or even place pictures in a cell.

Pressing the **Enter** key inside a cell puts a new paragraph in the same cell. Think of each cell as its own little document, which means the rules of editing and formatting apply.

One entry in a table is boring. It's time to move to the next cell. After filling in the first cell, you can move to the next cell by pressing the **Tab** key. If the insertion point is in the last cell of a table, pressing Tab adds a new row. To move backwards to a previous key, press the combination **Shift+Tab** keys. You can also use the Arrow keys to move around between cells inside your table, but you will find the **Tab** key is faster. Here are a few more navigational tips summed up in, what else, a table:

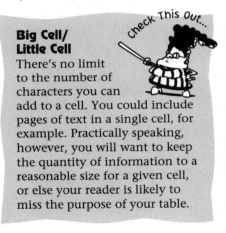

Big Cell/ Little Cell
There's no limit to the number of characters you can add to a cell. You could include pages of text in a single cell, for example. Practically speaking, however, you will want to keep the quantity of information to a reasonable size for a given cell, or else your reader is likely to miss the purpose of your table.

Table 14.1 Navigating Your Table

To....	Press...
To move to the next cell	Press **Tab**
To move to the previous cell	Press **Shift+Tab**
To move to the previous or next row	Use **Up** or **Down** arrow keys
To move to the first cell in the row	**Alt+Home**, or **Alt+7** on the numeric keypad

continues

Table 14.1   Continued

To....	Press...
To move to the last cell in the row	**Alt+End**, or **Alt+1** on the numeric keypad
To move to the first cell in the column	**Alt+Page Up**, or **Alt+9** on the numeric keypad
To move to the last cell in the column	**Alt+Page Down**, or **Alt+3** on the numeric keypad
To start a new paragraph	Press the **Enter** key
To add a new row at the bottom of the table	Press **Tab** at the end of the last row
To add text before a table at the beginning of a document	Press **Enter** at the beginning of the first cell

Formatting Tables Is Easy

Once you enter information into your table you may be so excited that you print your document to see it for real. Surprise! Not what you expected, I bet. No gridlines, no box around it, in fact, except for lining up your information, it doesn't look like a table at all!

We can fix that. This section explains several ways to improve the look of your tables. We'll start with the automated tools that format an entire table at once, then move into the tactical tools for formatting individual pieces of a table.

The Magic of Table AutoFormat

The easiest way to make a table fancy is by using another miracle of Word 97 called Table AutoFormat. Just click inside your table anywhere, it doesn't matter where. Now open the **Table** menu and choose the **Table AutoFormat** command. This is the dialog box you will see, and it's full of ideas for making your table the best it can be.

Scroll up or down this listing of preformatted sample tables using your **Up** or **Down** arrow keys. Watch the Preview box to see if any choices come close to what you want. Don't worry if your table is a different size; the formatting will apply to the size of your table. If the table you're planning will be much smaller than the samples, however, you may not get the heading or column format shown in the Preview screen. If you can't decide between a few of them, try them all! One at a time, of course, and you can always click the **Undo** button on the Standard toolbar to get rid of an end table that doesn't match the rest of the furniture in your document.

Scroll this list to see
preformatted tables.

*Fancy tables await
you in Table
AutoFormat.*

Look here to see an
example of how the
format will look.

If, at a later date, you decide you prefer another style of table, go get it! The information
you have already stored in your table will be preserved and placed in the new table
format. Select your existing table, open the **Table** menu, and run the **Table AutoFormat**
command. Choose a new table format from the list and press the **OK** button.

Creating Custom Table Borders and Shading Manually

If you're a perfectionist, you may not like any of the table format choices in Table Auto-
Format. Whether your table already has a border you don't like, or no border at all, you
can create your own custom border (or shading) for it. Start by selecting the entire table
(to add borders and shading to only specific cells, select only those cells, including the
end of cell mark). Open the **Format** menu and choose the **Borders and Shading** command. Click the **Border** tab to make sure it's in front. The easiest way to border your table
is to click the **Grid** box, and optionally change to a heavier line width by clicking a fatter
line on the right side of the dialog box. When you press the **OK** button, the custom
border will be applied to your table.

Shading can provide emphasis for important cells in your table. One or more cells can
stand out from the rest by giving it a background shading, color, or pattern. To give it a
try, select the cells, then open the **Format** menu and choose the **Borders and Shading**
command. Click the **Shading** tab to bring the options to the front. In the Fill area, click a
shade of gray or a color to appear as the background color. You can also choose to have a
background pattern for the selected cells by clicking and choosing the Style and Color
boxes in the Patterns area, and choosing from the palette that appears. The Preview box
will give you an idea of what it will look like. Click **OK** to apply the shading selections to
your table.

Adding a border is fast and easy; just choose Grid from the Borders and Shading dialog box.

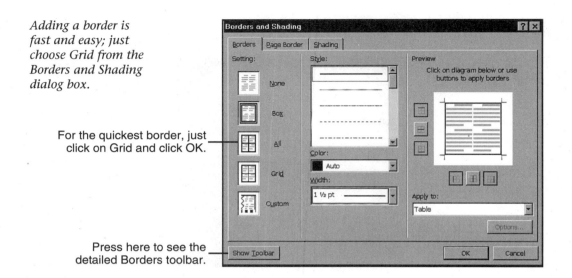

For the quickest border, just click on Grid and click OK.

Press here to see the detailed Borders toolbar.

Using the Tables and Borders Toolbar

Most tables you see in books and magazines are surrounded by crisply detailed lines called borders. Adding a border to your table can help call attention to it on a page. Borders are so common, in fact, that Word 97 includes an entire toolbar dedicated to creating these borders, The Tables and Borders toolbar. Just right-click on any toolbar and choose Tables and Borders. Here are the buttons you can use to format your table:

 If you prefer a fancy line (usually good for the outside borders or calling attention to special cells), click the **Line Style** button and choose a different style.

 Sometimes you'll want a thicker or thinner drawing line. In that case, click the **Line Weight** button and choose the thickness you desire.

To change the color of your table lines, click the **Border Color** button and choose a color from the palette. If you want to change the color of an existing line, click the **Border Color** button and choose the desired color, then drag on top of the existing line. The previous line will be selected and the color change will occur.

And Borders Aren't Limited to Tables Once you learn the method of placing a border on a table, you'll find that it also works on words, paragraphs, and entire pages.

To quickly add shading color to one or more cells, select those cells, then click the **Shading Color** button and choose a color from the palette. The background color of the cells will change to the selected color.

178

If you lose your creative spirit, you can always click the **Table AutoFormat** button on the Tables and Borders toolbar, and choose a predesigned table to suit your needs.

Removing Borders and Shading from Your Table

Regardless of how the border was applied to your table, there's an easy way to get rid of it. First, select the table by clicking anywhere inside of it. Open the **Table** menu and choose the **Table AutoFormat** command (even if you created the border using the Tables and Border toolbar or the Borders and Shading dialog box). In the Formats box, click **None**. Click **OK** to close the dialog box, and you will discover the borders have disappeared from your table.

Formatting the Contents of Cells

Once your table is formatted, you may still wish to format the individual contents of cells, or even whole rows or columns. No problem, just click and drag to select the portion of the table you wish to change. Anything you can type in a cell is fair game for the formatting tools of Word. You can apply any of the character formatting options to any cell, group of cells, entire row, entire column, or the entire table. First select the cell or cells containing the text or numbers you want to format. The following table can assist you in the selection process.

Table 14.2 Helpful Hints for Selecting Items in Your Table

To...	Do This....
Select a cell	Click the left edge of the cell.
Select a row	Click to the left of the row.
Select a column	Click the column's top gridline or border.
Select multiple cells, rows, or columns	Drag across the cell, row, or column; or select a single cell, row, or column, and then hold down the **Shift** key while you click another cell, row, or column.
Select text in the next cell	Press the **Tab** key.
Select text in the previous cell	Press **Shift+Tab**.
Select the entire table	Click the table, and then press **Alt+5** on the numeric keypad. Num Lock must be off.

When in doubt, you can also select rows, columns, or the entire table by clicking in the table and then using the Select commands on the Table menu, or by using keyboard shortcuts.

Rotate That Text!

A helpful tool for fitting more text into your tables is the new Change Text Direction button. If there's not enough room for the text in your table cells, rotate the text and fit it in vertically! You'll find this button on the Tables and Borders toolbar. Just right-click inside any toolbar and choose Tables and borders from the pop-up menu. Select the text in your table, click this button, and rotate the text instantly.

Once the cells are selected, you can apply any of the tools on the Formatting toolbar. Maybe the Bold, Italic, and Underline are growing old. Try changing the font or font size, or arrange the contents with the Center or Right Justify button, or even create a numbered list inside a single cell.

Merging and Splitting Cells

Some tables look better with a heading on the top row. But with multiple columns in a typical table, you always have those column dividers preventing a nicely centered title. You can get rid of column dividers on any given row using the **Merge Cells** command. To create a heading for your table, select the entire first row. Open the **Table** menu and choose the **Merge Cells** command (the **Merge Cells** button also exists on the Tables and Borders toolbar). The multiple cells will be merged into one across the width of a table. Now you can enter and format your title in this new cell.

On the other hand, sometimes you need to create two cells where only one exists. Select the cell you want to split and then click the **Split Cells** button on the Tables and Borders toolbar. You'll see the Split Cells dialog box, in which you can choose how many ways you want to slice your cell. Type in or click to increment either the columns or rows, or both, then click **OK**. Your table cell will now be split into the number of rows and columns you chose.

Editing an Existing Table

Tables hold information, and information changes. Therefore, your table is bound to change in the future. Good thing that Word 97 is packed with features and functions that assist you in your editing process. This section describes how you can add, delete, or move information from one part of your table to another, adjust the size or number of your rows or columns, and even sort the contents of those cells after you make a change.

Can't See Text in a Cell?

Sometimes you can't see some or all of the text in a cell. What should you do? It's important to check to see whether you have a row height or width that's smaller than the text you are trying to display. To adjust the height or width of a column or row, move your mouse pointer until it rests on the table line you want to adjust. The mouse cursor will change to the line adjusting symbol, and now you can drag the line in the direction you need. If you prefer a shortcut to adjusting your table, try this: On the **Table** menu, click the **Cell Height And Width** command. You can choose to either adjust the row height (click the Row tab), or the column width (the Column tab), or both. In the Height Of Row box, click **Auto** and the cells will be adjusted the proper amount to display text in the cells. For automatic column width adjustment, click the **AutoFit** button.

Moving Information from Cell to Cell

You can move or copy a cell's contents to a new location in your table. If you need to move a cell's contents, select the contents by clicking in the middle of the cell. Then drag the cell to its new location. You copy the contents of one cell to another with a similar technique. To copy a cell, hold down the **Ctrl** key as you drag.

Deleting Information in a Table

If you don't like the contents of any cell in your table, you can get rid of it easily. Your best bet for deleting a cell is to select it, then open the **Table** menu and choose the **Delete Cell** command. This opens a dialog box that provides you with deleting options. Since you don't want to leave a cell in the middle of your table blank, you have the option of shifting the cells around it to fill the space. The other option you can choose here is to delete either the entire row or entire column.

If you want to get rid of a larger amount of information in your table, you can delete one or more rows or columns at a time. Click and drag to select an entire row (or rows) and open the **Table** menu. You'll see the **Delete Cell** command has now changed into the **Delete Rows** command. Choose this command and the row will be deleted, and the remaining portion of the table will shift to fill the empty space. Likewise, to remove one or more columns, select the columns and open the Table menu. Choose the **Delete Columns** command and the table will shift to fill the empty space.

If you don't see the command you want on the **Table** menu, it probably means you haven't selected the row or column completely. Try again, or use the command **Select Row** or **Select Column** to help you.

Changing the Dimensions of Your Table

You may want to do more than simply change the format of the contents of a table cell or cells. You can also change the inside and outside dimensions of any part of your table.

To change the width of any column in your table, drag the column's right edge to its new location. The left edge can be moved, as well. If you want to let Word adjust the widths of columns automatically, you can double-click either edge of a column.

Unless you specify otherwise, the height of each row in a table depends on two things: the contents of the cells in that row and the paragraph spacing you add before or after text.

More Headroom in a Table You can also change row height by using the vertical ruler in Page Layout view. On the **View** menu, click **Page Layout**. On the vertical ruler, drag a row mark to the location that adjusts the size to your taste.

You can vary the height of each row, but all cells in the same row will have the same height. To make the row height fit the contents, open the **Table** menu, click **Cell Height And Width**, and then click the **Row** tab. Now click to choose the **Auto** option in the **Height Of Rows** box. If you don't select Auto and the cell contents exceed the listed height, Word cuts off the bottom of the contents. Not good.

You can add more space between the rows of a table if you want. First, select the rows you want to change. On the **Table** menu, click **Cell Height And Width**, and then click the **Row** tab. Now enter the exact measurement you prefer, or click to increment to measurement. When you click **OK**, the changes will be applied to the selected rows of your table.

Adding Columns and Rows

To add more rows or columns to your table, select the area where you want the new row or column placed, then choose either the **Insert Columns** or **Insert Rows** command from the **Table** menu. The new table addition will be added, and the table size will be adjusted to accommodate the new size. You can easily make a table bigger by moving the insertion point to the last cell (the bottom right) and pressing the **Tab** key. A new row of cells will be added.

Numbering the Lines in Your Table

Here's an easy method to number the cells in your table. First, select the range of cells you want to number. To number the beginning of each row, select only the first column in the table. Then click the **Numbering** button on the Formatting toolbar, and the Table Numbering dialog box will appear. You can choose between numbering your cells across rows or numbering down columns. Click **OK** and your cells will be automatically numbered. You may have to adjust the size of the column or row to accommodate the new numbering additions.

Sorting Table Information Automatically

Do you get the shakes when you need to prepare a table in alphabetical or numerical order? Shake no more, my friend, and say hello to the powerful sorting features of Word 97 that remove the pain of sorting—any sorting, in any kind of table, including sorts by date.

For important reasons known by logicians and the people who create the phone book, it's always a good idea to select your entire table, not just a single column, when performing a sort. Selecting only a single column in other word processors, including previous versions of Word, can cause misalignment of other related information in your table. By selecting the entire table, all related information contained in a row gets sorted at the same time, so it all stays together nicely.

Select your table and open the **Table** menu. Choose the **Sort** command, which opens the Sort dialog box. You can choose to sort on any column by clicking and selecting the column heading in the **Sort By** text box. The default is the first column, which is usually what you want anyway. Press the **OK** button, and a-sorting it will go. If the results look good the first time, save your work and quit while you're ahead. If not, click the **Undo** button and try again.

Sort This and Sum That

You'll notice that the Tables And Borders toolbar now includes **Sort Ascending** and **Sort Descending**.

As you edit your table, you may find these buttons helpful in sorting the contents. To use them properly, first select the range you wish to sort, then choose either ascending or descending. The cells don't have to be numeric—you can sort alphabetically just as easily.

And to turn your table into a fancy worksheet, the **AutoSum** button is at your service. Let's say you want to sum all the values of a column and put the total at the bottom. Just click in the bottom cell of the column (add an extra row if needed) and click the **AutoSum** button. The cell will now contain the sum value of the column.

Choose the column on which you wish to base the sort of your table.

To specify the type of data you want to sort, click Text, Number, or Date in the Type box.

You can sort your table in just about any way imaginable.

> **Sort**
>
> **Sort by**
> [Type of Pizza ▾]   Type: [Text ▾]   ◉ Ascending   ○ Descending
>
> **Then by**
> [▾]   Type: [Text ▾]   ◉ Ascending   ○ Descending
>
> **Then by**
> [▾]   Type: [Text ▾]   ◉ Ascending   ○ Descending
>
> **My list has**
> ◉ Header row   ○ No header row
>
> [OK]   [Cancel]   [Options...]

Click options to indicate whether you want to distinguish upper-case and lowercase entries.

Calculating Your Information

Σ You can also perform calculations in a table. To add a column of numbers, for example, click the cell below the column you want to add, and then click AutoSum on the Tables and Borders toolbar. The result will appear in the cell you clicked. For other calculations, use the Formula command on the Table menu.

Dealing with Tables That Spread over Multiple Pages

There's nothing worse than table headings appearing at the bottom of a page, with rows and columns of unlabeled data appearing at the top of the next page. Word provides protection from this sort of thing by either preventing smaller tables from being broken up in the first place, or by providing table headings on every page for large tables.

If Your Table Extends Beyond a Single Page

To break a table across pages, click the row you want to appear on the next page. Press **Ctrl+Enter**, and the table will be conveniently split between pages, including formatting and borders that may have been applied.

Preventing a Table from Breaking Across Pages

If your table fits comfortably on a single page, and you want to keep it that way, you can tell Word to take care of it. Then, if text editing ever pushes or pulls your table toward a natural page break, Word will push your table in its entirety to the next page.

To protect your table from ever splitting, first select it by clicking it. Open the **Table** menu and click the **Cell Height And Width** command. Now click the **Row** tab to bring it to the front. Clear the **Allow Row To Break Across Pages** check box by clicking it. Click the **OK** button, and your table will be forever protected (until you decide to fill that check box again).

Putting a Table Heading on Each Page

To repeat a table heading on subsequent pages, use the Headings command. First, select the rows of text, including the first row, that you want to use as a table heading. Then open the **Table** menu and click the **Headings** command. Word automatically repeats table headings only for tables that are split with automatic page breaks. Word will not repeat a heading if you insert a manual page break within a table. These repeated table headings are visible only in Page Layout view.

Messing Up a Table with Margins

If you change your margins with an existing table, you will notice the table isn't affected at all. It's stuck right where you put it. That's because existing tables are not affected by changes to the page margins. If you want to maintain the same relationship between table width and page margins after changing the margins, you will have to adjust the table width manually.

To change the width of columns in a table, first select the columns whose width you want to adjust. Next, on the **Table** menu, click **Cell Height And Width**, and then click the **Column** tab. You can specify an exact measurement by entering a number in the **Width Of Column** box, but there's an easier way: To make the column width automatically fit the contents, click **AutoFit**.

Don't forget that you can also change the width of a column by dragging the column boundaries in the table itself or by dragging the column markers on the horizontal ruler. To display column-width measurements, point to the horizontal ruler, and then hold down **Alt** while you click the mouse button. You will see the table markers appear in the Ruler.

Completely Blasting Away a Table Permanently

There is still no "delete the whole table" key in Word 97, which is bad news if you create lots of bad tables. You can still get rid of them however, but it takes an extra step.

To completely eliminate a table, first highlight the entire offending table. Then open the **Table** menu and choose the **Delete Rows** command. It's gone forever, unless you want to bring it back with the magic **Undo** button. But why would you?

The Least You Need to Know

Tables are the best way to organize and display multi-columned lists of information in your document. This chapter described the helpful tips that can be used when creating our tables.

Show me the fastest way to create a table in my document.

Click the **Insert Table** button on the Standard toolbar and drag it to the shape you need. When you release your mouse button, the table will appear, designed to your order.

Where are the tools I need to edit my table?

All the tools you'll ever need to edit a table can be found on the **Tables and Borders** toolbar, including alignment, merging, splitting, drawing, erasing, rotating, and formatting.

How do I move data from one part of my table to another?

If you need to move a cell's contents, select the contents by clicking in the middle of the cell. Then drag the cell to its new location. To copy a cell, hold down the **Ctrl** key as you drag.

I goofed. My table's too short. How do I make it longer?

To add either more rows or more columns, select the area where you want the new row or column placed, then choose either the **Insert Columns** or **Insert Rows** command, as needed, from the **Table** menu.

Okay, but my words are squished in the table cells. How can I give them more room?

You can add more space between the rows of a table by increasing the value found in the **Cell Height and Width** command on the **Table** menu.

I'd like a heading title that spans all of my columns. What should I do?

First merge the cells across the width of a table by using the **Merge Cells** command from the **Table** menu. Then insert your heading and center it as needed.

Chapter 15

Importing a Fine Piece of Text

In This Chapter

➤ Loading and saving a DOS text file

➤ Grabbing words from the Web

➤ Opening a WordPerfect file in Word 97

➤ Copying existing work from a DOS application

➤ Saving documents in other formats

Being human, we have to communicate with others. We can communicate using speech, our hands, even shaking our legs. If you understand the language, it's so easy you don't even think about it. If you don't, you stare in wonder and try to keep from laughing.

Computer files are like that. Pick up a disk with a document stored on it. Can you read the document? Even if you break it open and hold it up to a strong light? No, because that document is stored in a form unbeknownst to humans. We need a computer to translate those bits and bytes of magnetic ink into words and special formatting, and then splash the resulting document on our color screens.

But computers also have trouble understanding files that aren't stored in their repertoire of languages. So before you share a document with a friend who's using a different word processor or a very different type of computer, you might want to review these helpful tips on file formats. Or, if you've been given a file on disk that you can tell your computer is laughing at, fear not, for you can help your computer in the conversion.

Opening a Non-Word Document in Word 97

All word processors create documents and store them as files on hard disks or disks in something called a *file format*. Each word processor has its own format design, trying to be better than the competitors. The default file format for Word is different from the file format in WordPerfect, as you might expect. This sounds like it could lead to utter chaos in the world of computers, especially if you have to share documents between word processors. But amazingly, it works! The companies decided to make life easier for us by including *import filters* for most of their competitors' file formats. An import filter converts a document from one format to another. For example, the WordPerfect 6.1 import filter in Word 97 converts WordPerfect files into Word documents.

The good news for you is that Word does all the work! When you try to open a non-Word document, those import filters kick in automatically to examine and convert the file if necessary, after asking for your permission. Some formats are converted without telling you at all. And when you're finished, Word puts the document back into the format it came from, unless you request otherwise. So the next time someone hands you a disk with a document on it, you can feel reasonably confident that Word will be able to open and edit it.

What If You Can't Find It?

A trusted companion gives you a disk, explaining that the document it contains tells you how to make money while you sleep. You rush to your desk and pop the disk into your computer and start Word 97, hoping to double your salary by morning. You open Word, then click the **Open** button on the Standard Toolbar. You insert the disk into your computer and click the **Look In** box. Locate the icon of a disk labeled "3 1/2 Floppy" and click to select it. All the files stored on the disk should be displayed, right?

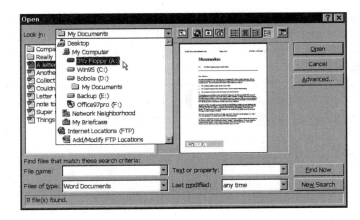

Select the floppy disk drive from the Look In window of the Open dialog box.

Looking for Files on Disk

Don't be discouraged if you don't see anything at first. It doesn't mean the disk is empty. This can happen often if you share documents with a friend who uses another word processor. Word is simply expecting Word documents, so if the file on the disk is in another format, Word won't immediately recognize it. You'll have to manually invoke one of those *conversion filters*, or all of them. You will find them at the bottom of the File Open dialog box in the **Files of type** field.

Open the **Files of type** drop-down box by clicking on it once. The drop-down box will list the available word processor products, so find yours and click to select it. If you aren't sure or want to see all of the files on the disk anyway, select the entry called **All Files (*.*)**. This option allows you to view all the files on your disk (and also your hard drive), not just the Word 97 documents.

Files on disks are found on "3 1/2 Floppy"

Scroll through list to view non-Word files

To see files on a disk, choose either the product type or just All Files.

If the disk contains folders, you can navigate through them by double-clicking them, or search through the whole disk using the searching tools found at the bottom of the file Open dialog box. Watch the preview window in the file Open box, because Word will actually convert and preview any non-Word documents it finds. This can also help you locate and identify documents even if you aren't familiar with the filenames. If these documents are large, the conversion could take several seconds, even for the simple preview. You can press the **Escape** key to quickly (and safely) ignore a preview at any time.

When you find the file you want, click the **OK** button and Word 97 will kick into conversion action. Word will do the best it can to maintain the contents and formatting of the original file, but if it can't, you will at least receive an informational message describing the problem. Most of the time, these problems relate to page formatting items, so you have to decide if it's worth the effort to continue.

Sometimes an external style file may be required, and you can either ask for the style from the person who gave you the document, or try to continue by clicking the **Ignore** button (it may not look great, but at least the words should show up).

Now that the document is open, you can enrich it with your talents and all of the features of Word 97. You don't have to know a lick about the original word processor product. For now, it's considered a Word document. And sooner or later, you will want to save it. Let's try.

Saving and Closing Non-Word Documents When You Are Finished

You can save your document at any time during the editing of a non-Word document (click the **Save** button on the Standard Toolbar), but you will see the Save As dialog box. Word knows you've been working with a different type of file format, and when you want to save it, Word wants to know *how* you want to save it—in Word format, or the other word processor format? The dialog box will present both choices as a button. Simply select the one you want. Remember that if you added any fancy formatting to this document while in Word, those items may not translate back to the other word processor format. Follow these tips to decide how to save your document:

➤ If you will be using Word to edit this document from now on, save it as a Word document.

➤ If you want to apply Word formatting to this document, you're better off saving it as a Word document.

➤ If the document has to be used again with the other word processor, avoid using any special formatting inside Word, and save the document in the other word processor format.

➤ If you haven't a clue, click **No** or **Cancel**. Your document will wait while you go find someone to help you.

You can also save your non-Word document in another non-word file format using the **Save As** command on the **File** menu. Click the pull-down arrow on the **Save As type** box and choose the file format you desire.

If you open a non-Word document, edit it, and attempt to close it before you have saved it, you will see the same dialog box. Once again, you have to decide in which *format* you want the document. You have two choices: It's either Word or the word processor format in which the file was originally created. Decide based on who is going to use the document next. If it's you and you always have Word 97 available, then save it as Word, of course. If you are returning the file to your friend using WordPerfect or WordPro, you'll be doing them a favor by choosing that format. Otherwise, they might not have a file converter for Word 97 documents and won't be able to open your document.

Decide on the format you want, then click the **Save** button on the Standard Toolbar and you'll see a dialog box similar to the one shown here:

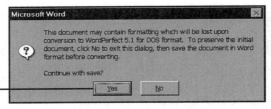

Click here to maintain the old format for others to use.

You decide what format to use before saving your Word 97 file.

Word Keeps Track of the Original Format, so You Don't Have To

Click either the **Yes** or **No** button, and the file will be saved. When it's time to close the file, Word will ask if you want to save your changes. Just remember that Word considers any open document a Word document (except for some plain text files), so you may be asked to save changes even when you didn't make any. That's Word asking one last time if you want to keep it as a Word document. If it's a WordPerfect document, for example, and you haven't made any further changes, you can click the **Cancel** button to prevent Word from replacing it in Word format.

Inserting a Whole File into a Word Document

What's the difference between opening and inserting a file? Glad you asked, because you can save yourself editing time if you choose correctly. The last few pages described how to open a file, regardless of the word processor that created it. When finished, that file is saved. One file is opened; the same file is closed. Inserting is taking the contents (some or all) of one file and placing it inside a Word document.

Take the Easiest Road to Inserting Text The Insert command is best used to copy the entire contents of a file into your Word document. If you only want part of the file, you can still insert the whole thing and then delete the portions you don't want. And don't forget Windows' Copy and Paste commands. You can bypass the Insert command entirely by opening and copying the portion of text in one file, then opening your Word document and pasting the contents into it.

With your Word document open, decide where you want the inserted text and place the insertion point there. Open the **Insert** menu and select the **File** command. Although you can insert other types of program files, such as spreadsheets or presentation graphics, the focus here is on text files, such as those created with other word processing programs. Locate the file you want, highlight it, and click the **OK** button. The file will be *imported*, which means the words and formatting will be automatically converted to Word 97 format and become a permanent part of your document. You may need to do some cleanup using Word's formatting tools, but the result is much improved over previous versions of Word. Remember to save your work when finished.

If you're shocked and disgusted by the inserted file, you can quickly remove it by clicking the **Undo** button. Maybe you inserted the wrong file. Try again, because the **Insert, File** command really works.

Lots of Formats to Choose From

In the earlier example, you used the Files of type drop-down box in the file Open dialog box to see the selection of available word processing formats. If you installed all of the *converters* available in Word 97, you'll be able to choose from many versions of WordPerfect and Word, and even Word for the Macintosh; over 20 converters are available.

If you can't find the converter you need, it may have been deleted or moved, or not installed in the first place. Run the Microsoft Word Setup program again, and install the converters you need.

Have You Been Converted?

A converter is used to take the text and formatting of a document created in one program and make it appear as similar as possible in another program. Microsoft Word 97 comes with converters for over 20 different programs, making it easy to convert documents created in those programs into Word 97 documents.

Formatting Issues

Nothing is perfect in life, and you may find that the file converter you used creates a document that looks different from the original. If the original contained a font you don't have in Word, Word will replace it with something else. A margin setting may be lost, causing heading locations and page counts to change. You may find that character formatting is changed. Page formatting like footnotes, headers and footers, and page numbers are often not converted due to the complexity. In these cases, headers and footers may show up as regular text, and page numbers may disappear completely.

If all the words are there, you should consider the conversion at least a partial success. Retyping words usually takes much longer than adjusting the formatting, so at least you saved *some* time.

Handling Graphics

If graphics are a part of the file you are inserting, you can kiss them goodbye. Although text is usually successful, graphics rarely make it through a file conversion. If yours didn't, don't give up hope; just look for a different way. Since graphics are usually individual components stored inside a file, you can try to find where the original graphic came from. Maybe it's clip art stored on a disk or CD-ROM, and you can copy it directly from the original source. Or you can copy and paste it from the original computer into another Windows program that might have better success, like Paintbrush, or another graphics program. Then you can store the graphic in a format you can insert using the **Picture** command on the **Insert** menu. Finally, if all hope seems lost, you can always print the graphic from the original computer and scan it in as a new graphic, using the scanner method described later in this chapter.

Inserting Only Portions of Text from Other Sources

Sometimes the information you want to insert is part of something bigger. Maybe it's a quote or a short paragraph from a large document, or a table or brief article. Maybe it's the reference section or an appendix from a useful instructional document—important information that you don't want to retype and risk accuracy or a deadline.

The source of the text information you need may be portions of documents created in other Windows or non-Windows programs, DOS applications like the DOS versions of WordPerfect or the DOS editor, or even words on paper that you don't want to retype. Here are some tips for making those words productive.

You Can't Beat Cut and Paste

Since you are running Word 97 using Windows 95 or Windows NT, you can do many things at once. You may have discovered that other programs, including other word processors, can run at the same time on your computer. Imagine having a document opened in Word, another opened in WordPerfect, WordPro, WordPad, Notepad, even a text file opened in the DOS Editor, all at the same time. With good eyes and lots of memory, you can even tile your screen with all your open windows at once. What can you do with such a mess? You can perform miracles.

Okay, maybe *miracles* is stretching it a bit, but to be able to move text so easily from one running program to another feels like a miracle if your only alternative is to import the entire document and edit out the parts you don't want. Just as you can copy and paste between two opened Word documents, you can copy text from another program into your Word document (and sometimes vice versa).

First, get your programs running and the documents or files opened in each. You don't have to tile and view all windows at the same time. The Task Bar makes it easy to switch between running applications. You can select and copy text in one full-screen program, choose another program from the Task Bar, and paste the text into that full-screen program. In fact, your computer remembers what you select and copy from any program, even after you close that program, so it's not absolutely necessary to have both programs running at the same time—it's just easier to explain and prevent mistakes.

If the other program happens to be a Windows program, you'll be happy to know your cut and paste keys usually work the same. Select the text in the other program and click the familiar **Copy** button to copy the text (or you can use the menu commands from that other program).

Check This Out...

Don't Cut Out on This Lesson Yes, the Cut button also provides the Cutting function, but don't use it; it's not worth the risk. It's like throwing a bag of food to a friend on the other side of a raging river. If your pal catches it, that's great; if not, your dinner's gone down the river.

The same rules apply to non-Windows programs. Only copy text from them—*never* cut text—to prevent losing it in case of an accident. But you've got bigger fish to fry using a non-Windows DOS-based program, like WordPerfect 5.1 or the DOS editor.

Once you switch back to Word 97, you simply place the insertion point where you want the text pasted and paste it, by clicking the **Paste** button on the Standard Toolbar. You can also open the **Edit** menu and choose the **Paste** command. The text is pasted into your document.

If the pasted text looks good, congratulate yourself and then save your Word document for safekeeping. If the pasted text looks different than you expected, you may have to do some adjusting.

Use the Mark button to select text.

Cut and Paste text between DOS applications and Word 97.

Windows 95 and NT provide copy and paste for DOS applications.

Grabbing Text from the Web and the Rest of the Internet

The Internet is a great place to find just about anything you can imagine. You can download text files from bulletin boards and newsgroups, e-mail from friends, and text from countless other sources. Find a friend who has experience downloading files from the Internet if you want to explore this subject further, or buy one of the 30-gazillion books available on the subject, such as Que's *Complete Idiot's Guide to Downloading*.

Your browser has Cut, Copy, and Paste functions built right into it. You can capture chats you have with other people, copy contents of e-mail and paste them into your document, and search bulletin boards and subject categories for things that are interesting or helpful in your work.

Just click and drag to select text from a Web page, then open the **Edit** menu on your browser and click **Copy**. Now you can return to Word 97 and click the **Paste** button to place the text into an opened document.

Grabbing text off the Web.

Click Copy in your browser, then...

...Paste the selected text into Word 97.

Click and drag to select text.

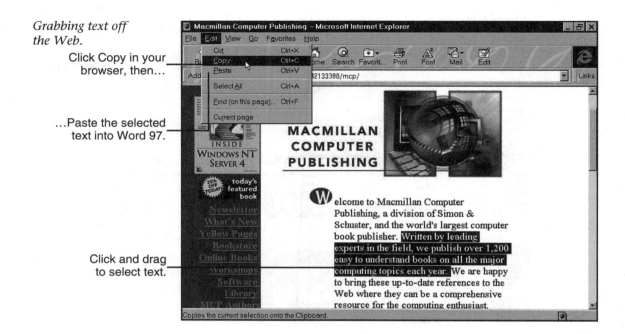

Obtaining Text from Older Files You May Have

If the file you want is on a disk or an older computer, chances are good that you will be able to recover at least some of the text contained in it, unless it was stored in a completely obsolete word processing package format and no other copies can be found. Before you give up on some text that you hope to save, review these quick tips:

➤ Try opening the file with the new Word 97 filter called Recover text from any file. Regardless of the format of your file, this filter will try to grab any text, and it might find what you need.

➤ You can convert files stored on 5.25" disks to 3.5" using a computer that has both types of drives; copy from one drive to the other.

➤ If you have only a 5.25" drive, you can still connect your computer to a modem and upload the file to a bulletin board. Then download the file to a computer with a 3.5" disk drive.

➤ If the file you need exists on an older computer, use the application stored on that computer to open it. If it opens, save it in a format you'll be able to import, like DOS text (or ASCII file).

➤ When a file exists on a minicomputer or mainframe at work, contact the support staff and request the file. They can usually provide the file you need on a disk in ASCII format.

➤ Does the file you need reside really far away? Have a person send it to you via e-mail, or as an attachment to e-mail, which you can then download and insert, or copy and paste.

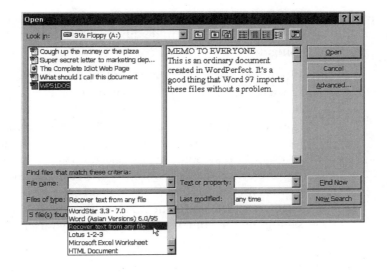

New import options recover text from just about anything.

Scanning In Your Own Text from Any Source

The sky's the limit. Well, actually the copyright laws are the limit. Here's how to take any piece of paper containing almost any kind of text and get those words into Word 97. This can be a real lifesaver if your computer crashes and the only remaining copy of your five hundred-page thesis is a draft you printed last week. Use this technique when the alternative—retyping all those pages—would be interminable hell.

The solution is called *scanning*. A *scanner* is a machine that comes in many shapes and sizes, with costs to match. It's usually attached to a computer. A scanner takes a paper document and turns it into a computer file. Think of it like a printer in reverse. You don't have to buy a scanner; you probably already have access to one, or at least have a friend who does. Many offices have scanners, and many computer stores offer scanning services for a small fee.

Here's the routine: You walk up to a scanner with your report and blank disk in hand, feed the scanner your document, and place the disk into the attached computer. You press a button or two on the computer (ask for help if you need to), and the scanner stores the file onto your disk.

Sound too easy? You knew there was a catch—and there is—because the scanner just takes a picture of your paper document, which might contain rips, folded corners, pictures, smudges, grape jelly, and what-have-you. That's why most scanners also come with a software program called *OCR* (*Optical Character Recognition*). The OCR looks at the scanned picture of your page, determines if there's any text on it, and reads only the text, or at least tries. So the single file saved to your disk is only the text found on all the pages (no pictures or jelly). Lots of smudges and folds will reduce the accuracy of the file, and it's always important to quality-check your file before using it.

Support for Your Scanner Yes, if you've got a scanner attached to your computer, Word 97 allows you to insert a picture directly from the scanner! Place the picture in your scanner, click to place your insertion point in your document, and start the engines. Open the **Insert** menu, point to **Picture**, and choose **From Scanner**. Your scanned image will be placed in your document automatically. And once it's inserted, you can move it, crop it, and resize it (and all the other editing features) just like any other graphic in your document.

When you scan pages of text and OCR is complete, your file is usually stored in ASCII format, and sometimes you have many more file format choices. That shouldn't scare you, now that you're equipped to handle such file formats. You know that Word 97 will have no problem converting ASCII to Word format. Some OCR packages will even try to capture the character formatting and save the document in a Word (or other) format, saving you even more time. Don't push your luck, and remember the real value in scanning is saving the time of retyping. Do the rest yourself.

All that's left is to take the disk back to your computer and import the file into Word. Once again, remember to check this new document for errors before using it. Word will help you catch lots of errors using the Spelling and Grammar Checker. See Chapter 6 for more information on proofing a document.

Saving Documents for Use in Other Word Processors

You've got the document that other people want, and you've created it in Word 97. But you've discovered that not everyone on the planet has converted to Word yet, and even two or three of those are a version or two behind. If you give a copy of your Word 97 document to a person who does not have Word 97, they will not be happy. A friend using another word processor like WordPerfect or WordPro may get an error trying to open your document, and the error message will be "unrecognizable file format."

But that doesn't mean you can't share your documents. In its infinite wisdom, Word 97 includes document converters, which take your document and create a copy in a different format, usually with a different name, that can be opened by others using those programs.

More Word File Converters Available

If you've browsed through the list of converters in Word 97 and don't see the one you need, don't give up hope! Try looking for the latest converters on the Microsoft Web site at **www.microsoft.com/office/ork/appa/appa.htm#ORKappaC2**.

Saving in Other Word Processing Formats

It's important to note that you always create and edit your document in Word 97 format, regardless of how you ultimately want it saved. The trick to saving your document in another format is in using the **Save As** command on the **File** menu (the **Save** button on the Standard Toolbar won't let you change file formats).

Even Word for Windows Version 2 is considered an outside format. A friend using Word 2 will not be able to open your Word 97 document unless you first convert your Word 97 document to Word 2 format, or another format that Word 2 can recognize, such as a DOS Text file.

DOS Text Files Are Easier to Identify
Locating and identifying DOS text files has been made easier because they are automatically converted and displayed in the Preview box before the file is even opened.

If you are using Fast Saves, turn them off before you forward a document to someone to use in another program, like desktop publishing. Other programs often have problems understanding the **Fast Save** format of Word 97. The details can be found in Chapter 7.

Saving Your Document as a Text File

If you want a reason to save your Word document as a text file, I've got one. There are over a billion DOS-based computers on our planet, and who knows how many on other planets, and they can all understand a DOS text file! That means you could take the file anywhere, even in the foreseeable future, and feel confident that your words will be recognized. A text file is considered the lowest common denominator of file formats.

Saving a DOS Text File

If your document is a DOS text file, you simply have to save it back to disk (or disk). Click the **Save** button. Word 97 will remember that you opened this file as a DOS text file and will keep it the same. If you made any formatting changes, such as using bold face type, you will be asked if you want the document saved in Word format.

If you started a new document in Word 97, it is automatically created in Word 97 format. To save this document as a DOS text file, you have to follow a few more steps.

Open the **File** menu and select the **Save As** command. You cannot use the **Save** command for this. The **F12** key also works. The Save As dialog box will appear. You must change the format, which appears in the Save file as type box. Click the down-arrow button next to the Save file as type box to see the drop-down list of choices. Click the **Text Only** option and press the **Enter** key. Now click the **File Name** box and think up a name for this file. Since this will be an ordinary-text file, you should follow DOS naming conventions, which are really restrictions. The restrictions are that the name must fit in eight letters, with no spaces or fancy symbols. Now click the **OK** button, and your file will be saved to disk.

If the file already exists, or you typed a name that is already taken by another file, you will be asked if you want to replace the existing file. Think about it for a second or two, and press either **Replace** or **Cancel**. Press **Y** (or the **Yes** button) to replace the existing file.

What Gets Lost When You Save as a Text File?

A lot of weight gets lost when you save a file as plain text. The file size drops to a mere fraction of its size in Word. That's because some things don't convert to this format called ASCII. Which, you ask? How about all of the character formatting you've learned (like fonts, font sizes, bold, italic, and underline), all of the paragraph formatting (like bullets and numbering, centering, spacing and margins), and certainly all of the page formatting (page numbers, pictures, borders and margins).

Hey, that's everything! Yes, basically, all the neat features of Word 97 that you choose to use are applied on top of a basic ASCII file. So if you want the plain ASCII file, you have to rip away all of the Word things. All word processors are like this, including WordPerfect, WordPro, Write, and countless others. They all create the same words; they just have their own way to make them interesting. Strip away those formatting features, and you have nothing more than a plain ASCII file.

Saving as Both Text and Word 97

You can save a document both as a Text file *and* as a Word 97 file. First, save the file normally as a Word file, then save the file as a text file by choosing **Text Only** in the **Save file as type** box in the **Save As** dialog box, which automatically adds the extension .TXT. You will then have a text file, which anyone can read, and also a Word 97 file, which can have all the formatting your heart desires.

The Least You Need to Know

Converting files and importing text is the way your computer acts like a language translator. You may become fluent performing these acts if you remember the highlights of this chapter.

Why can't I see a WordPerfect document that I need to open?

Word 97 can easily open documents created in other programs. Click the Open button on the Standard toolbar and be sure to change the file type to **All Files (*.*)** to allow you to see the names of non-Word files.

How can I grab just a small part of another document for use in my current document?

If you need only a few sentences or paragraphs from another document, it's often easiest to select the text in the first document, click the Copy button, and then click the Paste button in the second document. This even works for non-Windows programs running in a DOS box in Windows 95/98 or Windows NT.

How can I send a document to a client who doesn't have Word 97?

First find out what program your client owns. Saving a document for a client who doesn't have Word 97 is easy using the **Save As** command. The options in the **Save As** command allow you to save documents in other file formats, such as WordPerfect or generic DOS text.

What if I don't know what program my customer may use to read my document?

Remember that Word 97 offers **Save As** options such as ASCII and DOS text file (or just plain text file), and this is the special format that is supported by every major word processing package. Save a document as DOS text when you're sharing it with an unknown word processing partner.

Chapter 16

Working with Multiple Documents

In This Chapter

➤ Viewing multiple documents at once

➤ Viewing multiple parts of the same document

➤ Saving multiple documents at once

➤ Mail Merge for mere mortals

Sometimes one document just isn't enough. Sure, it's open on your screen and you're comfortable with all the controls, but you're sure there's more to life. You need more than this document. You probably need additional information stored in another document, and you want them both open at the same time.

If that's how you feel, this chapter will show you how to get not one, not two, but up to a gazillion documents open on your screen at once (if you have enough memory). You'll also learn how to copy or move information (or yourself) between them. And to keep things interesting, you'll also learn how to create your own form letters for fun or for profit.

Opening Documents

Why would anyone want to have more than one document open at the same time? An informal poll of the entire human population was taken last week, and here are the preliminary results:

➤ It's the easiest way to cut, copy and paste between them.

➤ It's quick when you need multiple reference documents available fast.

➤ It's easy to move graphics and text back and forth.

➤ It makes your boss think you're doing more work.

➤ It's the best way to slow down really fast computers.

Whatever your reason, having *multiple* opened documents on your screen is as simple as opening one document, then opening another, and so on. Although you probably see only a single document at a time, the rest are right behind it, waiting for you to bring them forward. You can see the list of all open documents by opening the **Window** menu (if you have more than nine opened documents, you will see the last entry as **More Windows...** which, if selected, takes you to a dialog box containing the complete list of all opened documents). Choose between any of the opened documents by clicking with the mouse, or use the keyboard and type the number of the document.

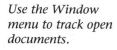

Use the Window menu to track open documents.

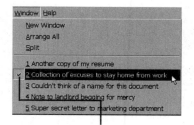

The check mark indicates the currently viewed document.

Opening Many Documents at the Same Time

If you need to have many documents opened at the same time, you can try this to save yourself some time: open the **File** menu and choose the **Open** command to see the **File Open** dialog box. Locate the folder storing the documents you need. This time, instead of double-clicking on a single document (which opens only that document), hold down the **Ctrl** key and click once on several documents to highlight them. All highlighted documents will be opened at the same time when you press **Enter** or the **Open** button. You can even highlight documents stored in different folders. You can also click **Advanced** and search for documents, and select several of them from the results listing. Finally, when you press the **Open** button, all selected documents will be opened, in the order you selected.

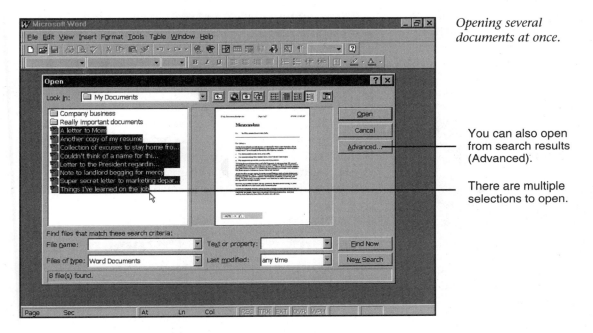

Opening several documents at once.

You can also open from search results (Advanced).

There are multiple selections to open.

You Opened Them, but Where Are They?

You're fairly certain you just opened 16 documents, but only one is staring you in the face. Where are the rest? In Word 97, each document is stored in its own window. Normally that window uses the entire screen, so a single document is all you see at the moment. You can see this list of windows by opening the **Window** menu.

Word 97 will display a numbered list of all opened documents for you to choose from. They are in alphabetical order, which was more helpful back in the old days of eight-letter document names.

Limited Only by Your Memory
Word for Windows lets you open as many documents as you want, as long as your computer has enough memory to support all of them.

Check This Out...

You can also switch between open documents by pressing **Ctrl+Shift+F6**, which takes you to the *next* window on the list. It's easier to press **Ctrl+F6** to go to the *previous* window on the list, however, since most people just switch windows until they find the one they want. The **Ctrl+F6** key combination is most helpful if you have just two documents open and want to switch between them.

So What Can You Do with Two Open Documents?

Probably the best thing you can do with multiple opened documents is easily cut, copy, and paste anything between them, and it can be anything stored in any of the documents. Just select the portion of text, figures, or objects you want to cut or copy from any document. Then click the **Copy** button to copy the selection to the clipboard. Now find the spot in any document you want to copy to, place the insertion point there, click the **Paste** button, and the selection will be pasted instantly. The **Cut** button works fine in moving selected text or graphics across multiple documents.

Check This Out...

Cutting and Pasting Over Multiple Documents Incidentally, multiple documents do not have to be open at the same time to cut, copy, and paste between them. You can select and copy from one document, close it, open another document, and paste it just fine. Fewer steps are required when both documents are opened.

Word 97 handles each window independently, in case you were wondering why only one document printed when you pressed the **Print** button. Each command affects only the current document, which is the one you're looking at. Spell checking, formatting commands, and printing are examples of tasks that are performed only on the current document.

Viewing Multiple Documents at Once

Instead of seeing a single document on the screen at a time, you may decide you want to see more than one, or all documents. Just open the **Window** menu and choose the **Arrange All** command. All opened documents will be placed on your screen, each in their own smaller window. This works best for two or three documents because each window has to share space on your screen, and too many open windows makes it difficult to work on any single document.

Although you can *see* more than one document on the screen at a time, you are still limited to working on one. Only one insertion point is active at a time. The active document has the highlighted title bar with the Title bar buttons and the Close, Minimize, Maximize, and Restore buttons. You can click the title bar of any of them to make it the current document. In fact, you can click anywhere in another window for its document to become active. You can also toggle through them by pressing the **Ctrl+F6** keys.

Clicking on the Maximize title bar button on the active document will cause that document to be maximized, moving its Title bar buttons to the Menu bar of Word 97. The remaining documents are still there, just covered up at the moment. You can get to them again by choosing from the Window list, pressing **Ctrl+F6**, or by minimizing the current window (press the Minimize Title bar button) or restoring it to a smaller window (press the Restore button, which toggles between Restore and Maximize) to expose the other active documents.

You can resize them and move them around just as you can any window. You can also minimize one or more of the documents, and you'll see a minimized Title bar for each near the bottom of your screen. A quick way to open all minimized documents at once is to open the **Window** menu and choose the **Arrange All** command. You will see all of your active documents sharing the available space. Once again, to return to focusing on a single document, you can maximize that window by pressing the **Maximize** button in that window's title bar.

> *Check This Out...*
>
> **See Multiple, Use One** It's easier to find the active window when you have many windows open. Word 97 places the Title bar buttons (Minimize, Maximize, Restore, and Close) on *only* the active window. This makes it much less confusing on a busy screen.

Viewing Multiple Parts of the Same Document

If you like working on two things at once, even if the two things are in a single document, then you'll love this screen manipulation. You can view different parts of a large document at the same time, in different windows on your screen.

Start by opening the document you want to work with. Open the **Window** menu and choose the **New Window** command. This creates another window on your screen where you will find another copy of the same document. These aren't two different copies—just two different views of the same document. Make a change in one, and it's instantly updated in the other view also. Your documents are also labeled in the Title bar with something extra—a colon and a number after the filename—which helps you identify the views. For example, you may have Quarterly Summary Report:1 in one window and Quarterly Summary Report:2 in the title bar of the second window.

What's this dual view good for? It is good for cutting and pasting in very long documents. Clicking the different views or using **Ctrl+F6** pops back and forth between them.

When you are finished editing either part of this document, save it and close it by opening the **File** menu and choosing the **Close** command. You'll only have to do this once because closing one will close both.

Splitting Your Viewing Screen

You can save some space on your viewing screen and still have two views of the same document by using a slightly different feature of Word 97 called *screen splitting*. To view two parts of a document simultaneously, open the **Window** menu and choose the **Split** command. A horizontal bar will appear about halfway down your screen. Now just click your mouse button and you will have a split screen. The bottom window will contain an exact duplicate of your document. Try clicking in this new window and scroll around. The other window will remain still, allowing you to see different parts of the same document at the same time.

Seeing double using the old Split-Screen trick.

Place the cursor here to drag up or down for a new window size.

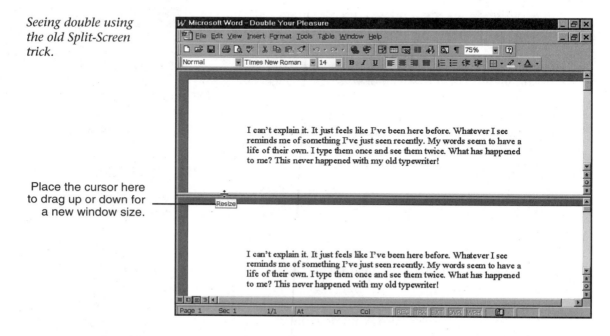

Split screen view is often used to copy or move text between parts of a long document. Display the text or graphics you want to move or copy in one pane and the destination for the text or graphics in the other pane, and then drag the text or graphics across the split bar. Instant success and feedback. What a concept.

When you are tired of this view, you can quickly get rid of it by double-clicking the split bar in the vertical scroll bar, or by simply opening up the **Window** menu and choosing the **Remove Split** command. Or if you have lots of time to waste, you can try to click and drag that little arrow shape on the vertical scroll bar all the way back up to the top.

Saving Multiple Documents at Once

You can save all open documents at once by opening the **File** menu and selecting the **Save All** command. Any document containing any new changes since it was last saved will now be saved. You'll be able to watch each document flash in the status bar at the bottom of your screen (if your status bar is hidden, you can bring it back to see this action, but it's not necessary. Open the **Tools** menu, select the **Options** command, click the **View** tab to bring it to the front, and click to check the **Status Bar** box).

Of course, if you are going to be away from your computer for more than a few minutes, it's best to close all of your documents.

Closing All Documents at the Same Time

Press and hold down the **Shift** key (either one) and use the mouse to open the **File** menu. It changed! There's now a **Close All** command, and by selecting it, all of your documents will be closed. Of course, if any documents have changes not yet saved, Word will stop before closing them and ask if you want to save the changes. These dynamically changing menus may have you wondering what else might change if you hold down a key and open a menu.

Mail Merge

You may not know what *mail merge* is, but you have experienced the results of a mail merge. Anytime you receive junk mail with your name pasted next to the possible winner of $1,000,000, you have experienced a mail merge.

If it's done well, a mail merge is ideal for communicating more personally to a large number of people, like your friends during the holidays, the customers of your business, or the tax base of your country.

What Is a Merge?

Mail merge is the process of taking a single form letter, mixing it with another containing a bunch of names (or other information), and then *merging* both to create several documents. Each of the documents is customized by using the list of names and information that you provide.

First some definitions. The document that contains the names, addresses, phone numbers, and so on is called the *data source*. The file that contains the form letter is called the *main document*.

Now the process. You start by creating the *main document*, your form letter, complete with formatting. But leave blank the places you would normally enter a name or address, or anything else that might change from document to document. In these blank spaces, you add something called a *field*. Each field is replaced with a real name or address during a merge.

Next you find or create a *data source*. The *data source* is a document that contains a collection of the names and addresses (or anything else) that you want. Unlike a regular document, however, this one is created in a different format called a *database*. For example, this could be a database of all your customer names and addresses. Got it? One database file, many names and addresses. Each combination of name, address, and other information in this data source is called a *record*.

When you say go, Word 97 creates a bunch of customized documents (as many as you have *records* in your data source), one form letter for each customer in your database. Then it's very easy to print all of these custom documents as a final step, without the need for saving all of them (or you can save them all—in fact, you can e-mail them all if the names came from your address book provided with Word 97).

Using the Mail Merge Command

This won't be so bad, I promise. If you follow the steps to the end, I'm certain your sentiments will be something like "Wow!", "How about that!", or "Who cares, I'm hungry."

The easiest way to explain mail merge is to use an example. You just had a birthday and got lots of presents. You know you'll keep getting presents in the future if you send a personal thank-you note to everyone. But that's a lot of work. You decide to send the same note to everyone since they all live in different parts of the country. Only the names and addresses will change.

What's first? Building the basic thank-you note. Start by opening the **Tools** menu and choose the **Mail Merge** command. You see the Mail Merge Helper dialog box. The large numbers 1, 2, and 3 make you guess you'll be finished in a snap. Guess again! This example goes on for pages! See the **Create** button? Push it. Now select **Form Letter** from the list. You can press **New Main Document** next, to begin the creation of your form letter.

After pressing the **New Main Document** button, two new buttons will appear—an **Edit** button and a **Get Data** button. Now you're ready to gather the names and addresses of the friends who will be getting this letter. You can either gather these names from an existing electronic address book, or create a new list from scratch.

The Mail Merge
Helper dialog box
steps you through
the process.

Already Have Names and Addresses Stored in Your Computer?

If you already have your friends' names and addresses stored in your computer, you can use that file as your data source for a mail merge. Word 97 automatically accepts entries in the personal address book of Microsoft Exchange server, Outlook, or Schedule+ 7.0 contact lists, and many other third-party address lists. To use one of these as your data source, click the **Use Address Book** command found on the list that appears when you click the Get Data button. Choose the appropriate address book and then select as many names as you require. You can also open address list files created in Microsoft Excel or Microsoft Access. To use these alternate data sources, click the **Open Data Source** command found on this same list appearing when you click the Get Data button. Locate and open the desired file, then choose the entries you wish to include in your mail merge.

Creating Your Data Source

Press the **Get Data** button to reveal the pull-down listing of potential sources of data. Choose **Create Data Source** for now. We're going to build a list of our generous friends from scratch.

Creating the data source (the names and addresses for your form letter).

Build your list of names by choosing Create Data Source.

In the **Create Data Source** dialog that appears, just press the **OK** button. It's a shortcut for quickly creating the file that will contain your names and addresses. You are now asked to save what you've just created. What have you created? Nothing yet, but call it **People Who Gave Me Presents This Year** to give you an idea. Press the **Save** button in the Save As dialog box to continue.

Next you will find a dialog box asking what you want to do next. It says that the data source you just created contains no data records. No kidding. So let's add some. Choose the **Edit Data Source** button to begin adding names to our mailing list.

Adding to a list of names for your merge.

These are called Fields.

Press OK when you finish adding all your names and addresses.

Press here when you finish adding one name, and then you can add another.

What's this, you ask? It's called creating your *data source*, and it's easier than it looks. Think of the best present you got. Now think of who gave it to you (Stumped? Don't worry; everyone is getting the same letter anyway. Guilty? You should be, since you should have done this sooner!) Type your friend's first name right next to the **First Name** box. That's it! Unless you want to add more information about this person (by pressing the **Tab** key to move to each field), you are ready to move on to the next person. Do this by pressing the **Add New** button and don't panic. Although it looks empty again, you can relax because the first entry was saved. Fill in the second person's name. Press **Add New** for the third person, and so on.

When you've finished adding everyone's name, press the **OK** button, and your database will be saved, and you will be returned to the document screen.

Creating Your Form Letter

Now be creative as you compose a generic thank-you note. When it's time to add something personal, like a first name after Dear so-and-so, click that **Insert Merge Field** button on your Mail Merge toolbar (the Mail Merge toolbar appears automatically when you choose Mail Merge from the Tools menu). Choose **First Name** from the list of fields. This ties directly back to those names you entered earlier.

Don't worry about the formatting, those silly <<things>> will be replaced later. Keep on creating the thank-you note.

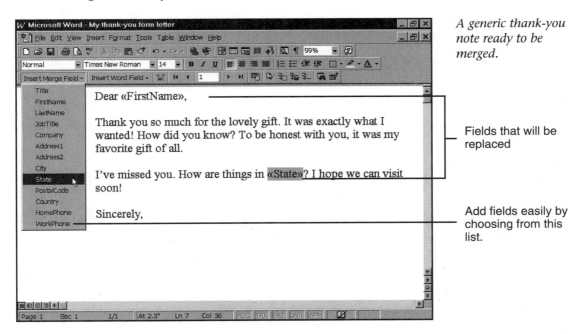

A generic thank-you note ready to be merged.

Fields that will be replaced

Add fields easily by choosing from this list.

Merging at Last

You're so close to the end of this example, you should be able to taste it. Open the **Tools** menu and press **Mail Merge** for the third (and final) time. Press the **Merge** button to see the Merge dialog box. The most common defaults are already selected in this dialog box, like the option to merge to a new document. You can also choose to merge directly to your printer, or even e-mail, by pressing the **Merge To** pull-down arrow and choosing another destination.

Now press the **Merge** button in the **Merge** dialog box to finally start the merging process. You may be surprised how quickly your computer can accomplish this merging, and you will want to inspect the results to make sure the proper merging took place. If the merge was less than spectacular, you can press **Ctrl+Z** to undo the previous step, or simply delete the merged results (by closing them without saving) and trying again. All of the tedious merging steps have been saved, so you are taken to the very last step to try again.

The finished product.

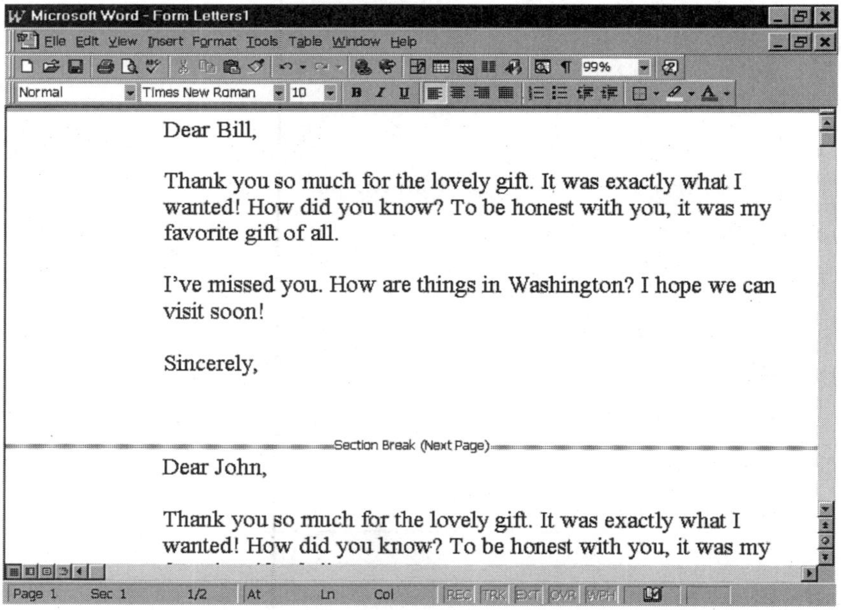

Microsoft Word - Form Letters1
File Edit View Insert Format Tools Table Window Help
Normal
Times New Roman
10
99%
Dear Bill,
Thank you so much for the lovely gift. It was exactly what I wanted! How did you know? To be honest with you, it was my favorite gift of all.
I've missed you. How are things in Washington? I hope we can visit soon!
Sincerely,
Section Break (Next Page)
Dear John,
Thank you so much for the lovely gift. It was exactly what I wanted! How did you know? To be honest with you, it was my
Page 1 Sec 1 1/2 At Ln Col REC TRK EXT OVR WPH

The Least You Need to Know

Humans have no problem doing 50 things at once. Now our documents can keep up with us. This chapter reviewed ideas on using multiple documents.

How many documents can be open at the same time in Word 97?

As many as you require. You'll run out of space long before Word 97 runs out of gas. Open as many documents as your heart desires and track them by opening the Window menu.

I've opened two documents but I can't see them at the same time. What should I do?

You can view two (or more) opened documents at once by opening the Windows menu and choosing the Arrange All command.

I need to see two different parts of the same document at the same time. Am I crazy?

Not at all. You can work on two sections of the same document by splitting the window into panes. Double-click on the **Split Box** or open the **Window** menu and select the **Split** command. Click in each pane as needed to control that area.

What's the easiest way to send the same letter to lots of people?

A mail merge takes a single master document and mixes it with another (usually an address list) to create many new documents (also known as "form letters"). Find the **Mail Merge** feature of Word 97 under the **Tools** menu.

Part 3
Pushing Word 97 to the Limit

There's more to Word 97 than just great word processing. It's packed with more tools than a hardware store, and you don't have to wait in line to use them. You'll find tools from A to Z that help you with everything from headings to footnotes; a wide variety including e-mail, sharing documents, changing a template, finding documents you've misplaced, building your own toolbars, auto-this, auto-that—it's enough to rouse tears of joy just imagining the productivity gains you'll experience.

Before we embark on this journey into the land of Word 97 tools, I have one question for you. Is that the kitchen sink I see on the toolbar?

Sharing Your Word 97 Documents

In This Chapter

➤ Revising an original document

➤ Commenting on a shared document

➤ Tracking different versions of a document

➤ Using e-mail to send and route shared documents

➤ Comparing documents for changes

➤ Protecting documents before sharing them with others

One person usually has enough problems keeping an important document up to date; imagine sharing and updating the same document with others! Relax, you've got Word 97 and this book. We'll make it easier with document sharing tools. And if you've got a network, you'll discover ways to make life even easier by using e-mail to route shared documents and by saving documents to common storage areas so everyone can find them.

Keeping Track of Changes in Shared Documents

Let's say you and a friend have to work on the same document. You're given enough time to finish the task, so you plan to share a disk with the stored document. Each of you builds and edits the document, while trading the disk back and forth. It's important for each of you to know what the other person has done, especially if there's lots of moving and deleting of text. Otherwise, suspicion and tension may rise, wars may begin, and hunger and famine may spread.

Luckily for you, Microsoft Word 97 provides several options for tracking, incorporating, and keeping a record of all these changes. Let's start with simple and common ways to track changes.

Highlighting Text in Color

An easy way to identify a change is to highlight it. Click the Highlight button on the Formatting toolbar, then click and drag to select text you want to highlight (you can also highlight graphics).

You can highlight in one of fifteen different colors, even more than the famous marking pens. To change the highlighter color, click the arrow next to the Highlight button, click the color you want, and then select the text or graphic you want to highlight. When you highlight parts of a document that you intend to print, be sure to use a light color for best results on laser and dot matrix printers.

Find Those Highlights Fast Want to focus your reviewer on the key sections only? Tell them to open the **Edit** menu, click **Find**, and click **Highlight** in the Format box. Now they can browse the document, stopping only at your highlights.

Anyone opening your document will immediately see your highlighted text. If it bothers them, they can switch it off without removing it. Open the **Tools** menu, click **Options**, and click the **View** tab to bring it to the front. To display or hide highlighting (but not the text itself) on the screen and in the printed document, set or clear the **Highlight** check box.

Please Leave Your Message at the Tone...

Yes, voice comments are a reality in today's multimedia world, and you can add them to your Word 97 documents with ease. Chapter 13 provides all the details like sound cards and microphones to get you started. Once you're up and talking, you can talk to your document and it will listen.

To put voice comments in your document, place the insertion point where you want to add a comment. Open the **Insert** menu and choose the **Comment** command. Click the **Insert Sound Object** button and talk away! Press the **Close** button to save it, and a small set of initials will appear, representing the person creating the comment.

Just as a reminder, if you want to record or listen to comments inserted into your document, your computer must have the necessary hardware. All you need is a sound card, external speakers or headphones, and a microphone to record the comments. All of these components are usually included when you purchase a "multimedia" computer, and they can also be purchased individually at your local computer store if you don't own them yet.

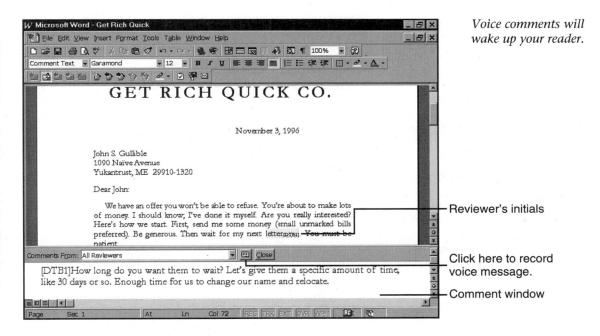

Voice comments will wake up your reader.

Reviewer's initials

Click here to record voice message.

Comment window

Your friend may prefer to browse through your entire document just listening to your comments. Word 97 assists them with the Select Browse Object, because it includes the Browse By Comment button. Use it and you'll be able to zip back and forth finding only the recorded comments.

Incidentally, you don't have to have sound to put Comments to great use. You can type your message (it will automatically be spell checked) in the Comment pane and press the **Close** button to save it. The very same set of small initials will appear, representing the initials of the person creating the comment.

View comments by pointing at them with your mouse.

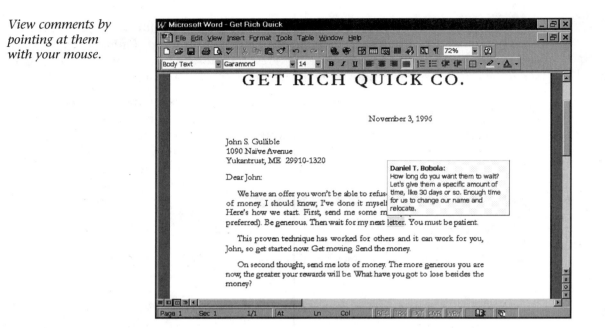

Wrong Initials? If the initials are not set correctly on your reviewer's computer, have them open the **Tools** menu and select the **Options** command. Click the **User Info** tab to bring it to the front. Correct the user initials in the text box, and press the **OK** button to save the changes and close the **Options** dialog box.

To get rid of comments in your document, you must select them first (you can't just backup over them with the backspace) and then delete them with the **Cut** button or the **Delete** key. You can also click in the **Comment** pane and delete your message there.

Interested in printing your documents, comments included? Open the **File** menu and choose the **Print** command. Click on the **Options** button and under **Include with Document**, use the **Comments** check box. If you are interested in printing the comments only, select **Comments** in the **Print What** list on the Print dialog box, and then press the **OK** button.

Is This the Latest Version?

Instead of filling a document with comments or highlights, you may prefer to work with documents as if they were in final form. You just reconcile changes by calling each new updated document a new *version* of the same document. Yes, Word 97 makes this easy using the **Version** feature. This allows you to save different versions of a document as a separate file.

To turn on the version feature for a document at any time, open the **File** menu and click **Versions**. In the Version dialog box you see the history of saved versions for this document. Click **Save Now** and you'll be asked to comment on this particular version. These comments help you further identify a version if you need it in the future. You'll also have the exact time, date, and name of the person who last saved a version of this document. After typing a comment, click **Save**. Provide a name for this document and a folder to store it in.

Each time you want to save another version of this document, open the **File** menu, click **Versions**, and click **Save Now**. To open any previous versions of this document, just select them from this Versions dialog box.

Click here to automatically
save a new version each time.

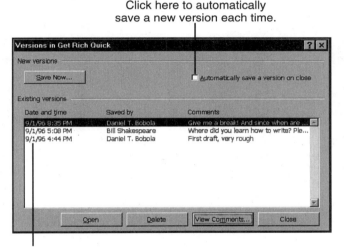

What version of my document do you want?

Time and date of each saved
version are listed here.

You can also set up versioning to automatically save a version each time the document is closed, which can provide a great audit trail for paranoid schizophrenics. Open the **File** menu and click **Versions**. Select the **Automatically save a version on close** check box. Click **Close** and sleep peacefully.

Experience the Reviewing Toolbar

To experience the full impact of editing and reviewing tools available in Word 97, you must try the Reviewing toolbar. Open the **View** menu, point to Toolbars, choose the Reviewing toolbar, then sit back and let me tell you about them.

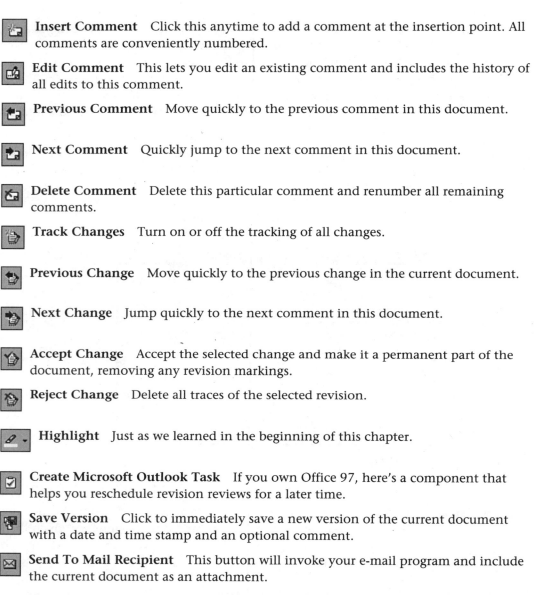

Insert Comment   Click this anytime to add a comment at the insertion point. All comments are conveniently numbered.

Edit Comment   This lets you edit an existing comment and includes the history of all edits to this comment.

Previous Comment   Move quickly to the previous comment in this document.

Next Comment   Quickly jump to the next comment in this document.

Delete Comment   Delete this particular comment and renumber all remaining comments.

Track Changes   Turn on or off the tracking of all changes.

Previous Change   Move quickly to the previous change in the current document.

Next Change   Jump quickly to the next comment in this document.

Accept Change   Accept the selected change and make it a permanent part of the document, removing any revision markings.

Reject Change   Delete all traces of the selected revision.

Highlight   Just as we learned in the beginning of this chapter.

Create Microsoft Outlook Task   If you own Office 97, here's a component that helps you reschedule revision reviews for a later time.

Save Version   Click to immediately save a new version of the current document with a date and time stamp and an optional comment.

Send To Mail Recipient   This button will invoke your e-mail program and include the current document as an attachment.

Now let's use all these buttons on the Revising toolbar by revising some real live documents. Try these along with me; it's good to get the feel of these tools before you're committed to working on something like a peace treaty or a lunch order.

Adding, Editing, Reviewing Comments in a Document

Start the revision process on an opened document by clicking the Track Changes button on the Revising toolbar. Now make the changes you want by inserting, deleting, or moving text or graphics. With each change you'll see revision markings like bars in the margins, text color changes, and lined-out text. These make it easy to find and understand changes.

➤ All changes will be identified by a bar in the margin to help you quickly find them.

➤ Inserted text will be a different color.

➤ Deleted text will be lined out, but still visible and readable.

➤ Moved text will be lined out in the old location, and a different color in the new location.

➤ All formatting changes may not be noticeable but will still be identified by a bar in the margin.

If you don't like any or all of these revision formats, you can change them. Open the **Tools** menu and click **Options**. In the Options dialog box, click **Track Changes** to bring it forward, and you'll see all the revision format options. Change them as you like, then click **OK** to save your changes in the current document.

Remember, you can add comments to help clarify any changes you might be making. Comments are a much better way to communicate changes to a document. You don't clutter the actual change with a description that could be confused as part of the change.

Accepting or Rejecting Changes from Others

After your friend returns a revised document, you'll be ready to negotiate the changes. Revisions can either stand as they are, or become merged into your document. You control what happens with the Revision toolbar.

 Like a particular change? Click anywhere inside this particular revision marking and click the **Accept Change** button. Revision markings will disappear and the change is smoothly integrated into your document.

 Don't agree with a change? Then click the **Reject Change** button and the change will be returned to its previous state. Revision markings will disappear.

Likewise, comments can be added, edited, and deleted using the Comments portion of the Revision toolbar (you can even cut and paste comment text into the document). And you can speed through a document using only the Next or Previous Change buttons. At any time during the process you might decide it's time to call this document a new version by clicking the Version button.

Comparing Different Versions for Changes

What if someone forgot to turn on Revision markings before they made changes to your document? Do they run and hide as you hunt them down? Give them a break and test your wits with the Compare feature. Just find an earlier copy of the same document (go hunt them down) and compare the two. Any differences between the documents will be the most current revisions, right?

Make sure that the documents you are comparing have different filenames by renaming one of them (or, if you insist on the documents having the same name, make sure they are in different folders). Start by opening the latest version of your document. To start comparing, open the **Tools** menu, point to Track Changes, and choose **Compare Documents**.

Now find the other document you want to compare and double-click the name of the document to start the comparison process. Comparisons can take many seconds, even minutes, so be patient. When the comparison is completed you will see a single document on your screen with all differences between the two documents fully identified. You can save this as a new document, or discard it after reviewing the change. Lawyers often use features like this to determine if any changes have been made to a contract.

Protecting Your Work Before You Share

If you plan to share your document with lots of people, on a network for example, you may want to protect your document to prevent unauthorized changes. This section will describe the different levels of security available to you.

Passwords Can Protect Your Secret Files

Word 97 provides multiple ways to restrict access to your document. You'll find all of them by opening the **File** menu and choosing **Save As**. Click the **Options** button and examine your **File Sharing Options** near the bottom. You can do any of the following:

➤ Assign a password to open the document, which prevents unauthorized users from opening the document.

➤ Assign a password to modify the document, which allows others to open the document but not to save changes without the password. If someone opens the document without the password to modify and changes the document, that person can save the document only by giving it a different filename.

➤ Recommend that others open the document as a read-only file. If someone opens the document as a read-only file and changes it, that person can save the document only by giving it a different filename. If someone opens the document as a read-write file and changes it, the document can be saved with its original filename.

➤ Assign a password when you route a document for review, which prevents any changes except for comments or tracked changes.

Protect your document with a password.

This password is required for opening.

Changes must be saved with a new name if this is checked.

This password is required to edit this document.

What If You Forget the Password?

If you assign password protection to a document and then forget the password, you can't open the document, remove protection from it, or even recover data from it. Pretty bad, huh? It's a good idea to keep a list of your passwords and their corresponding document names in a safe place, so you can refer to them at a time like this.

Preventing Virus Attacks

Be certain to protect yourself from "macro viruses." These may be hiding inside documents you receive from friend or foe, and once unleashed they can do damage such as erasing information stored on your computer. Word 97 offers some built-in protection: It can warn you about the presence of a macro in a document before it is opened. You'll get the chance to disable any macros and still open the document.

To make sure this level of virus protection is turned on, open the **Tools** menu, click **Options**, and choose the **General** tab. Make sure the **Macro Virus Protection** check box is checked. Click **OK** to save this setting.

It's also a good idea to invest in a full-featured antivirus program such as McAfee VirusScan or Norton AntiVirus to protect all of your programs from the wide range of virus threats.

Word 97 can warn you about the presence of macros in documents and templates.

Sharing Documents on a Network

Now we're ready to share our document with just about anyone, because we know how to use revision markings and we can protect our document from unauthorized changes using passwords. It's time to trust technology and send your document off to be poked and prodded by your assortment of bosses, secretaries, and other work associates, until one day finally returning to the warmth of your loving computer.

If you want your document reviewed by several people and you want final control over which changes to accept or reject, you can prepare a copy of your document and distribute it to others for revision editing. Instead of the old method of passing a single disk from one person to the next, you might try putting the network to work. Here are two alternatives you might want to try:

You can place the document in a shared location on network and have your team members access it one at a time. Each reviewer can take turns opening and revising the document as needed, and all changes are tracked automatically. When team members complete their reviews, the document is up-to-date.

Or, you can route a single document through your e-mail system so each team member opens and revises the document, and then forwards it to the next person on the distribution list. After reaching each member, the document is then returned to you for review of all previous reviewers' changes and comments.

Setting Up Your Document for Sharing on the Network

Open the document you want set up as a shared document. For best results, make sure the document doesn't have multiple versions (or else your reviewers might open previous versions) by clicking Versions on the File menu. If multiple versions exist, save the current version as a separate document with a different name, and use this copy as the review copy. If this happens to be a newly created document, save it before performing these steps.

Techno Talk

Can Two People Edit the Same Document at the Same Time? Unfortunately, no. In an emergency, a document can be opened and edited while someone else has it opened, but the second person to open a document must save the changes using **Save As**, and provide a different name for the document. The result is two documents that may have to be merged manually.

It's almost a given that you'll want to have reviewers' changes and comments automatically appear as tracked changes, so turn on revision marks by opening the Tools menu and choose Protect Document. Click **Tracked Changes**. To let reviewers insert only comments but not change the contents of the document, click **Comments**.

Now place a copy of this document on a shared network drive where your team members have appropriate network access. Your network administrator can help with this, but generally it's a drive letter and a directory, or a folder, where users have read and write access. Now each team member can open and revise the document, and revisions will be identified with the initials of the reviewer.

If a team member opens the document while another has it open, Word will alert them that it is currently opened by another user. Only one person can revise a document at a time, so this member can try to access it again later, when the document might be available. Or, if this person just wants to view, not edit, this document, they can click the **Open As Read-Only Copy** button. This allows full viewing of the document currently opened by someone else.

Sending Shared Documents by E-mail

The best method of routing a document to each member of the team for revisions is to use the e-mail capabilities of your network. Instead of sending the document to all team members at once, you should route the document to each member, one at a time.

Are All E-mails Created Equal? To send or route documents through e-mail, you need an e-mail system compatible with the MAPI (Messaging Application Programming Interface) or VIM (Vendor Independent Messaging) standards. The most popular e-mail programs work fine, including Microsoft Exchange, Lotus cc:Mail, and Novell GroupWise. And if you plan on sending Internet Notes, be aware that sending and routing documents through e-mail may not work across all electronic mail gateways.

You can accomplish this by including a note telling the reviewer to send it to the next team member when his revisions are complete, or you can use the automatic routing capabilities built into many e-mail packages. After all of the recipients have reviewed the document, it should be returned to you with the accumulated revisions of all team members.

To e-mail your document to one or more people, just click the **Send to Mail Recipient** button on the Revision toolbar, or use the following commands found in the File menu:

E-mail delivers— come rain or shine.

Routing Slip

From: Daniel T. Bobola

To: 1 - Martha O'Sullivan
2 - Melanie Palaisa
3 - Barry Pruett

Add Slip
Cancel
Route
Clear

Move

Add names quickly from your address book. → Address... Remove

Subject: Routing: Document2

Message text: Don't sit on this. We need an answer soon. Take a day, then route it to the next person on this list. Thanks.

Type a short instructional note here. The document will be attached to the e-mail.

Route to recipients
◉ One after another
○ All at once

☑ Return when done
☑ Track status
Protect for: Tracked changes

➤ **E-mail a document to another person**   Open the document you want to mail. Open the File menu, point to **Send To**, and click **Mail Recipient**. Address and send the mail message to whomever you want to receive the document.

➤ **Route a document to multiple people**   Open the document you want to route. Open the File menu, point to **Send To**, and click **Routing Recipient**. To select recipients to route the document to, click **Address**. In the **Type Name Or Select From** list box, type a recipient's name, and then click **To**. After you entered the last recipient name in the To box, click **OK**. Select any other routing options you want, and then click **Route**.

The Least You Need to Know

Word 97 offers several features to help you share your documents with others. You just have to learn how to use them. Some of the better ones are reviewed in this chapter.

My yellow highlighter dried out last week. Am I out of luck?

Not if you use the new Highlight button on the Formatting toolbar. You can quickly highlight a document with a click and a drag of the mouse. If you need a different color, click the Highlight color option button right next to it and choose between the color options.

How can I control updates from several people on a single document?

Open the **Tools** menu and turn on **Track Changes** to initiate revision controls for that document. After that, all changes to a document are easily visible, manageable, and traceable to the originator.

Instead of changing the content of a document, I just want to add a comment. Can that be done?

Yes. Comments can be added to a document during revisions, and they can be either text or actual voice recordings. Click the **Comment** button and create them in the Comment pane.

What buttons or controls do I use once I'm in revision mode?

The Revision toolbar contains all the quick buttons you'll need to revise your document. Click the **View** menu, point to **Toolbars**, and choose the **Revision** toolbar.

Is there an easy method to route this document during the revision process?

You can use e-mail to conveniently send or route shared documents during the revision process. You'll find the **Send to Mail Recipient** button on the Revision toolbar.

How can I protect my document from unauthorized personnel?

You can protect your shared document by including different levels of passwords that any reviewer will need to know before viewing or editing your document.

Chapter 18

Using Word 97 Tools

In This Chapter

➤ Using AutoFormat and AutoSummarize tools

➤ Working with footnotes and endnotes

➤ Using WordMail

➤ Adding a table of contents to your document

➤ Using Word 97 Document Search features

Here's the place you'll find the leftovers. But some of these powerful Word 97 tools could be the main course to help you solve difficult formatting problems, or make life easier with automated correction of errors as they appear. Bon Appétit!

A Hands-On Introduction to AutoFormat

If you are new to the whole subject of formatting styles, there's a quick way to jump in and immerse yourself. It's called the **AutoFormat** command. The **AutoFormat** command *sounds* like a miracle worker—garbage in, beautiful document out, right? Not so, my friend. A better suited phrase for AutoFormat is garbage in, garbage out. And that's good enough, because it gets rid of the garbage most of us (who don't use styles) put into our documents as we create them.

Take a look at your **Style** box in the **Formatting** toolbar. Does it say Normal? Does it *always* say Normal? If so, then you aren't making use of styles. The **Normal** selection is the epitome of boring text. Now let's find the garbage produced by using nothing but the Normal style.

How do you separate paragraphs to make them look better on your page? Most people press **Enter** twice. In the Style world, that second **Enter** is considered useless, and there-fore, garbage. How do you indent the first line of your paragraph. Sure, you are to be congratulated for moving up from the **Spacebar** to the **Tab** key, but both are considered unnecessary (garbage) when using styles. Do you create numbered or bullet lists manu-ally? Do you always center the page heading on the page, and make it bold or under-lined? All of these formatting tasks needlessly chew up your valuable time.

Training Wheels: AutoFormat While You Type and Watch

In your mind, AutoFormat probably exists as a command on the Format menu that is applied *after* you create a document, right up there with Print and Save. That's correct; your mind has tuned into the default setting of the AutoFormat command. But there's more! Try something really different using AutoFormat.

With AutoFormat, Word 97 analyzes each paragraph within your document (even as you create it) to determine its purpose (such as a heading, a bullet or number list, regular text, and so on), and then applies an appropriate style from the current template.

Open the Format menu and choose the AutoFormat command. Click the **Options** button. Click to select the **AutoFormat As You Type** tab. Notice the box labels in the dialog box change from merely Apply and Replace to Apply as you type, and Replace as you type. Go ahead and click to select the **Headings** box, also. Now start a new document and have some fun.

Type the title at the top of your page as you would normally, and then press **Enter** twice. How about that? Word watches you press Enter twice and determines the text is impor-tant enough to become a style heading, and it picks a style called Heading 1. It also gets rid of the spare blank line above your insertion point.

Now press three underline symbols (_) and press **Enter**. An instant underline appears across the entire page! Actually, you always have this feature regardless of AutoFormat, and it even works with the equals symbol (=) and the hyphen (-) as well. Try using the Tab key to begin your second short sentence and press **Enter** twice. AutoFormat kicks in, and you are pleasantly surprised with a Heading 2 style applied (you must be using a Tab stop on your ruler for this one to work).

232

AutoFormat while you type.

Keep going. Start a list by typing something like: **1) My first option** and press **Enter**. Instant numbered lists! AutoFormat presumes you will want a 2 next, and gives it to you. It also removes any spaces or tabs you might have included between the number and your text. Not a bad way to create numbered lists in a hurry. As long as you include a closed parenthesis or a period (some form of punctuation) after the first number, AutoFormat is aroused and adds new numbers and applies an appropriate style for you. To make it stop, just press **Enter** again, and you'll be returned to normal text waiting patiently for your next command.

You can also create quick bulleted lists this same way. Type an asterisk (*****) or the letter **o** (the one after n) and a space. Then type some text and press **Enter** once. The asterisk or letter **o** will be converted to bullet symbols automatically.

Automatically Summarize Any Document

Got lots of large documents that you need to read, but you don't have the time? Feeling wild and crazy? How about letting Word 97 automatically read those documents for you, and present you with a brief summary of the most important information. Sound like science fiction? Well, sometimes it borders on humor, but the new AutoSummarize tool is worth a look.

AutoSummarize A tool that might save you lots of time summarizing large documents is AutoSummarize. It analyzes and summarizes any document automatically.

Build Large Web Sites Faster Auto-Summarize can be a great help in building large Web sites, when you've got oodles of large documents that need to be condensed to provide abstracts and hyperlinks from the home page. Let this tool take the first stab at it, then you come around and check for accuracy and perform any needed edits.

If you want to read a summary of an online document, you can display the document in AutoSummarize view. In this view, you can switch between displaying only the key points in a document and highlighting them in the document. As you read, you can also change the level of detail at any time.

Keep in mind that AutoSummarize works best on well-structured documents, like reports, articles, and scientific papers. And for the best quality summaries, make sure that the Find All Word Forms tool has been installed in your computer, because AutoSummarize recognizes and uses past, present, and future tenses of words in making its judgment of what belongs in the summary.

Okay, the first time you try this you might laugh yourself silly, because maybe the summary isn't quite what you expected. Remember that AutoSummarize is only a tool, and you should review the accuracy of any summary because it is, after all, just a summary or your entire document.

Create Your Abstract Automatically

Don't forget to save your document before trying this at home. With the document slated for analysis opened on your screen, open the **Tools** menu and click **AutoSummarize**. Immediately, this feature will start chugging away for a few moments, doing its thing. If you get worried and change your mind at any time, just click the **Escape** key and it will stop. Upon completion, you'll be staring at the AutoSummarize dialog box, asking you how you want it. Under Type Of Summary, click the way you want to display your summary: **Insert An Executive Summary Or Abstract At The Top Of The Document** or **Create A New Document And Put The Summary There**. In the Percent Of Original box, type or select the level of detail to include in the summary.

As soon as you get your summary, spend a few moments to analyze it yourself. This summary text is nothing more than a "rough draft" and you should treat it as such. Make sure it covers the key points in your document. If it doesn't, click the **Undo** button to delete the summary, and then repeat the process, but this time choose a higher percentage of the original document. You can also keep a rough summary and modify it yourself later.

AutoSummarize can be the judge of your work.

How to View Different Levels of Detail

If you just want to view different levels of summarized details, follow this same process. Open the document you wish to analyze, then open the **Tools** menu and click **AutoSummarize**. When it's finished (longer documents may take a few seconds), in the Type Of Summary area click one of the four ways you can view the summary of the document.

➤ **Highlight Key Points** maintains the original layout of your document, but highlights the words and sentences that express the major themes of the document.

➤ **Create A New Document And Put The Summary There** leaves your original document untouched, but copies and consolidates the major themes of the document into a single summary, which is then placed in a newly created document, completely separate from your original document.

➤ **Insert An Executive Summary Or Abstract At The Top Of The Document** Choose this to insert the automatic summary at the beginning of your document, where you can edit or save it as part of your document.

➤ **Hide Everything But The Summary Without Leaving The Original Document** Here's a way to easily view only the summary of the main themes of your document without creating an additional document. When you choose this option, only the summary text will be displayed. All other text will be hidden.

235

With each of these options, you have the capability to control the amount of summary information you receive. In the **Percent Of Original** box, type or select the level of detail to include in the summary. This level is expressed as a percentage of your document, so if you choose 25 percent for the summary length of a four-page document, your summary will be one page long. Then click **OK**. You'll see the basic summary screen (prepared according to the option you've chosen), and the AutoSummarize toolbar.

If you aren't satisfied with the length of the summary, you don't have to start again from scratch. To show more or less summary detail, use the options on the AutoSummarize toolbar. To adjust the level of detail, drag the yellow Percent of original slider (or click the arrows) in the AutoSummarize toolbar. To switch between displaying only the key points or highlighting them, click the **Highlight/Show Only Summary** button on this same toolbar. After you've finished viewing this summary, click the **Close** button on the AutoSummarize toolbar.

How Does AutoSummarize Really Work?

AutoSummarize searches the document for keywords and sentences that represent the most frequently discussed topics. AutoSummarize then assigns a score to each sentence in your document. It gives a higher score to sentences that contain words used frequently in the document. When it completes, you decide what percentage of the highest-scoring sentences to display in the summary.

AutoSummarize then copies the keywords and sentences to the Keywords and Comments boxes on the Summary tab. To see this for yourself, open the **File** menu and click **Properties**. With this information stored here, you can easily locate the document by searching for the keywords or comments it contains. If you don't want AutoSummarize to replace your existing keywords and comments, clear the Update document statistics check box in the AutoSummarize dialog box.

Got the New Mouse with the Wheel?

If you're using the new Microsoft IntelliMouse, you can use it to adjust the level of detail displayed in AutoSummarize view. To display more or less detail in five percent increments, hold down the Shift key as you rotate the wheel forward or back.

Creating Footnotes

If you really want to impress your boss, try placing *footnotes* in your status reports, referencing conversations you've secretly recorded. It's easy to make simple documents look impressively professional by following these tips on creating footnotes.

You remember footnotes from high school or college. The little numbers are strategically placed to interrupt your reading by sending subliminal messages to your brain urging you to look down to the bottom of the page to see what was so important that it warranted this number. Maybe you were tricked and didn't see anything at the bottom of the page, because they weren't footnotes, they were *endnotes*, which appear at the end of a document.

Your First Footnote Is the Hardest

If you have trouble making decisions in life, stick with the defaults, and you won't go wrong. This philosophy also applies to footnotes because the hardest part about creating them, besides writing them, is deciding where they should appear on your page. Some people like them at the bottom of the page (the default), some

Endnotes are a special form of footnotes that are placed at the end of the section or the end of the document.

prefer just below the current paragraph, still others at the bottom of a table or the end of a document (but technically, that's called an *endnote*); the rest of us don't bother with footnotes.

Don't Confuse Footers with Footnotes

Footers appear at the bottom of each page (in the margin) of a document, regardless of the content of that page (see Chapter 11 for more details on footers). A footnote is an extended explanation of some detail expressed in the content of that particular page. Reference to a footnote in a document is usually indicated with a superscript number. Footnotes generally appear at the bottom of the page, and are typically preceded by the corresponding superscript number from the document.

You can have multiple footnotes per page, and you can have both footnotes and a footer on a given page.

When you're ready to create a footnote, start by placing the insertion point where you want the footnote to be referenced. It can be a word or a sentence (or paragraph). For a word, place the insertion point at the end of an individual word, and Word will automatically place the footnote mark in the conventional location—slightly raised and to the right of the word. If you want to footnote an entire sentence, place the insertion point at the end of the last word of the sentence. Open the **Insert** menu and select the **Footnote** command. You will see the Footnote and Endnote dialog box.

Deciding where a footnote should be seen.

Click here to have your footnotes automatically numbered.

Make sure you leave **AutoNumber** selected so your footnotes are correctly numbered and organized.

You may also want to try the **Options** button, which helps adjust the placement of notes, set note numbering and formatting options, and convert notes to footnotes or endnotes (or vice versa). And if you would prefer to use a different symbol as a custom note reference mark, click the **Symbol** button.

Graphics in Footnotes?

If you're serious about sticking things like pictures, charts, or graphs in your headers, footers, or footnotes, you need to see a doctor soon. In the meantime, you can review Chapter 15, which shows you how to add pictures just about anywhere, including in footnotes.

When you press **OK**, you will be transported to the footnote area at the bottom of the page. You normally don't see this part of your page because your view is set to Normal. If you insert a footnote while in Normal view, the window splits and the cursor is transported to a footnote editor. Working in Page Layout view will move the cursor to the bottom of the page, where the footnotes are located.

Now start typing your footnote. You can place almost anything in a footnote, including text, pictures, and charts (and even sounds and video for multimedia buffs). Footnotes can be long, and can exceed a page in length. Don't fret, because Word 97 will take care of the formatting.

When you are finished typing, click the **Close** button. If you happen to be in Page Layout view, you don't have to do anything—you're finished. Now admire your work. Little numbers appear properly, and the page is adjusted to fit the footnote.

The good news is that once you've set your footnote options, you don't have to come back to this dialog box each time you add another footnote or endnote.

Spewing Forth Footnotes After That

After the first footnote has been placed, the rest are easy to create—even if you have to place one earlier in your document. Place the insertion point at the next point of text you want to reference, and select the **Footnote** command from the **Insert** menu. You are now in the footnote editing area. Type away and press the **Close** button when finished. No more menus to worry about, and the numbering is taken care of for you.

Editing Footnotes

If you need to change the wording of a footnote or two, they can easily be edited. All you have to do is double-click the little footnote number and the handy footnote editing window will appear, with the cursor already at the start of the footnote text. Or, if your aim is not so good on those little numbers, you can switch to Page Layout view and see the footnotes directly. Open the **View** menu and choose the **Page Layout** view, and if you move to the bottom of the page you will see your footnotes. Either way, once you are inside the footnote area you are ready to edit your footnote directly.

Once the cursor is inside the footer area, you can update the footnote text by using any of the editing or formatting tools you are comfortable with. When you have finished editing the footnote, click on the **Close** button. You will be returned to the Normal view of your document. Or, if you are in Page Layout view, simply click in the main body of your document to return to it.

Deleting Footnotes

Now here's a demonstration of Word 97 doing something really helpful for you. Let's say you've got 27 footnotes in your research document on the livers of aquatic emus, and you just realize the first one is incorrect and has to be deleted. Word not only blasts it away and reformats the entire document, but more importantly *renumbers* and *re-references* the remaining footnotes automatically. Now *that's* what you bought a computer for.

To delete a footnote, you must go to the footnote number in your document, not the header and footer area. You don't have to be in Page Layout mode when you delete a footnote. Select the footnote's number (it's called a *reference mark*) in your document (it will appear highlighted) and press the **Delete** key.

To delete all automatically numbered footnotes or endnotes, open the **Edit** menu and choose the **Replace** command. Click **Special** and then click **Endnote Mark** or **Footnote Mark**. Make sure the **Replace With** box is empty, and then click **Replace All**. You cannot delete all custom footnote reference marks at one time.

Cutting, Copying, and Pasting Footnotes

Power users will be amazed that you can even cut and paste a footnote from one area to another if you need to. Select the footnote and click the **Cut** button. Find the proper location for the footnote and click the **Paste** button. If you pass another footnote during the move, everything will be renumbered automatically and referenced correctly for you.

Copying is just as easy for those popular *IBID*s and *See Footnote #1*s. Select the footnote and click **Copy**, then go find the next location. Click the **Paste** button and you've got a newly numbered visitor here to stay.

Try WordMail

What's this? E-mail in my word processor? Not just any e-mail, mind you, but WordMail! Yes, when you installed Word 97, WordMail is installed by default as one of its features. Lots of you have been clamoring for this (keep it down) because you wanted full formatting capabilities in your e-mail. WordMail works in conjunction with your e-mail system and enables you to create mail messages with all the formatting capabilities of Word 97. Well, at least the ones that apply to e-mail messages. Don't forget, you can also send Word documents as attachments to e-mail.

Start WordMail from Your Web Browser!

Any recent version of Web browser, including the Microsoft Internet Explorer and Netscape Navigator, includes access to e-mail through a button or menu command. Choosing this command will automatically start WordMail. If WordMail doesn't start automatically, check the options for setting the default e-mail editor inside your browser.

Improve the Look of Your E-mail Messages

Word 97 includes several e-mail templates to help you compose your e-mail when you use WordMail as your mail editor. Each template has a different theme. For example, you might use the urgent theme template to compose an urgent mail message.

In addition, Word automatically formats headings and lists in your plain text WordMail messages when you open them. You can easily distinguish the current message from the previous messages in the e-mail conversation.

Word 97 as Your Microsoft Outlook E-mail Editor

Open Microsoft Outlook, click **Options** on the **Tools** menu, and then click the E-mail tab. To turn on Word 97 as your e-mail editor, click to put a check in the **Use Microsoft Word As The E-mail Editor** check box. To turn off Word as your e-mail editor, clear this check box.

Automatically Format Your WordMail Messages

To automatically format your WordMail messages, open the **Format** menu and click **AutoFormat**. Click the **Options** button in the AutoFormat dialog box. Under Always AutoFormat, select the **Plain Text WordMail Documents** check box. When you select this option, Word 97 automatically formats unformatted e-mail messages that you open using WordMail. To help you even more, Word automatically formats all Internet addresses in your WordMail messages as hyperlinks. That means you can click on the hyperlink and jump right to that destination.

Several WordMail formatting features don't appear in other e-mail editors. If recipients of your messages aren't using WordMail as their e-mail editor, then borders, highlighted text, numbered lists, and floating drawings in your messages may not appear. Also, other editors may display tables as tab-delimited text and reduce all fancy bullets to plain round bullets.

Adding a Table of Contents Automatically

If you've paid your dues, then you can reap your rewards, and the automatic Table of Contents generator in Word 97 is a big reward. The only dues required is a consistent use of heading Styles throughout your document. For example, use Heading 1 for the big chapters, Heading 2 for sections in those chapters, and so on (even including a heading for tables or figures if you like). You'll get a great-looking document anyway, even if you don't use the TOC function.

Once your document has Heading styles for all the important parts, you can generate a table of contents. Start with a click in your document telling it exactly where to place this table of contents. Open the **Insert** menu, click **Index and Tables**, and then click the **Table of Contents** tab.

Generate a table of contents for your document automatically.

Choose different styles of TOCs here.

Decide how many different levels of headings to include.

Click to choose from the different appearances available for your table of contents. Also decide how many levels, and which levels, you want to include in your table of contents. For example, maybe your document title is the only Heading 1; you might choose to ignore that heading. Or maybe skip other headings to keep the size down, but perhaps leave in a lowly heading that you've used for figures or tables, because you'd like to include them. Experiment! You can always delete a table of contents and try again.

Afraid to try a TOC because you forgot to use styles, and you think it's too hard to apply them now? Try this tip when no one is looking—have Word 97 automatically format your document with AutoFormat. The result might be close enough to a result that allows for a decent table of contents. If not, you can also Undo an AutoFormat.

Using Word 97 Document Searching Tools

It's tough enough to find your car keys in this day and age—you don't need the extra headache of a complicated search for a particular document. Thank goodness Word 97 provides the kind of searching tools we've been asking for since the industrial age began. Too bad it can't find car keys, too.

Where to Look

All the searching capabilities you need to find documents are included in the Open dialog box. This includes the capability to browse, perform simple searches, and perform very complicated searches, all in one screen.

To begin your search for a document, open the **File** menu and choose the **Open** command (or you can press **Open** on the **Standard** toolbar).

Look on your computer's hard drive.

Look on disks you may have.

Starting your search by deciding where to look.

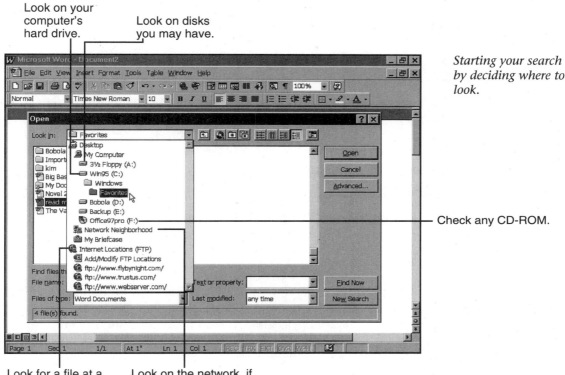

Check any CD-ROM.

Look for a file at a site on the Internet.

Look on the network, if you're connected to one.

The start of a search for any document usually begins with the Look In box at the top of the Open dialog box. On the right side of the attached box is a down arrow, which reveals a drop-down list when you click it. Click the **down arrow**. This list contains all the possible places your computer can search for your documents.

By double-clicking any of these icons, you can dig deeper into the folder levels to find your documents. For example, double-clicking Desktop displays My Computer, and double-clicking My Computer reveals all the folders at the very top level of the computer's hard disk. Double-clicking any of these folders displays files and other folders that may be stored inside them.

Up One Level

A folder can contain documents and other subfolders. When you double-click a folder, you go *down* into it, and see the documents and folders that might be stored inside. To move to a parent folder, click the **Up One Level** button. Press this button once and you will move up a folder level. Press it again and you will move up another, and so on, until you are at the top level of your computer. You can also click the **Backspace** key, which has the same function as **Up One Level**.

Search the Web from a New Starting Point

There's a new button in your File Open dialog box called Search The Web. If you need to find a source of information on the Internet, just click this button to open the search page of your Internet browser.

Your Favorite Hiding Spot

Two other new buttons on the Open dialog box can help you store and find documents: the **Look In Favorites** and **Add To Favorites** buttons. This Favorites folder could become your *favorite* place to store the documents you create.

To find out if the document you want is in the **Favorites** folder, just click the **Look In Favorites** button. You can also create folders inside of **Favorites**, and you probably should if you plan to store more than a handful of documents here. Organize your documents by storing them in several logical folders, and name the folders so you will recognize them, such as Weekly Reports, or Client Contracts, and so on. It will be much easier to find what you're looking for in the future.

Exactly where is this mysterious Favorites folder stored? It's usually stored in the default Windows folder, but you really don't have to worry about it. Just be comforted in the fact that Word 97 knows where it is, and you can build your own structure of personal folders starting in Favorites. And since the File Open dialog box has a button called Look In Favorites, doesn't it make sense to store your documents here?

Looking on Disks

Lots of people save their documents to disk—with good reason. There's a lot of comfort in the fact that you can carry the documents wherever you go, on a single disk that's easy to protect. If you have all your documents *backed up* to a disk, you can take them to any computer and continue working. Open the **File** menu and choose the **Open** command. Near the top of the dialog box, click to open the **Look In** text box. Click on the **3_ Floppy** to display the contents of your disk. The documents will be displayed in the Name box. If you have folders on the disk, you can double-click them to look inside, and then press the **Up One Level** button to return to where you started from.

If you don't see any documents, it could mean that the files stored on disk were not created with Word 97; in that case, your best bet is to view all possible file formats on the disk. To view all types of files on disk, click the down arrow connected to the **Files of Type** box near the bottom left of the Open dialog box. In the drop-down text box that appears, scroll to the top of the list and choose **All Files**. This option will enable you to see the name of any file, no matter what word processor may have created it. You might also see lots of other files that aren't documents at all, and it's best not to waste too much time on them. Be sure to check once again in any folders that might be included on your disk.

Searching All Over for Your Documents

Still can't find your document? It's time to get creative. Word allows you to throw in some curious information to assist in the search for a document. Do you know when it was last used? Can you guess at any part of the name or summary information? Do you know any words that might be inside the document? It might be enough to locate your document.

You can specify any additional search criteria you want in the bottom of the Open dialog box. You can type the name of the document in the **File Name** box, if you know it; or you can type partial names, and it's no longer necessary to use the wild card character * (asterisk) at all. Just type as much of the word as you know (for example, just type gold to search for any document name containing the word *gold* anywhere in its name).

Now you must tell the computer where to search. To search all subfolders from where you start the search, click the **Commands and Settings** button (near the top right of the Open dialog box), and then click **Search Subfolders**.

To display the folders that contain the files found, click **Commands and Settings** button again, and then click **Group Files By Folder**. Otherwise, you'll see only the names of the files found, and not the folders containing them.

With your search criteria entered, click the **Find Now** button. The search may take a few seconds, or longer, depending on your search criteria and the size of your computer's hard drive. If you ever want to stop a search, just press the **Stop** button.

If the search works well, and you want to use it again in the future, you'll find it at your fingertips. To use an existing saved search to find the files you want, click the **Commands and Settings** button in the **Open** dialog box, click **Saved Searches**, and then click the name of the search. Your original entries are loaded and ready for you to press the **Find Now** button.

The following is a summary of options (in the Open dialog box) for finding files:

➤ **File Name**   If you happen to know the name, type it here so searches through folders won't display anything but the document you're looking for.

➤ **Files of Type**   To specify the type of file you want to open, like a Word document or WordPerfect, or any other type of document.

➤ **Text or Property**   To find all files that contain certain text, either in the contents of the file or as a file property, such as the title, enter the text in the **Text Or Property** box. For example, to find only files that contain the phrase "fresh hamburger," type **"fresh hamburger"** in this box. You must enclose what you type in quotation marks (" ").

➤ **Last Modified**   To find all files that were saved during a specific time period, like any files created in the last day or week.

Using Advanced Searching Features of File Open

If the list of files found does not contain the file you want, you can specify even more detail in your search criteria. In the Open dialog box, click **Advanced** to open the Advanced Find dialog box.

Advanced searching helps you find all documents containing any word you remember.

You can even find forms of the word if you aren't sure how it exists.

Select Contents from the pull-down list in the Property box.

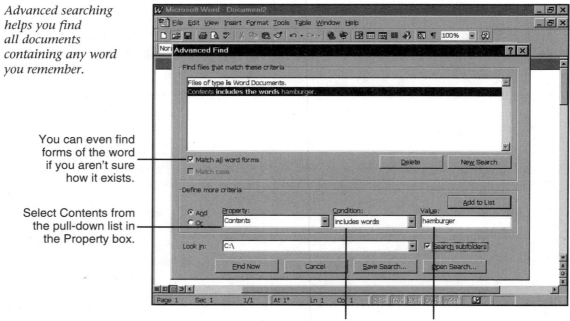

Leave this alone.

Type the word contained in the document.

This dialog box looks intimidating, and it is sort of, but it's worth the investment of learning a simple and important search feature. See the Property box? Click the arrow to expose the pull-down list of possible properties to search on. If you ever bothered to enter the summary information when previously working with a document, you can quickly find those documents now, and you'll be pleased that these properties are among the fastest things to search for. For example, if you filled in the Company or Keywords fields (or any of the other fields) in the Properties dialog box for any documents you have created, you can now perform searches like finding all documents related to XYZ Company.

If you want to try a more complicated search, give this a try. If you ever want to find a particular word inside of a closed document, no matter what the word or where the document might be, follow these steps.

In the Advanced Find dialog box, click the **Property** down arrow to display the list of choices. Find the word **Contents** and select it; it will appear in the Property text box. Leave the Condition box alone, as long as it has the words Includes words in the box. Now click in the **Value** box and type the word you are looking for. Once the boxes are filled in, press the **Add to List** button. You will see a sentence describing your search in the display box.

Before starting the search, you may want to narrow down or expand it with further available options. Click on **Match All Word Forms** if you want to find similar forms of a word (for example, choosing this option on a search for the word "sell" will also locate documents containing the words "selling" and "sold." Or you might want to click **Match Case** if you are certain of the case of letters in your word search. Also, be sure to put a check mark in the **Search Subfolders** check box if you are interested in checking the folders beneath the current one.

When you are ready to go, click the **Find Now** button. This type of searching takes significantly longer than other types, so be prepared to wait many seconds or minutes, again depending upon the complexity of your search and the number of documents it has to look at. During the search, the **Find Now** button turns into the **Stop** button, which can stop a search in progress if you've changed your mind.

After a successful search, you may want to save your searching parameters for the next time you need to search. You can save your search criteria by pressing the **Save Search** button and providing a name for your search.

The Least You Need to Know

At last, we found the tools we were looking for in this chapter. Word 97 comes loaded with productivity helpers that have now been explained.

I need to add a footnote in this exact location. What do I do?

A footnote is easily created by first clicking where you need it, then open the **Insert** menu, and choose **Footnote**. To move or copy a footnote, use the **Cut**, **Copy**, and **Paste** buttons.

I'm a real beginner and my document looks boring. What can I do?

Use the **AutoFormat** features of Word 97 to improve the appearance of your document and to correct typos on-the-fly. Open the **Format** menu and choose **AutoFormat**.

This document is huge and I'd like to summarize it. Any features hiding in Word 97 that might help me?

The **AutoSummarize** feature can help you analyze a document even before you read it—by automatically creating an abstract, or summary report. Try it by clicking **AutoSummarize** on the Tools menu.

My e-mail package lacks a decent editor. Can I use Word instead?

WordMail is a helpful tool that provides full formatting features as you compose e-mail. It's automatically installed with Word 97, and is waiting to be your e-mail editor of choice. Just open the **File** menu, click **Send To**, and choose **Mail Recipient**.

When is it best to add a table of contents?

Most people wait until a document is complete before adding the table of contents. When you've finished your document, open the **Insert** menu and choose the **Index and Tables** command. A table of contents will be generated automatically. If you've used Style Headings consistently in your document, your new table of contents may achieve a status of perfection.

I've lost my document. What kind of searching tools are available?

Powerful searching capabilities are built into the File Open features of Word 97. You can search your entire computer for details about your document, such as date ranges that may have been created, words that may be in the document name, or even text that may be inside the document.

Chapter 19

Desktop Publishing Techniques

In This Chapter

➤ Fast and easy newsletters

➤ Creating columns like a newspaper

➤ Flowing text from one location to another

➤ Using WordArt and Drawing

➤ How to create a drop cap

➤ Special character formatting

Read all about it! All the tips that are fit to print (the ones related to newsletters, anyway) are located in this chapter. And these features aren't just for newspapers alone—you'll find uses for some of these features in all your documents, especially formatting your text into columns, flowing text around graphics, and using some unusual character formatting tools.

Instant Newsletter Guaranteed!

You can't go wrong with a wizard on your side. Although this entire chapter covers details about creating your own newsletter, here's an example that might be enough to

Check This Out...

Where's the Wizard?

If you don't see the Newsletter Wizard, you can install it using the Setup program for Word 97. Choose the option to install Wizards and Templates and they will be installed and available to use.

satisfy your requirements. Word 97 comes with a *Newsletter Wizard* that walks you through the creation of something good enough to sell on the street corner.

Start a new document by opening the **File** menu and choosing the **New** command. You must use the *menu*, and *not* the **New** button on the Standard toolbar, to find the Wizard. In the **File New** dialog box, click the **Publications** tab to bring it to the front. Double-click on the **Newsletter Wizard**.

Working with a wizard is kind of like ordering fast food at the drive-thru. You don't see what's behind the wall creating your lunch. You get bombarded with lots of simple questions like, "Do you want lettuce? Tomato? Fries? Milkshake? Mustard?" All the answers you provide are used to create your meal and determine how happy you are with that meal. Wizards do the same thing. They help you create a beautiful document by asking a few simple questions.

Instant newsletter success using the wizard.

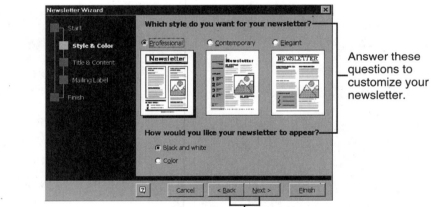

Answer these questions to customize your newsletter.

You can always move forward or backward with these buttons.

When the wizard starts, you'll see an attractive finished newsletter in the Preview box. Your first question is if you prefer the Classic or Modern style. I haven't the foggiest idea, but since the **Classic** button is selected, it must be Classic. Click the **Modern** option and watch the change in your preview box. These changes are subtle, some parts moving around, but it is a different style. Click the **Next** button to continue to the next question. That's all there is to talking to your wizard.

Continue answering the following questions. Notice that a default appears in all of them, so you can easily get through the process by pressing nothing more than the **Next** button.

➤ How many columns do you want?

➤ What's the name of the newsletter?

➤ How many pages do you think it will be?

➤ Would you like any of these options—Table of Contents, Fancy First Letters, Date, Volume and Issue?

When you click the **Finish** button on the last Wizard dialog box, a completely formatted professional-looking newsletter will appear on your screen.

Fast and simple Newsletter in seconds.

Notice that Page Layout View is used to see columns.

With the formatting completed, you are left with the task of entering the contents of your newsletter articles. You can click directly in the heading of a column and type your headline, then click in the text area to type your news article. You never have to worry about paragraph formatting because it has already been created for you.

When you save your newsletter, it will be saved as a regular document, albeit one with loads of formatting. The point is that it's no longer related to the wizard that created it. You can use the wizard over and over again to create different newsletters.

If you always choose the same options in the Newsletter Wizard, you can save even more time by opening a previously created newsletter and saving it with a new name. Then you can simply make changes to it. Or if you want to get fancy, you can create your own custom newsletter template. The details for creating your own template are found in Chapter 20.

Doing Columns

Which would you rather read, a supermarket tabloid claiming that the President is Bigfoot, or the novel *War and Peace*? Probably the tabloid, but not for the reasons you might think (the President just isn't that big and hairy). Newspapers in general, along with magazines and newsletters, align their text in multiple columns on a page. Why? It's easier to *read* that way. You don't have to move your eyes as much, or turn your head, shoulders, or entire body to keep up with the text running across the pages of a book.

Creating Columns

Believe it or not, you are already using columns in your documents. It just happens to be one large column that stretches the width of the margins. So much for trivia. At any point in your document, if you want to include two or more columns, you can change the number of columns by creating a section to contain the columns. Without sections declaring the start and finish of multiple columns, your document will appear with a consistent number of columns throughout.

Check This Out...

Column or Table? A different type of column is the *parallel column*, which is just a fancy way of saying *table*. With a table, you read across (instead of down) several columns of text and numbers. If you prefer to have a table in your document instead of creating newspaper-style columns, see Chapter 14.

When you add columns to a document, the width of the columns is adjusted automatically so they fit between the margins. For instance, if you add three columns, the width of your paper is divided into three equal parts. You can also decide to create column widths that are uneven, if you want a different effect.

The absolute fastest way to create columns on your page is with your mouse. Click the **Columns** button on the **Standard** toolbar. Drag to select the number of columns you want (from two to six), and then release the mouse button. This method is a bit restrictive because you're limited to up to six equally spaced columns (in portrait mode, or up to nine columns in landscape mode), but that's usually good enough for most people.

To learn more about what's happening, you should use the **Columns** dialog box to create your columns. There's hardly any limit to what you can do with columns when you create them this way.

Start by moving the insertion point to the section in the document where you'd like to change the number of columns. Open the **Format** menu and select **Columns**. Select any of the preset column patterns by clicking on the examples. As an alternative, you can enter the number of columns you want in the Number of Columns text box. If you need to create a section break so you don't affect earlier text, select the number of columns you want and then choose **This Point Forward** in the Apply To list box. You'll see a preview of your choices in the Preview screen. When you are finished, press **OK** and you will return to your document, now formatted in columns.

If you want to try creating columns of different widths, remove the check from the **Equal Column Width** check box by clicking on it. Now you can enter the width and spacing desired for each column. The numbers you enter are in the default unit of measure, in this case, inches. Try entering different numbers and watch the effect in the Preview box.

Editing Columns (Making Them Bigger or Smaller)

Your columns should be wide enough to have at least a few words on each line for readability. If you find you're averaging less than one, you have a problem.

To change the width of your columns using your mouse, first expose your horizontal ruler. If your ruler isn't visible, open the **View** menu and make sure the **Ruler** is checked by clicking on it. To change the width of a column, drag the column marker on the horizontal ruler to the right or left, until the column meets your approval.

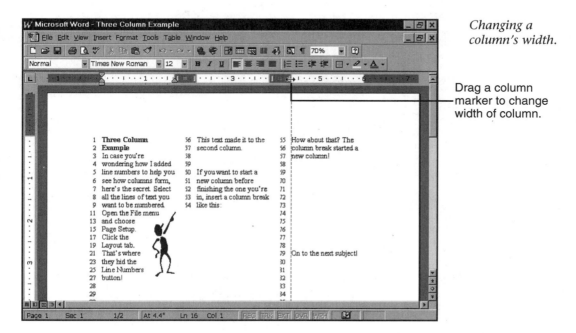

Changing a column's width.

Drag a column marker to change width of column.

253

To make precise changes to your columns, open the **Format** menu and choose the **Columns** command. Enter a new measurement in the Width box. If column widths are even, the other columns will adjust automatically. If you are using uneven columns, enter new measurements for each column. You can also change the spacing between columns.

Viewing Your Columns

Each viewing mode displays columns a little differently, with each view offering its own advantages. You will learn more about different views in Chapter 21, but for now understand that the most common view won't do. At least when it comes to columns, the Normal view (most common all-purpose view) doesn't do a good job of displaying columns. You need to change your view.

To change to a better view for viewing columns, press the **Page Layout View** button on the Horizontal scroll bar. You can also open the **View** menu and choose the **Page Layout** command.

Columns appear differently in different views.

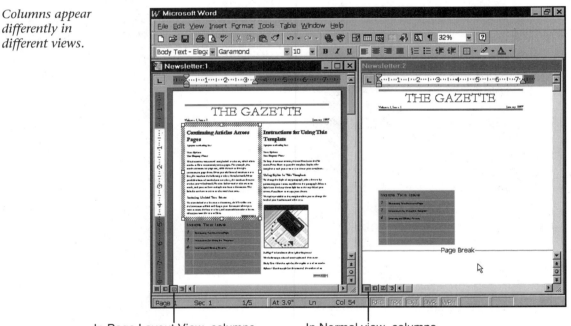

In Page Layout View, columns appear as they will print.

In Normal view, columns appear as one long column.

Within either view, you can zoom in to get a closer look at text or zoom out to get a bigger overall picture of your work. Just click the **Zoom** box down arrow on the Standard toolbar and select a magnification from the drop-down list box. You can also zoom by opening the **View** menu and choosing the **Zoom** command.

Dividing Your Columns with Lines

Sometimes it helps to keep those eyes where they belong. Truckers call it white line fever when you start hugging the middle of the road. Reading can be boring sometimes, just like driving, but instead of blasting the radio to stay awake (or improving your writing), you can draw lines between your columns of text to help contain them. It's especially helpful when your columns are close together.

Remember that you should be in Page Layout View when working with columns, and especially when creating these lines. Place the insertion point into the section where you want to add lines. Open the **Format** menu and choose **Columns**. Then click the **Line Between** check box. Using the **Apply To** box, select how much of the document you want the line to appear in.

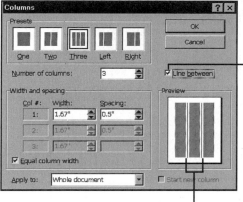

Vertical lines make your columns easier to read.

Check to include lines between columns.

Vertical lines improve readability of columns.

Techno Talk

Other Ways to Draw Lines

The **Line Between** option will place lines between all the columns in that section. There is no way to place a line only between two columns in a three-column section using this option. You can always create a line yourself by using the Drawing toolbar and place it between just two of the columns. Word 97 does a decent job of creating newsletters and columns, but other products exist and specialize in the subject. Examples of these types of products are Microsoft Publisher 97, Ventura Publisher, or PageMaker.

Straightening Out the End of Those Columns

Take a look at the last page of your newly columned document. When real newspapers or magazines can't fill a page, at least they balance the remaining text across the multiple columns. You can, too—and it's easy. Just insert a section break at the end of the document. Open the **Insert** menu and select **Break**. Under **Section Breaks**, choose **Continuous**, and then click the **OK** button.

You Want to Add Pictures?

Sure you want to add pictures to your newsletter or columns. It would be boring without them. Chapter 12 provides all the details about how to insert pictures and scanned photographs (called imported art or graphics) from other programs. To insert a picture or clip art, open the **Insert** menu, point to **Picture**, and then click the type of picture you are inserting. Once the picture is in your document, you can use the Picture toolbar to crop the picture, add a border to it, and adjust its brightness and contrast.

You might also be wondering how to get text to flow around a picture or graphic. That's in Chapter 12 also. There's no secret to this skill; just right-click your graphic, choose **Format Picture**, and click the **Wrapping** tab. The top row displays five different wrapping styles, click the one you prefer. The next row provides options for side margins of wrapping. Use these with larger graphics to keep text flowing on one side only.

Flowing Text to Another Part of Your Document

Want to make that story from page one finish in a column on page three, skipping two altogether? You can make text flow in a continuous story from one location in your document to the next by creating *text boxes*. You place your text in these boxes and then create text box links throughout your document, even if the locations aren't adjacent.

One Document at a Time
Linked text boxes must be contained in a single document. You cannot create text box links from one subdocument within a master document to another subdocument. You also cannot split subdocuments that contain linked text boxes belonging to the same story.

When you add lines of text to a linked text box, the text flows forward into the next text box. When you delete lines of text from a text box, the text in the next text box moves backward. You can link several text boxes in a document, and you can have multiple sets of linked text boxes. The links can flow forward or backward through your document.

Creating Text Boxes for Flowing Text

Open the **Insert** menu and click **Text Box**. Click or drag in your document where you want to insert the first text box. The instant you create your first text box, the Text Box toolbar will appear. Now click and drag your second text box, where you want the text to flow. Click the first text box to select it.

On the Text Box toolbar, click **Create Text Box Link**. Now click in the text box that you want the text to flow to. The text boxes are now linked. To link to more text boxes, continue these same steps to create the box and then link them. Once two text boxes are linked, you can create text that flows. In the first text box, type text that you want. As the text box fills, the text will flow into the other text boxes that you've linked. The text box that you link to must be empty (and not previously linked somewhere else). To use the Text Box shortcut menu, move the pointer over the border of the text box until the pointer becomes a four-headed arrow, and then right-click the border.

Click the chain to link text boxes.

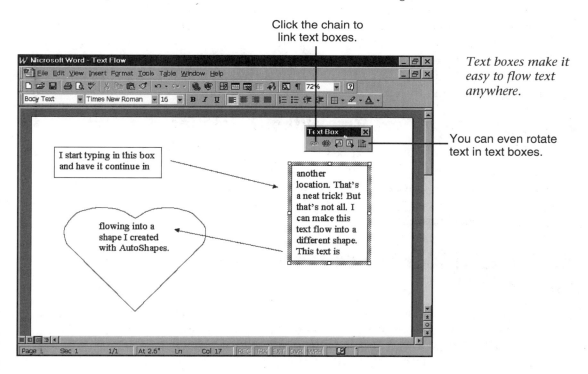

Text boxes make it easy to flow text anywhere.

You can even rotate text in text boxes.

To restore the Text Box toolbar if you accidentally close it, click a text box in your document, point to Toolbars on the View menu, and then click **Text Box**. (Your document must contain a text box for this toolbar to be available on the list.)

How Do I Stop This Thing?

If you click **Create Text Box** Link and then decide you don't want to link to another text box, press the **Esc** key to cancel the linking process.

If you want to make your text box more interesting, you can remove the borders, change borders, or add background colors or textures. First select the text box, then click the **Text Box** command on the **Format** menu (it only appears if a text box is selected).

Creating Flowing Text to an AutoShape

It's just as easy to create text box links between different shapes, such as circles, diamonds, flowchart shapes, even stars and banners. First create your drawing object, then right-click the shape. Click **Add Text** on the shortcut menu. Now select the first text box or drawing object containing the text you want to flow. On the Text Box toolbar, click **Create Text Box** Link. Finally, click in your drawing object (when you move the upright pitcher over a text box that can receive the link, the pitcher turns into a pouring pitcher) and the text will flow.

Deleting a Linked Text Box Without Deleting the Text

If you need to delete a linked text box but you want to save the text inside, click the text box to see the border handles. Carefully move the pointer over the border of the text box until the pointer becomes a four-headed arrow, and then click the border. Press the **Delete** key and the text box will vanish. The text, however, will be stuffed back into the previously linked text box.

Playing with Your Words (Special Character Formatting)

Work hard. Play hard. Sleep in. Being the life of the party is hard work. So is coming up with ideas to make your words more interesting. The tools to accomplish this task, however, are easy to use and work quite well in Word 97. You'll now learn how to take your best stuff and make it even better.

Dropping Your Caps (but Not in Your Soup)

You've seen them all over the place, in magazines, books, and newspapers. Big letters. Really big. But only one, and it's the *first* letter of the *first* word of the reading. They have a name for this kind of thing. It's called a *drop cap*.

258

The drop cap used to be a special effect reserved for highly talented artists, editors, and monks. Now with Word 97, mere mortals can create them in a fraction of the time once required. Not much to learn here except how to choose the Drop Cap command from a menu.

To create a drop cap, move to the paragraph where you want to place it, then open the **Format** menu and choose the **Drop Cap** command. In the Drop Cap dialog box, you can change the font and point size in the text boxes provided. Then choose whether you want it **Dropped** or **In Margin**. You can also change the number of lines to drop by clicking **Lines to Drop**. This determines the size of the drop cap letter. You can even change the distance between the drop cap and the paragraph text by clicking on **Distance from Text**. Then press the **OK** button (or **Enter**) to close the dialog box.

Staying Young and Playful with WordArt

Have you ever been so mad at a word that you wanted to gut it all over the page? Relax, they're only words. Find another. Or if the idea appeals to you, use WordArt, which actually helps accomplish these tasks. In fact, with Word 97 you have even more features, such as 3-D effects and textured fills.

WordArt is a tool that lets you manipulate words artistically, and it goes beyond the normal text attributes you learned about in Chapter 10. Take a look at some examples, and you will agree that they could have a place in your newsletter:

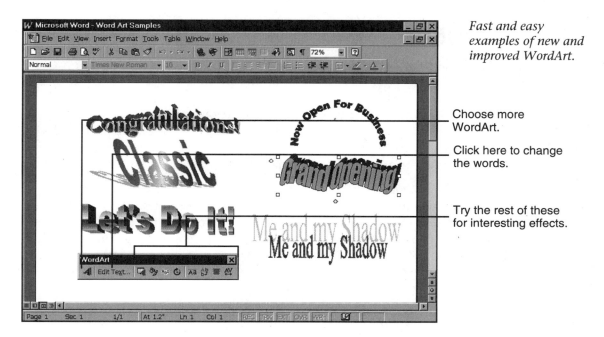

Fast and easy examples of new and improved WordArt.

Choose more WordArt.

Click here to change the words.

Try the rest of these for interesting effects.

To give WordArt a try, place the insertion point where you want the creation. Open the **Insert** menu, point to **Picture**, and choose **WordArt**. Here are actual WordArt samples; you just select the one you like and click the **OK** button. You'll see the Edit WordArt Text dialog box waiting for you to type in the words you want to display as art. Type some text, then click the **OK** button. The text you've entered is converted to WordArt and is placed in your document, along with the new WordArt toolbar, in case you want to customize it further. Click the **Edit Text** button on the WordArt toolbar if you need to change this text. That's all it takes!

Since your new WordArt is a graphic, you can change the size and shape by clicking and dragging the handles that appear when the graphic is selected.

The WordArt toolbar contains helpful buttons to assist you even more, by letting you twist, rotate, color, fill, and more. It's easier to experience than to describe, so give them all a chance to impress you. If something happens that you don't like, you can always click the **Undo** button.

Entering Strange Characters That Aren't on Your Keyboard

Sometimes you need to enter a character that isn't on your keyboard, such as the trademark symbol, the cent sign, or an umlaut. Word 97 makes it easy to insert these symbols wherever you need them. Just open the **Insert** menu and choose the **Symbol** command.

In the dialog box that appears, double-click any symbol to insert it into your document. If you want to insert additional symbols, simply repeat the process. To close the dialog box, press **Esc** (Escape key) or press the **Close** button.

Drawing Your Own Pictures

You can also draw your own pictures by using tools on the Drawing toolbar. Word 97 comes with a new Drawing toolbar you can use to create objects like lines, circles, flow-chart shapes, arrows, stars, and other shapes. You can also fill these objects with colors or patterns, and place them behind text or in the margins. Want more? You can then rotate, squish, flip, and turn it into a three-dimensional object.

To display the Drawing toolbar, click the **Drawing** button on the Standard toolbar. Don't worry about the large number of buttons; you probably only need a few, but you should try many of them. To use a tool, click it. Then use your mouse to create the object or effect in your document. Click to establish the upper-left corner of the object. Drag downward and to the right, and the object will form as you drag. Release the mouse button to create the object.

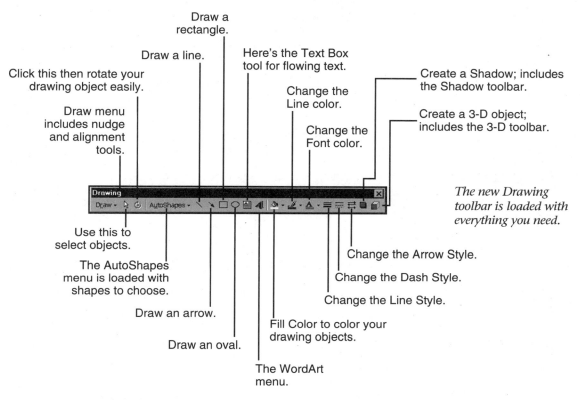

Draw a rectangle.

Draw a line.

Here's the Text Box tool for flowing text.

Click this then rotate your drawing object easily.

Create a Shadow; includes the Shadow toolbar.

Change the Line color.

Draw menu includes nudge and alignment tools.

Create a 3-D object; includes the 3-D toolbar.

Change the Font color.

The new Drawing toolbar is loaded with everything you need.

Use this to select objects.

Change the Arrow Style.

The AutoShapes menu is loaded with shapes to choose.

Change the Dash Style.

Change the Line Style.

Draw an arrow.

Fill Color to color your drawing objects.

Draw an oval.

The WordArt menu.

Boxing Your Words and Shading Them Well

Warning labels had trouble in the 1950s and 1960s. Nobody was reading them. Dying continued to be the major cause of death around the world. But then, almost like magic, someone decided to draw a box around a warning label. People started reading them. Lives were saved. And now you can do the same in Word 97 (draw a box, that is—not save lives).

You can draw a box around anything. It will call attention to whatever is inside the box. Need more attention? Shade your box, or else wear baggy lime-green pants and cluck like a chicken.

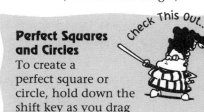

Perfect Squares and Circles
To create a perfect square or circle, hold down the shift key as you drag the mouse.

Drawing a Box Around Your Words

Start easy. Write some words first. Then box them up. You won't find the word *box* anywhere, however, because Word refers to them as *borders*. Borders are lines placed on any (or all) of the four sides of a text paragraph, the cells in a table, or a graphic such as a picture or a chart.

Check This Out...

Easier Than Ever to Border Your Work!

Horizontal borders can now be created quickly with a shortcut in Word 97. Just press three or more special characters in a row and then press the **Enter** key, and a perfect horizontal border will appear. The special symbols are === (equal), --- (dash), or ___ (underline). Each provides a slightly different version of horizontal border, so you'll want to try all three and see for yourself.

Placing a border around text or a graphic is fairly easy. Start by selecting the text or table cells. A graphic (a picture or a chart) can be selected by clicking on it.

After making your selection, open the **Format** menu and select **Borders and Shading**. On the left side of the dialog box, you see a make-believe page with two paragraphs. The choices you make in this box will be reflected in this little page as a sample. If you want to add a box (a border around all four sides), click **Box** under **Presets**. To get rid of a box, click **None**. Really upscale boxes have a shadow effect, giving your words a three-dimensional appearance. You can try it by clicking **Shadow**.

Shading Really Important Boxes

You should avoid boxes in your document. If you really need to have several, and still want to call special attention to one or more of them, try *shading*. In fact, forget about how many boxes you may have; shading is so great that you can do it anywhere!

It's important to understand that shading is the background color of your text. You'll want to know that in case you plan to include a picture or two because any picture existing in a shaded area will disappear on you. It's still there, of course; it's just hidden behind the shading.

Carefully select the text or table cells you want to shade. The shading will occur exactly where you highlight (unlike boxes, which were still square, even if a paragraph was indented). Then open the **Format** menu and select **Borders and Shading**. Click the **Shading** tab to bring Shading to the front.

Use the **Shading** box to select the percentage of gray that you want. If your letters are small, choose a lighter percentage, like ten percent. Larger letters can withstand larger percentages to become more striking and yet remain visible. The result is really determined by the type of printer you have and how well it handles shading; therefore, you might need to experiment until you get the results you like. Use a font with clean, crisp lettering, such as Arial, or apply bold formatting for better results. Now press the **OK** button to return to your document and witness the shading of your selection.

Headlining with Fancy Titles

It's probably time to put a *banner* on this thing and go home. A banner is a *headline* or a major title across the top of a page. It's usually on the first of your document. If you already tried this on a multiple column section, you may have been frustrated if you couldn't figure out how to spread the title over the multiple columns. The answer is coming up.

Banners should be fancy. If you haven't used any of the fancy character formatting capabilities of Word yet, now is the time. How else will you capture the attention of your audience, unless they see a startling and teasing title like *Elvis Seen with Mars Probe* or *Pumpkin Crushes Building*?

The Tables and Border Toolbar
If you want to apply borders and shading to a lot of areas within your document, use the Tables and Borders toolbar. To display the tool bar, open the **View** menu, select **Toolbars**, and then select **Tables and Borders**. You can also click the *right* mouse button while pointing to any displayed toolbar, and select **Tables and Borders** from the list.

Get Rid of the Border Fast! If you want to remove a border completely, select the same text or graphic, open the **Format** menu, and select **Borders and Shading**. Click **None**, and then click **OK**.

Type the words first. Short and interesting. They will become your heading text, which can span multiple columns. Now change to Page Layout view (open the **View** menu and choose the **Page Layout** command). Select the heading text, using your favorite selecting technique learned in Chapter 6. Click the **Columns** button on the **Standard** toolbar and drag to select a single column. The result will be your heading centered in what's basically a single column above multiple columns.

Next click the **Font Size** box, also on the Formatting toolbar (in fact, all of these tools are found on the Formatting toolbar, so you will get to know them well). Pick a large number, like 26 or so. If the text flows to the next line, it's too big; try something a little smaller. Although you can justify this text to spread evenly across the page (using the **Justify** button), it's better to choose the proper size with natural font spacing.

Oh, yes; next is the choice of the actual font. Click the **Font** box to see the many fonts you can choose from. Scroll down the list and try different fonts to see what's available. Make sure your text is selected before trying this, or else you won't see much. You should be able to find a font that matches your mood or style. Don't forget the basic font attributes of **Bold** and *Italic* that can also help the appearance. You might even want to shade the background, put a border around it, or both, using the skills you learned earlier in this chapter.

Adding a Caption or Callout to a Picture or Table

Some pictures are informative enough to stand by themselves in your document. Others need help. Help can come in the form of descriptive text added nearby, to identify the picture itself, or something specific inside the picture. Tables of information can often use this help, too. Word 97 provides an easy way to add descriptive text to either a picture or a table, and they are called captions and callouts. Captions are words used to describe the name or subject of a picture or table. Callouts are words pointing to a specific place inside the picture or table.

Captions Capture Your Attention

Adding a caption to a figure enables you to make a simple statement that summarizes your point. Adding a caption to a figure or table is easy. Start by clicking on the object to select it. Open the **Insert** menu and select the **Caption** command. Select the type of label you want from the **Label** list. You'll see a label such as "Figure 1" appear in the Caption text box. If you want to add something more, just type in the space after the label. Click the **OK** button (or press **Enter**) when you're done, and that figure will have a caption.

Using the **Numbering** button, you can change the numbering system of your figures to include chapter numbers, for example, or create your own label, by using the **New Label** button. You can even create automatic captions when you insert certain items into your document that increment automatically. Just click **AutoCaption** and click an item to select for automatic captioning.

Callout and Touch That Figure

You can also add a note of explanation for a figure or table using another tool called the *callout*. The callout tool is a button on AutoShapes, which is located on the **Drawing** toolbar. To display the Drawing toolbar, click the **Drawing** button on the **Standard** toolbar.

To add a callout anywhere inside your document, click the **Callout** tool and choose the shape of your callout from the wide variety displayed. Now move to your document area and click at the point where you want the callout line to begin, then drag to create the callout. Enter your text and click outside the callout box when you are finished. For more information on creating callouts, review Chapter 12.

Adding captions can help clarify pictures or tables.

A caption to summarize the figure.

Printing Your Newspaper

You can publish yourself with little effort or cost, and the quality will equal or exceed many professionally produced newsletters for which people pay good money. Just compose your thoughts in columns with pictures, boxes and borders, give it a title, and send it to the laser printer. If you want to impress people, you can also use a dot matrix printer.

Previewing Prevents Paper Cuts

Good thing that in the last chapter you learned how to Preview a document before you print it. Desktop publishing is one of those things that you can't get a sense for until you see the whole page. Maybe it's too crowded, unbalanced, and confusing, and that's what life is like—but your document doesn't have to be. Take a good visual browse at it before you print to catch the bigger mishaps.

Changing Your Margins in Print Preview

It's very common in desktop publishing to change margins based on the amount of space your words take up. While you are in this print preview state, remember the easy way to change margins. All you do is drag a margin handle to its new location (point at the margin handle, then press and hold the left mouse button as you move your mouse). As you drag, you'll see an "invisible" guideline to help you get it right. When the margin is set, release the mouse button, and the text will flow automatically.

The Least You Need to Know

If you ever need to make your document look more interesting, this is the chapter to review.

What's the quickest way to create an entire newsletter from scratch?

Use the Newsletter Wizard. Find this wizard by opening the **File** menu and choosing the **New** command. Click the **Publications** tab to see the Newsletter Wizard, and double-click this icon to start the process.

How can I quickly create three columns in my document?

To create any number of columns in your document, press the **Columns** button on the Standard toolbar and drag to select the columns you desire.

What tools should I use to create special effects?

To create special effects with text, use **WordArt**, which is available as a button on the Standard toolbar.

I found the dollar sign, but now I need the cents symbol. Where can I find it?

You'll find hundreds of standard character symbols in Word 97. To insert a special character into your document, open the **Insert** menu and choose the **Symbol** command. Locate the symbol you need and double-click to add it to your document.

How can I sketch a quick picture in my document?

Try using the tools found on the **Drawing** toolbar. Just click one of the many tools, and then drag around in your document to create your sketch.

How do I put a box around my words?

Word 97 refers to boxes as borders. First select the text you want to contain, open the **Format** menu, and choose **Borders and Shading**. Click **Box** found under **Presets** and you'll get the job done. You'll also find border-customizing features in this dialog box, along with fancy shading features.

Chapter 20

Templates, Styles, and Add-Ins

Computers have been promised to make our life easier. Yeah, right; I'd like to get my hands on the neck of that salesperson. But the promise has been delivered in key features of Word 97 called *templates*, and *styles*, and if this is news to you, this chapter is guaranteed to make you happy. That is, of course, if creating beautiful documents in a fraction of the time (so you can get home earlier) makes you happy.

What Is a Template?

Creating any document takes time, especially if you want it to look good. There are lots of tedious steps. You type the date, enter the addresses and the salutation, and maybe create headers and footers (such as a company logo or a page number). Maybe you change the margins, paragraph formatting, or add borders or lines to improve the appearance.

When you use a *template*, most of this groundwork is already done for you, so you can focus your attention on the words you want to say. You don't have to start a document from scratch.

Think of a template as a blueprint for the text, graphics, and formatting of a document. Templates in Word 97 are predesigned, ready-to-use documents into which you put your own information. You order a template, and the template automatically creates the foundation for your document. Those tedious details, like margins, dates, salutations, and so on, instantly appear on your screen. All you do is type the words of your memo or report. When you're finished and it's time to save your work, you provide a name and your creation is stored as a regular document. The template you chose is safe and sound for the next time you want to use it, and it will be just as helpful the next time.

Templates come in a variety of subjects and complexity levels. The simplest may do nothing more than set the margins and a font for your page, while the more complex may include dialog boxes that guide you through the document creation process. These are often called wizards, and you'll find more information on them later in this chapter, along with Chapter 3.

Word 97 includes more than 30 professionally designed templates for you to use, but the story doesn't end there. With a connection to the Internet you can find hundreds more on the Microsoft Office Web site and download free templates and wizards to your heart's content.

Nice Documents Word Can Create for You

Here are the categories that already exist to help you create common documents with the least amount of work:

More Free Templates! Want more? Open the Help menu, point to Microsoft on the Web, and then click Free Stuff. Your Internet connection will take you to a Web page loaded with templates and wizards. Choose what you want, then copy the files you want to your Templates subfolder (usually found in C:\Program Files\Microsoft Office\Templates, or find out for yourself by opening the **Tools** menu, click **Options**, click the **File Locations** tab, and the User Templates location will be displayed).

➤ **Letters & Faxes**   Business letters in several styles, personal letters, Fax cover sheets.

➤ **Memos**   Three different styles (simple and elegant to contemporary or professional) of memorandums.

➤ **Reports**   Three different styles of casual and professional reports.

➤ **Publications**   Brochures, Directories of names and addresses, Manuals, Newsletters, Press releases, Theses.

➤ **Other Documents**   Agendas for meetings, Award certificates, Calendars, Invoices, Purchase orders, Résumés or curriculum vitae, Weekly time sheets.

Templates can also be changed, and you can change them. New templates can also be created, and you really should consider taking your most common document type and saving one as a template to make your life easier the next time. Before we get too daring, let's test drive an existing template.

Using a Template for the First Time

Take a look at all the templates Word has to offer by opening the **File** menu and choosing the **New** command (unfortunately, pressing the **New** button on the **Standard** toolbar will not display the New dialog box. It's just a fast way to create a new document using the current template). With the New dialog box open, notice the list of tab titles across the top. This is how Word organizes the templates so you can find the one you want faster. Click the **Letters & Faxes** tab to bring it to the front. What you see are all templates, waiting to be chosen.

Don't See Any Templates? If you don't see these templates, run Setup again, and click the **Custom** button to find and install additional files. If you have the Word 97 CD-ROM, insert the disk and double-click on the **ValuPack** folder to see what other templates and wizards are available.

Press these other tabs to see more ready-to-use templates.

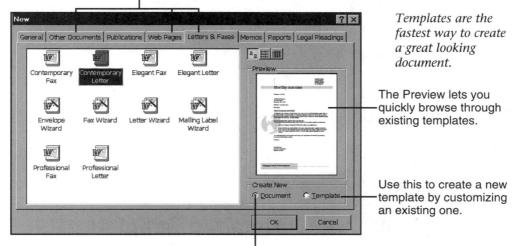

Templates are the fastest way to create a great looking document.

The Preview lets you quickly browse through existing templates.

Use this to create a new template by customizing an existing one.

Use this to create a new document from a template.

Double-click the **Contemporary Letter** to start using it. Be sure that **Document** is selected in the Create New box near the bottom. Your screen will fill with an interesting preformatted letter just waiting for you to fill in with your own information.

Easier Web Pages from a Template
Another great use for a template is in helping you create Web pages. Word 97 includes the Blank Web Page template and the Web Page Wizard to get your Web site filled fast. Find out more about these in Chapter 24.

Click in any of the areas you would like to fill out, and start typing. The text you enter is formatted automatically for that part of the letter. Click your way through the rest of these text fields to complete the letter. When you're finished, press the **Save** button (or open the **File** menu and choose **Save**). You are given a chance to save this completed letter as a regular document—it's no longer a template.

So remember, creating a document with a template does not change the template. Your new document is simply an automatic copy of the template's styles and any text it already has.

Templates guide you to perfectly formatted documents.

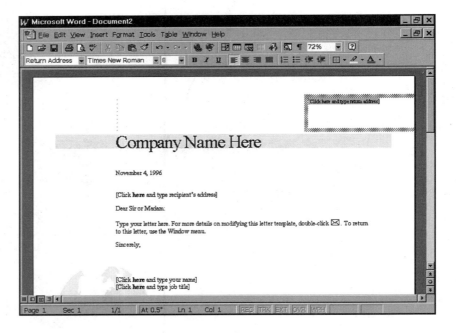

Creating Your Own Customized Template

You probably have documents you already use as unofficial "templates." Maybe it's a weekly report that you open and change a few words, then save it as a new document. Whenever you open, copy, and adapt the contents of an existing document, you're using that document as a template. Protect your time investment by formally saving these documents as templates.

The easiest way to create a new template is by saving an existing document as a template. To create a new template based on an existing document, open the **File** menu and choose the **Open** command. Locate and open the document you want.

Before making any changes, save your work. Open the **File** menu and choose the **Save As** command. In the **File Name** box, type a name for the new template. In the **Save In** box, open the Templates folder (it should be labeled Templates). If you want the template to appear in a particular template group, open that folder. In the **Save As Type** box, click **Document Template**, and then click **OK**. Congratulations! You've just created your own template, and now you can customize it.

Add the text and graphics you want to appear in all new documents that you base on the template, and delete any items you don't want to appear. Don't forget to make the changes you want to the margin settings, page size and orientation, styles, and other formats. When you finish, click the **Save** button, and your customized template will be saved.

Where Should You Store Your Templates?

Save your custom templates in the appropriate folder inside of the Templates folder, such as the Letters and Faxes folder, or the Memos folder. (The Templates folder is found in the same folder where you installed Word.) Templates that you save in the Templates folder or any of its folders appear in the New dialog box when you open the **File** menu and choose **New**. Any documents that you save in the Templates folder (or below) also acts as a template.

You can add a folder to the Templates folder to store your custom templates. When you first save the template, click **Create New Folder** in the **Save As** dialog box. Templates in the new folder appear on a separate tab in the New dialog box. To list a template on the General tab, save the template in the Templates folder, not in a subfolder.

You should always save your new templates in this standard Word Template folder, which is the default location that appears when you click the **Save File As Type** text box and choose **Templates**.

If you choose to store your template anywhere else, you can, and it will still work and act as a template. But to use it next time, you will have to remember where you put it.

> Check This Out...
>
> **Protect Your Originals** If you happen to click any of the templates in the New dialog box with the right mouse button, be careful not to choose the Open command. The original template is opened for modification, and you might accidentally change the original. Always use the **New** command to create new documents based on templates.

Modify an Existing Word 97 Template

Like that Newsletter template? Wish it had your company's name and logo on it, to save you the trouble of changing it each time? It can, by modifying the original template (or any other, for that matter).

Check This Out...

What's Normal About My Normal Template?
Everyone using Word 97 has one of these. The *Normal* template is a general-purpose template for any type of document. When you start Word or click the **New** button, Word creates a new blank document that is based on the Normal template. It's possible, but not advised, to modify this template to change the default document formatting or content. Word also uses the Normal template to store the AutoText entries, macros, toolbars, and custom menu settings and shortcut keys you routinely use. Should you customize any of these elements and store them in the Normal template, they become available for use with any document.

The process is simple enough, but first a word of warning: It's best not to change the Normal template (that's what you see when you first start Word 97), because any change you make to the Normal template will affect all other templates that you use. That means you first open the template you want to change before making any changes.

Open the **File** menu and choose the **New** command. Be sure to click **Template**, not **Document**, in the **Create New** area (lower right on your screen). Find the template you want to modify, click to select it, and click the **OK** button.

Now go ahead and make changes. Change any of the template's text and graphics, styles, formatting, macros, AutoText entries, toolbars, menu settings, and shortcut keys. When you have finished, press the **Save** button. Provide a name you'll recognize in the future. The template will be saved with your changes, ready to provide customized service in the future.

Once again, any changes to the template's content and formatting are reflected in any new documents you choose to create from this new template; existing documents aren't affected.

Styles: What Templates Are Made Of

Before leaving the subject of templates, you should know about styles, because if a whole template won't do the trick, maybe a style will. Styles are combinations of character, paragraph, and other formatting all saved in one easy-to-remember name. This goes beyond the bold, italic, or underline formatting that you give to individual words. Think of styles as a broader collection of interesting details brought together to become the default formatting of what you type.

Is It a Style or a Template?
What *is* the difference between a style and a template? Basically, a *template* is made up of several *styles*. A single *style* is a collection of paragraph and character formatting used in a document. A collection of styles can be saved as a template.

Are You Really Interested in How the Normal Style Works?

Up until now, every paragraph you've typed probably starts its life in the Normal style: Times New Roman 10-point font in a left-aligned paragraph. If you hate Times New Roman font, all you have to do is modify the Normal style to use some other font.

Changing your Normal style can, and often does, change the rest of your styles. Whether or not the change affects another style in that document depends on what Normal attributes the other style has. For example, suppose you create a style called *Title* that is centered, specified at 24-point size, and used the same font as Normal style (Times New Roman). The size of these fonts do not match, so if you change the size of your Normal font, your Title font will not change. But the *font* used in Title matches the Normal style, so your Title *will change* if you change the Normal font to something other than Times New Roman.

When you create a style, you usually start with the Normal style as a model. Therefore, any formats that you change will no longer be affected by subsequent changes to the Normal style. Formats that you leave at Normal's default *will change* if you change the Normal style. Got it?

Exposing the Styles on Your Screen

When the insertion point is placed in a paragraph, the style you are currently using appears in the **Style** box on the **Formatting** toolbar. If a character style is applied to a word, its style will appear in the **Style** box when the insertion point is placed *within the* *word*. To keep you from straining your neck looking up at that Style box all the time, you can show the paragraph styles right next to each paragraph in your document. To do this, turn on the **Style Area**.

You should be in Normal view for this trick. To display the Style Area on your screen, open the **Tools** menu and choose the **Options** command. Click the **View** tab to bring it to the front. Look for the **Style Area Width** box and replace that zero with a positive decimal number. You can just type over it, or click the up/down arrows to increase or decrease the width. A number like 1 (inch) will do just fine; this is temporary (remember to change this back to zero after you've experienced the Style Area). Now press the **OK** button and look at your screen.

Exposing the secrets of styles.

Temporarily enter a small width to view the style area column.

The extra margin to the left now displays the style applied to each paragraph on the screen. You can see that templates can be made up of many different styles, each serving a useful purpose. Remember the names of styles you like, because you can apply them to your own paragraphs whenever you wish.

Style labels leaking out on the left.

```
W Microsoft Word - Get Rich Quick                          _ ð x
File Edit View Insert Format Tools Table Window Help        _ ð x

Body Text    Garamond      14   B I U      90%

Company Name         GET RICH QUICK CO.
Return Address          PHONE: (900) 555-1212 • FAX: (900) 555-5050

Date                                          November 4, 1996

Inside Address Name   John S. Gullible
Inside Address        1090 Naïve Avenue
Inside Address        Yukantrust, ME 29910-1320

Salutation            Dear John:

Body Text                 We have an offer you won't be able to refuse. You're about to make lots
                      of money. I should know; I've done it myself. Are you really interested?
                      Here's how we start. First, send me some money (small unmarked bills
                      preferred). Be generous. Then wait for my next letter. You must be patient.

Body Text                 This proven technique has worked for others and it can work for you,

Page 1    Sec 1    1/2    At    Ln    Col    REC TRK EXT OVR WPH
```

Style commands are exposed.

Applying Styles to Paragraphs

With that introduction out of the way, and before you think styles are too complicated, let's apply a style to a paragraph.

Find a boring paragraph and place the insertion point anywhere inside the paragraph. Select several paragraphs if you want to format multiple paragraphs at one time. If it's your first time, however, you might want to start with a very small, perhaps single-line paragraph, so you can see the whole thing. Using your mouse, click the down arrow in the **Style** box on the **Formatting** toolbar. All of the currently available styles can be seen and selected from this drop-down scroll box. Click one of them, such as the **Heading 1**, and watch your paragraph jump into action and transform itself into something that looks like a major heading of a magazine article.

Try another style. Click on the drop-down **Style** list and choose **Heading 2**, and then **Heading 3**, for example. Keep trying different styles to get a feel for how styles convert your paragraph into impressive, consistent formats that can improve the look and feel of your document.

I Want More Styles! If a style you want to use isn't listed, press the **Shift** key, then click the same down arrow. A box will appear displaying all of Word's built-in styles, instead of the mere sampling you usually see.

Check This Out...

Now click the **Undo** button on the **Standard** toolbar, and watch your paragraph change to the previous style. You can always undo an applied style, so don't be afraid of experimenting with them!

Copying Styles from One Paragraph to Another

If you have a paragraph that looks really good and you want to copy the style (the formatting) to another paragraph inside your document, you can use a helpful feature of Word 97, even if it has a silly name. It's called the *Format Painter*. Click anywhere in the preferred paragraph and then click the **Format Painter** button on the Standard toolbar. Listen carefully, because the next thing you select will be modified to this preferred formatting. Find the target paragraph and select it (it's usually easiest to use the selection bar on the left). That's it. The formatting is copied to the target paragraph.

When you click once on the **Format Painter**, it works once. To copy style formatting to several paragraphs, *double-click* the **Format Painter** button. Now you can go click on as many paragraphs as you wish, and they will all have your preferred style applied to them. When you want to stop this activity, press the **Esc** (Escape) key to end the repetitive style applications.

Using the Style Dialog Box

You can also create and modify existing styles using the Style dialog box, which contains every possible paragraph formatting function under the sun. It's useful to take a peek at it to give you an idea of the wealth of formatting options available. Open the **Format** menu and choose the **Style** command. You will see the Style dialog box.

The Style dialog box helps you create and save styles.

Bold names contain font and paragraph formatting styles.

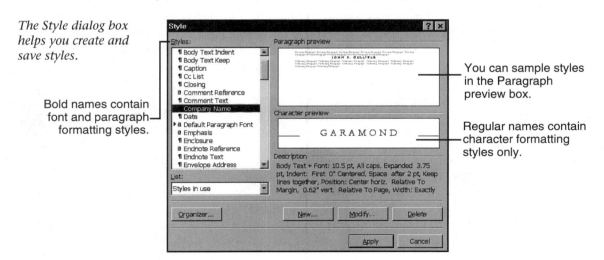

You can sample styles in the Paragraph preview box.

Regular names contain character formatting styles only.

The Style Gallery

The *Style Gallery* is a fun place to play and learn. It's basically a workshop where you can experiment applying various format styles to your documents. To get to this playground, open the **Format** menu and choose the **Style Gallery** command. You will see one of the largest dialog boxes Word ever dreamed up. A list of styles are on the left, and a preview of what they look like is on the right. If you are the curious type, this is a great place to experiment with the different styles and see how they change your document.

If you aren't the curious type, it can still be helpful to press the **Example** button. This way you will see a preview of the style effect on a finished sample document instead of your own text.

Press the **OK** button when recess is over to return to your document. Any style changes you discover and apply will remain with your document, as long as you save your document before closing it. Press the **Save** button to enjoy this style tomorrow.

Click different templates to see how your document looks with them applied.

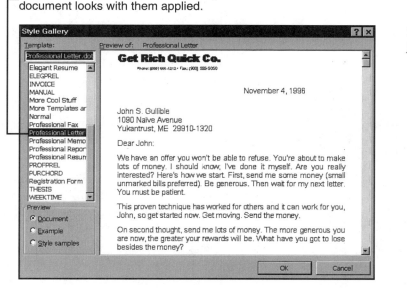

The Style Gallery playground.

What Are the "Add-Ins" in Templates and Add-Ins?

If you think you're comfortable with templates and styles, including that everyday one called Normal, then you're ready for this trick. Open the **Tools** menu and choose the **Templates And Add-Ins** command. You'll see an intimidating dialog box, but have no fear!

Use Templates and Add-Ins to customize your session of Word 97.

Check this box for up-to-date style formatting.

Templates and Add-ins

Document template
Normal.dot   Attach...

☐ Automatically update document styles

Global templates and add-ins
Checked items are currently loaded.

☐ HTML.DOT
☐ Elegant Letter.dot   Add...
☑ Professional Memo.dot   Remove

Full path: C:\...\Memos\Professional Memo.dot

Organizer...   OK   Cancel

This changes the default template for the current document only.

Click these to add or remove a favorite template to your documents.

Remember when you start Word 97, the Normal template consisting of the Normal style appears first. If you find yourself always opening another template, changing a style, using AutoText entries, macros, or customized things (toolbars, menu settings, or shortcut keys), why not add those changes automatically from the start of your session? If that's what you want, then you've opened the right dialog box. You're about to "add-in" your favorite settings to Word 97. Most of the time, you'll do this by adding a template to your document, but you might also purchase things called "Add-ins" and examples include insurance form creators, document assemblers for legal or medical industries, and so on. You can load these following the same procedure given here for loading templates.

Techno Talk

blah blah blah bla bl

Global Template
This is a document template that you have loaded into Word by using the Templates and Add-Ins command on the Tools menu. You can use the macros, AutoText entries, and custom toolbar, menu, and shortcut key settings stored in a global template while you work with any document, not just documents based on that template.

For example, the Normal template is by design a global template. Customized items you store in the Normal template are available to all documents.

To use any favorite items that are stored in a favorite template, you can either *attach* that template to the current document, or *load* that template as a *global* template.

To attach a template to a document, click the **Attach** button and locate the template you want. When you've located it in the Attach Template dialog box, click the **Open** button. The template name should appear in the Document Template text box, and by clicking **OK**, you can return to your document and start using the features of the newly attached template. This template will remain attached to this document forever, unless you choose to remove it by opening the Templates And Add-ins dialog box, clicking and deleting the template name in the Document Template box, and clicking the **OK** button.

To load one or more templates to be available to all documents during this session of Word, click the **Add** button. Locate the desired templates one at a time, clicking

OK for each one, and they will show up in the Global Templates box. The check box next to each template tells you if that template is currently loaded. If the box is checked, the features of that template will be available to all documents you open or create during this session of Word. If you happen to load too many templates, Word performance can get sluggish. In that case, click the check box to unload a template you no longer need.

So what do you do to load a favorite template automatically, each time you start Word 97? For starters, you won't need the Templates and Add-ins dialog box, you'll need something like Microsoft Explorer to copy a file from one folder to another. To load a template each time you start Word, copy the template to the Word 97 (or Office 97) Startup folder, whose location is specified on the File Locations tab (find yours by opening the **Tools** menu, choosing the **Options** command, and finding the folder for User Templates on the list).

Whizzing to the Finish with Wizards

Wizards take the idea of templates one step further. What if you had an assistant that could help you one step at a time in the creation of a complete and customized document, using information that you supply? That's how a wizard can help you. Word 97 includes more than 10 automated wizards for creating letters, memos, Web pages, fax cover sheets, newsletters, résumés, calendars, tables, meeting agendas, award certificates, and even legal pleading documents.

Using a wizard is like hiring a contractor to build your house. You don't want to know all the details about construction—you just want a kitchen over there and a fireplace over there. And you don't want to be bothered by too many questions because then you start second-guessing yourself. You just want it done.

And don't think that using wizards stifles creativity. The formatting of the finished document is not set in stone; you can change any bit of it by modifying the styles of the document, or even the template, on which the wizard bases the document.

Ready to try to whiz through the creation of a document? Open the **File** menu and choose the **New** command. Click the different category tabs to bring a selection of wizards to view. They live side-by-side with their template friends. Wow, if you are interested in creating a spectacular newsletter, you should click the **Publications** tab and choose the **Newsletter Wizard**. Click the **OK** button, and the wizard will kick into action.

You might see a single dialog box or many dialog boxes during the "wizarding" that ask you for general information about what you're looking for. Don't pressure yourself! Casually click each option button appearing on the right, and you will see and understand what it does by watching the Preview box included for each decision. When you are ready to move to the next step, press the **Next** button. You can step backwards also, right up to the very end, to change any of your previous requests. Try doing that with your house contractor. At the very end, you will see a **Finish** button. Push it. You will land in the middle of a completely formatted document awaiting your content. You can save it at any time, and you will have to give it a name and a folder to live in.

The Least You Need to Know

Templates and styles can make your life a whole lot easier by automating your favorite formatting. You can write home about some of these template and style tips learned in this chapter.

I'm afraid of messing up a template. Any advice?

Word 97 comes with lots of templates, and they exist to make your life easier. A template is a predesigned, ready-to-use document into which you put your own information. Just remember to save your finished work as a new document and you can't go wrong. To get started, open the **File** menu, click **New**, and try choosing a template from the **Template** list box.

This document is good. Can I make it a template?

Yes, you can create a template based on your document by opening the **File** menu and choosing the **Save As** command. Enter a name for your new template, then select **Document Template** under **Save File As Type**.

How can I tell what style is applied to a paragraph?

Word 97 provides the Style Area to enable you to see the complete details of how styles are being used. Open the **Tools** menu and choose the **Options** command. Click the **View** tab and temporarily change the **Style Area Width** setting to 1 (or .5 to save space). You'll now see the style details.

How do I make changes to an existing style?

To make changes to any style, change a paragraph with that style, and then select it. Make sure the style name is correctly displayed in the **Style** box on the Formatting toolbar, then press **Enter**. Click **OK** to confirm that you want to make these changes to the style.

Chapter 21

Customizing Word 97

In This Chapter

➤ Add or remove buttons on your toolbars

➤ Add or remove commands on your menus

➤ Create a new toolbar

➤ Changing your right-click shortcut menu

➤ Adjust the view of your workspace

If you don't like something, change it! That's the rule in this chapter, demonstrating the new flexibility in Word 97. Discover how to add or customize a button on your toolbar, a command in your menu, or create your own unique toolbar. And if that's not enough for your creativity, try customizing your own shortcut menu that pops up when you right-click!

Customize Your Toolbars

Toolbars in Word 97 were created by Microsoft to organize the most common commands so you can find and use them quickly. But take a look at them. Do you really need the button to insert an Excel worksheet on your Standard toolbar? Maybe not, and Microsoft provided the means to easily customize toolbars. For example, you can add and remove menus and buttons, create your own custom toolbars, hide or display toolbars, and move toolbars.

Put Anything on Those Toolbars!

In previous versions of Word, toolbars only contained buttons. Now toolbars can contain buttons, menus, or any combination of them.

Add a New Button to a Toolbar

You can add toolbar buttons for commands and frequently used styles, AutoText entries, and fonts. First display the toolbar you want to change. Now open the **Tools** menu and choose **Customize**. In the Customize dialog box, click the **Commands** tab. In the Categories list, you see names for each group of buttons classified by function. The buttons grouped in that category are displayed in the Buttons preview box. For instance, the Table category has 24 buttons for creating tables (and you currently have *only one* on the Standard toolbar). If you don't see the command you want under a particular category, click **All Commands** in the Categories box.

Customize your toolbars by clicking to choose any of these commands, then dragging them onto any visible toolbar (if the target toolbar isn't visible, click the Toolbars tab, find the toolbar you want and click to make it visible). If it doesn't land in the exact spot you want, just click and drag it to a new location.

You can also remove buttons while the Customize dialog box is open. Click to select the offending button, then drag it off the toolbar into some empty area and just let go. It vanishes. If you feel badly and want to bring it back, just find it in the Commands box and drag it up again.

Edit Any Toolbar Button

You can edit the specifics of your new button, or any existing button. What kind of specifics? Things like changing the picture on the button, or the ScreenTip words that appear when your mouse hovers over it, or resetting back to the original button.

Make sure the button is visible on your screen, then open the Tools menu and choose Customize. Briefly ignore the Customize dialog box and right-click on the actual button you wish to change in your toolbar. You'll see the shortcut menu of changeable options.

Commands are organized
in categories here.

*Add a useful button
to your favorite
toolbar.*

New button will be
placed at this marker.

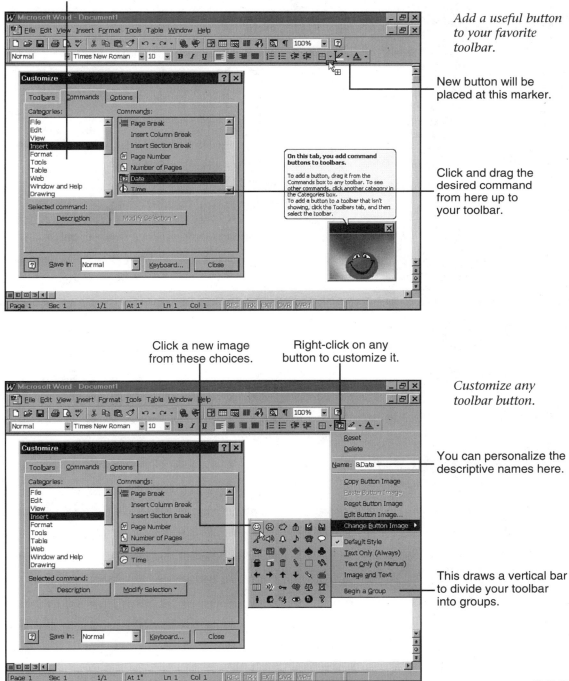

Click and drag the
desired command
from here up to
your toolbar.

Click a new image
from these choices.

Right-click on any
button to customize it.

*Customize any
toolbar button.*

You can personalize the
descriptive names here.

This draws a vertical bar
to divide your toolbar
into groups.

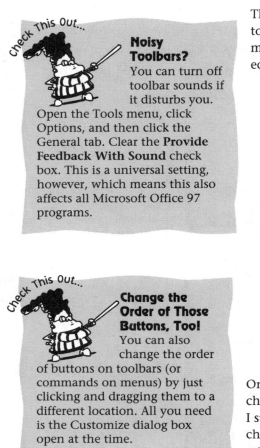

Noisy Toolbars?
You can turn off toolbar sounds if it disturbs you. Open the Tools menu, click Options, and then click the General tab. Clear the **Provide Feedback With Sound** check box. This is a universal setting, however, which means this also affects all Microsoft Office 97 programs.

Change the Order of Those Buttons, Too!
You can also change the order of buttons on toolbars (or commands on menus) by just clicking and dragging them to a different location. All you need is the Customize dialog box open at the time.

The Customize dialog box must remain open to perform toolbar button editing, and sometimes you might need to move it out of your way to see the button you want to edit.

➤ To change the button icon to one of 42 new icons, click **Change Button Image** on the shortcut menu and choose one from the palette of images that is displayed.

➤ To change the button icon to something completely different, click the **Edit Button Image** and you'll open a graphics editor giving you almost complete freedom in drawing your own icon.

➤ You can divide your buttons into groups using separator lines. Click **Begin A Group** to add a line in front of this button.

➤ If you prefer words to pictures, choose Text Only. Sometimes a short word might be more helpful.

➤ To reset this button to the original settings, click **Reset**.

Once you see how easy this is, you might be tempted to change all of your toolbars. That's not recommended. I suggest you create a new toolbar and keep all of your changes limited to that single toolbar. Then you can always return to the original toolbars if someone else needs to work at your computer.

Create a New Toolbar

If you can think of a handful or more of important buttons you can't live without, then you're ready to build a whole new toolbar! You already know how to add the buttons to it; you just need to know how to create the toolbar itself.

If it's not already up on your screen, open the **Tools** menu and click **Customize** to open the Customize dialog box. Click the **Toolbars** tab to bring it to the front. Click the **New** button, and in the **Toolbar** name box, type the name you want. In the **Make Toolbar Available To** box, click to choose the template or document you want to save the toolbar in, or leave it at **Normal** (the Normal Template), which makes it available all the time.

Voilà! Your new toolbar appears, even though it looks a little squished. You need to make it grow by adding buttons. Follow the same steps as before, clicking the **Commands** tab and dragging favorite commands to your new toolbar. When you have added all the buttons you want, click **Close**.

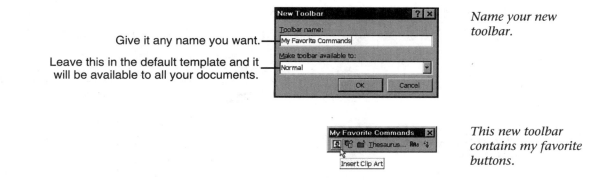

Give it any name you want. ⎯

Leave this in the default template and it will be available to all your documents.

Name your new toolbar.

This new toolbar contains my favorite buttons.

Restoring Original Toolbar Buttons If You Change Your Mind

There's an easy way to put back the original toolbar buttons in Word 97, just in case you change your mind. Open the **Tools** menu, click **Customize**, and then click the **Toolbars** tab. Select the toolbar you want to restore by clicking a toolbar name in the Customize dialog box. Click the **Reset** button. Finally, in the Reset changes box, click the template or document that contains the changes you want to reset.

Customizing Your Menus

Remember what your menu bar looks like? It's that special toolbar at the top of the screen that contains menus such as **File**, **Edit**, and so on, with **Help** pulling up the rear. Yes, you can customize your menu bar the same way you customize any built-in toolbar, by adding and removing buttons and menus. You can also add frequently used styles, AutoText entries, and fonts to menus (just as you did with toolbars) to customize them.

Add a New Command to Your Menu

The menu bar is really nothing more than a list of commands. Some commands display a list of more commands. Many of these commands now have images next to them so you can quickly associate the command with its purpose.

Unlike your other toolbars, you can't hide the menu bar. It's always visible on your screen (with the one exception of the Full Screen View, when nothing but your document is in view). That takes care of the first step in customization. Now open the **Tools** menu, click

Customize, and this time click **Commands**. Find the command you want to add, then click and drag it up to the menu bar. When you drag on top of the existing menu bar commands like File and Edit, you'll find that they open right up, enabling you to place the new command anywhere you want in the list.

Right-click a menu bar to open it first (it will stay open for you).

Customize any menu command.

You can also right-click on any command to edit it.

Drag a new command from here up to the menu bar.

Edit Your Menu Commands

Just like your toolbar buttons, you can edit the specifics of your new menu command, or any existing menu command. You can change the wording, paste an icon next to it, or add lines to divide commands into groups.

First open the **Tools** menu and click **Customize** to open the Customize dialog box, which must be open whenever you edit menus or toolbars.

Getting to the desired menu command to edit it might be tricky the first time you try. Left-click to open a menu if you need to get to a command inside. Right-click on the menu command you want to edit. You'll see the shortcut menu full of customization options. To add a menu command image, click **Edit Button Image** and choose from the palette. To change the name, click in the **Name** box and start typing. When you finish, click the **Close** button and your customization will be saved.

What's That Ampersand All About?

You may notice the ampersand symbol (&) wedged somewhere inside the name of your menu command. It's the secret keyboard shortcut, and you can create them yourself! Word 97 enables you to add a single ampersand anywhere inside a menu command name, with no spaces. The letter immediately following the ampersand is the shortcut key letter, and will be underlined in your menu (the ampersand disappears). Now when you see this menu command, you can press the **Alt** key along with this key letter, and the command will be executed. For example, the letter F is the key in the File menu command name (it's underlined), so when you press Alt+F your File menu opens automatically. Some people think these shortcut keys are faster than using your mouse. One word of advice—don't choose letters that have already been taken, like Alt+F for example, or else you'll never be certain which command will execute when you press the shortcut key.

Create a New Menu in Your Menu Bar

Instead of adding commands to an existing menu, you can also create a whole new menu. The steps are slightly different than those used to add a new toolbar.

Open the **Tools** menu and click **Customize** to bring up its dialog box. Click the **Commands** tab to bring it to the front. Scroll to the bottom of the Categories and choose the **New Menu** command. In the Commands column, drag the **New Menu** command up to your menu bar and drop it where you prefer. If it doesn't land where you want, click and drag it to a different spot.

Your menu bar will shine with its new entry! Of course, it doesn't do anything yet, because no commands are assigned to it. You know the routine; find commands in the available categories and drag them up to this new menu. Afterward, you can edit them with a right-click and a selection from the shortcut menu that appears. When you have added all the commands you want, click **Close**.

Hey look, a new menu option!

Add a new menu to your menu bar.

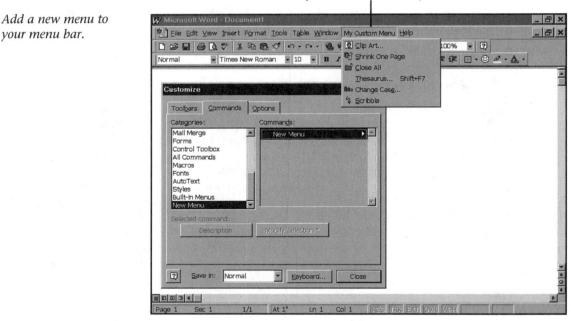

Impress Your Friends, Change Your Right-Click Shortcut Menu!

Here's a new trick that's sure to impress your geekiest of friends and perhaps make you more productive at the same time. By now you should be using the shortcut menus that pop-up when you click the right mouse button. They often contain helpful commands like cut, copy and paste, and it's faster to click them here rather than sending your mouse up to the toolbars or menus. Well, how would you like to customize these shortcut menus, to contain your all-time favorite commands, just like we did with the toolbars and menus? The Customize dialog box makes it a snap.

Open the **Tools** menu, choose **Customize**, and click the **Toolbars** tab. Scroll to the bottom and click to select the **Shortcut Menu**. You'll see the Shortcut toolbar.

Keep this Shortcut toolbar up on your screen while you click the **Commands** tab on the Customize dialog box. Right now you're setting up the playing field.

Ready? Click to choose the **Text** column on the Shortcut toolbar, and then choose the shortcut menu you want to edit. For this example, click on **Text** near the bottom of this list, and you'll see a menu pop-up that displays the actual shortcut menu you see every day.

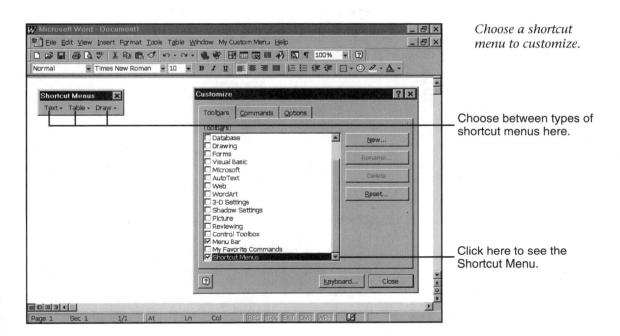

Choose a shortcut menu to customize.

Choose between types of shortcut menus here.

Click here to see the Shortcut Menu.

This menu will stay open while you reach over to see the commands in the Customize dialog box. Browse through the categories to find the command you want, then click and drag this command to the Text shortcut menu. You can click and drag it (or any of the commands) to a different position in this menu. When you finish, click the **Close** button and your work will be saved.

Now it's time to test your new shortcut menu! Open up an existing document or create a new one. Point to anywhere you want using your mouse, and click the right mouse button (since we changed the Text shortcut menu, you need to right-click a text area, not on graphics or tables). There's your new command sitting inside the menu!

If you want to go beyond this example, you need to remember that shortcut menus tend to offer different commands depending on what you're doing at the time. This is how they got their other name—the Context menu—because they change based on what you're doing at the time (your context). Why do you need to know this? Because each different context menu has a different name, and if you plan to change one, you'd better know its name!

But It's Covered Up! If you can't see the Commands area because it's covered up by this shortcut menu, click **Text** again to close this column temporarily, then drag the Shortcut toolbar further out of the way of the Customize dialog box.

Customize the shortcut.

Click and drag a new command to your shortcut menu.

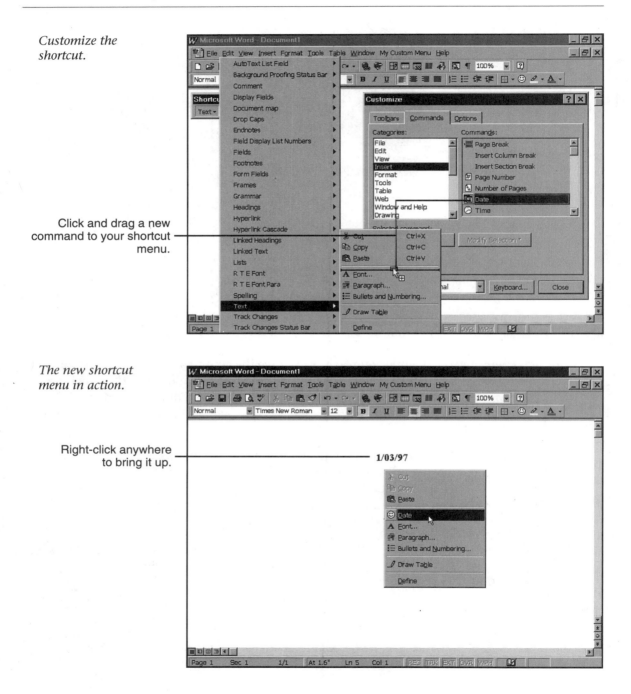

The new shortcut menu in action.

Right-click anywhere to bring it up.

Other Word 97 Custom Options

The remainder of this chapter brings you other helpful ways to customize Word 97 in an effort to make you more productive. Some change the way you see things, others change the way you do things.

Tips for Making Your Workspace Larger in Word 97

If you find yourself constantly squinting at your screen with bloodshot eyes, why not give yourself a break? Here are some tips on how to make documents easier to see on your computer screen.

➤ **Run Word 97 full-screen**. Be sure you can see the Restore, not Maximize button, in the Title bar. If it's not maximized, click the **Maximize** button in the Title bar.

➤ **View only a single document at a time**. Make sure the document window is maximized inside of Word, and don't waste space working in a split screen unless you are moving and copying information from one to the other.

➤ **Hide any toolbars you don't need**. Most people can get along fine without the Ruler or Status bar (or even the scroll bars).

➤ **Adjust Zoom control to maximize your comfort level**. You can choose Page Width to prevent horizontal scrolling. You can also type a number directly in the Zoom box for custom viewing sizes.

➤ **Switch to Full Screen view**. Everyone should experience this at least once in their lifetime. Open the **View** menu and click **Full Screen**. You'll see nothing but your document (and a small Close button), even though the menus are still there! To prove it, slide your mouse pointer to the very top of the screen and the menu bar will be exposed temporarily. To leave full-screen view, click the **Close** button (or press the **Esc** key).

➤ **Resize a floating toolbar**. To resize a floating toolbar, move the pointer over any edge until it changes to a double-headed arrow, and then drag the edge of the toolbar. Didn't know toolbars could float? Click and grab the left border of any docked toolbar, and you can drag it anywhere around your workspace.

➤ **Change the size of your toolbar buttons.** This might not make your workspace larger, but it might save your eyes so you can work longer. Open the **Tools** menu, click **Customize**, and click the **Options** tab. Select the **Large Icons** check box.

Changing Your View on Documents

Here's an important point before we start: Your document doesn't change just because you change your view of it. Why have more than one view? To help you and your computer perform at their best, depending on the task at hand. The only reason to change the view of your document is to help you see parts of it better, or work with it in a different manner. There is a suggested document view for each of the tasks you are trying to accomplish, whether it's editing (Normal view), reorganizing or working in very large documents (Document Map or Outline view), creating a Web page (Online Layout view), manipulating graphics or pictures (Page Layout view), working with Headers and Footers, or preparing to print (Print Preview). There's even a special view for performing tasks that include multiple documents (Master document view). You can even hide everything with Full Screen view.

If you want to customize the way Word 97 displays your document, open the **Tools** menu, click **Options**, and browse the select options on the **View** tab. For example, you can display or hide items in your document (such as graphics, animated text, and field codes) or screen elements (such as scroll bars). The options that are available on the View tab depend on which view you're in.

Check This Out...

When Should I Use Document Map? This is a new feature of Word 97. The Document Map view provides you with an extra window on the left of your screen that displays the current document's headings. Just click on these headings to quickly navigate your way around a large document. It's also a quick way to tell where you are inside a large document at a given time. Word 97 automatically displays the Document Map in Online Layout View, but you can also display it in any view by choosing it from the View menu.

Techno Talk

Speeding Up Scrolling If You Have Pictures

Pictures are more difficult than text for your computer to display. If you have several in your document, you might notice sluggish movements when you scroll. If this bothers you, you can speed things up, if you don't mind temporarily ignoring those pictures.

To increase the speed of scrolling through graphics-ridden documents, open the **Tools** menu and choose the **Options** command. Click the **View** tab to bring it to the front. Now click the **Picture Placeholders** to place a check in the check box. Press **OK** to return to viewing your document. Now Word displays a box to represent each graphic in the document, which is as fast as text to display.

Check This Out...

Viewing What Does Not Print

To view special characters on your screen that do not print, make changes to your View options. Open the **Tools** menu and choose the **Options** command. Click the **View** tab to bring it to the front. Select the check boxes for the characters you want under **Nonprinting Characters.**

Changing Your Default Colors in Word

The color of your work area is a very personal thing, and as creatures of habit we depend on them. Most of us had a word processor in the past that displayed white text on a blue background (and *real* old-timers remember green on black). In other words, color. With the advance of technology, we now have black and white. Black letters on a white background (that's much harder for your computer to do, if it's any consolation) is the current rage, but before you drag out that old PC-XT or Kaypro, if you demand color, try changing the *default colors* in Word 97.

You have lots of color choices in Word 97. For the background, you can choose between white and blue. For the text, you can choose between, well, nothing. You don't get a choice for your text color—if you pick the blue background, you get white text. Otherwise, the text is black. Viva la Word 97!

Open the **Tools** menu and choose the **Options** command. Click the **General** tab to bring it to the front. Find the **Blue Background**, **White Text** box and click it to insert a check mark. When you press the **OK** button, your screen will be magically transformed.

Check This Out...

Change Your Units to Match Your World

To set the default unit of measurements that you type in dialog boxes and on the horizontal ruler, open the **Tools** menu and choose the **Options** command. Click the **General** tab to bring it to the front. Near the bottom of this box, you will find a place to enter your default unit of measure. Click the **Measurement Units** box to select the standard unit of measurement you prefer from the drop-down list.

Create a New Keyboard Shortcut

Shortcut keys are ways to quickly accomplish a task without using your mouse. For instance, if you want to open your Edit menu without using your mouse, you can press the **Alt+E** key combination, and have it open instantly. Touch typists love these shortcuts, because they can type much faster without stopping to touch the mouse.

You can assign a shortcut key to almost any command, macro, font, AutoText entry, style, or a commonly used symbol. Give it a try by opening the **Tools** menu and click

Customize. Click the **Keyboard** button to see the Keyboard dialog box. In the **Categories** box, click the category that contains the desired command, and then click the name of the command to select it. In the **Press New Shortcut Key** box, type the shortcut key combination you want to assign. Any shortcut keys that are currently assigned appear in the Current keys box, to prevent you from changing existing shortcuts. Next, in the **Save Changes** in box, click the current document name or template in which you want to save the shortcut key changes, or leave it at the Normal template to make it available everywhere. Finally, click the **Assign** button and then **Close**, and your new shortcut is ready and waiting for you.

A new custom keyboard shortcut to speed you along.

Choose the command that will execute.

Type a new key combination here.

You'll be warned if that combination is already in use.

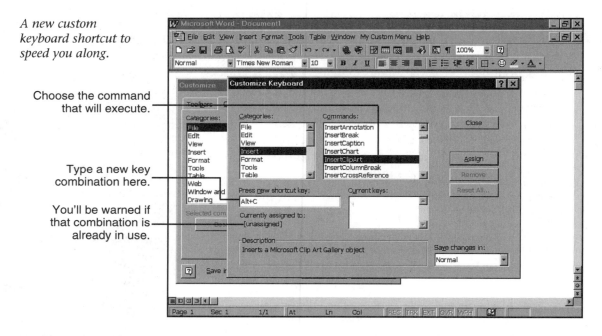

For WordPerfect Lovers Only

If you are familiar with WordPerfect commands, you can customize your Word 97 to react intelligently when you accidentally press those old key combinations. Word will stop you at that instant and say, "Hey, that's not how we do things here. Try it this way…" If you're interested, open the **Tools** menu, click **Options**, then put a check in the following boxes:

➤ **Help for WordPerfect Users**   Choosing this option prepares Word for the next time you need help. With this box checked, the first help thing you'll see when you ask for help will be a modified help screen slanted towards WordPerfect commands.

➤ **Navigation Keys for WordPerfect Users**   Once again, the WordPerfect command you know by heart won't actually work, but a help screen will pop up and explain the rules of the road for Word.

For that matter, WordPerfect lovers coerced into using Word 97 will be pleasantly surprised with an option on the Status bar. See the one called **WPH**? It stands for **WordPerfect Help**, and if you double-click it, you will get the Help for WordPerfect Users dialog box. It's full of all the standard commands you may remember from WordPerfect, and by selecting each command you get directions on using the Word equivalent. There's also a demo button for each command, allowing you to sit back and watch as the computer demonstrates the new command for you. Now if you could only get it to write that report.

WordPerfect Commands Don't Work in Word 97
So what's the big deal about having these two check boxes if they won't make the WordPerfect commands actually work? Well, if you're an experienced typist with WordPerfect commands memorized, it's better to be forced to stop and read a help menu rather than being allowed to continue typing, thinking your command was executed.

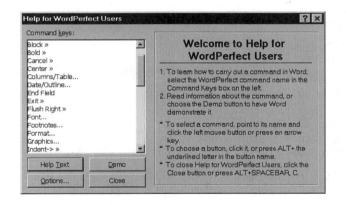

So that's what the WPH button is doing on my status bar!

WPH ——————— WordPerfect Help

Where's Reveal Codes?   Sorry, Word 97 still does not allow you to view and edit formatting codes directly, as you can in WordPerfect, because Word 97 stores many of these codes inside the paragraph symbol at the end of a paragraph. You can, however, choose to view many of the non-printing characters in Word by checking the appropriate box in the **View** tab of the **Options** command on the **Tools** menu.

The Least You Need to Know

I now have 23 custom toolbars dancing on my screen with no room left to work, and I click randomly using my joystick (I now enjoy Word 97 more than Space Invaders). I hope you have also been more productive in customizing Word 97 to suit your needs, especially if you gleaned some of the tips from this chapter.

I forgot to read this chapter. How do I customize a toolbar?

You can customize toolbars by opening the **Tools** menu and choosing **Customize**. Click the **Commands** tab to display what's available, then click and drag new buttons on or off any toolbar (or menu).

Can I also customize a menu?

Sure, it's just as easy using the same **Customize** dialog box. Click the **Commands** tab to display what's available, then click and drag new commands on or off any menu (or toolbar).

How about that shortcut menu when I right-click? Can I customize it?

Absolutely. Open the **Tools** menu, choose **Customize**, and click the **Shortcut** toolbar found on the **Toolbars** tab. Drag and drop commands to any of the many shortcut menus available in Word 97. To run a shortcut menu, just click the right mouse button at the desired location for the command.

I hate using the mouse. Can I speed things up using the keyboard?

Try creating your own keyboard shortcuts. Open the **Tools** menu, click **Customize**, then click the **Keyboard** button. Assign a new shortcut key combination to any of the commands in Word 97.

Can I get rid of everything on my screen and see nothing but my document?

It's called Full Screen view, and you can find it quickly. Open the **View** menu and click **Full Screen**. Spend as much time as you like. When it's time to return, press the **Esc** key.

Chapter 22

Using Word 97 Along with Its Other Friends in Office 97

In This Chapter

➤ Different ways to share information in Office 97

➤ Hyperlink to Office 97 programs

➤ Displaying Excel data inside your document

➤ Sliding a PowerPoint slide into your document

➤ Beefing up your document with database information from Access

➤ Storing related files in an Office Binder

Now that you've mastered the basics of Word 97, you might want to know more about complementing its use with the other Office 97 programs—Microsoft Excel worksheets, Microsoft PowerPoint presentations, and Microsoft Access databases. Even if you aren't expert at those other programs, this chapter describes how you can combine the very best parts of them into Word, all to make your document the very best it can be.

Learning All the Ways to Share Information Between Programs

Not too long ago, if you wanted to share information from one program to the next, you usually ended up retyping that same information into the second program. It was bad news all around, because information changes with the times, and then we were left with two or more files filled with that same old information. It was hard to keep up-to-date.

Microsoft now provides lots of different tools to make it easy to share information between the Office 97 programs. Each tool serves a slightly different purpose, so you should learn when to use which. You'll be glad to hear these tools work the same way in each of the different programs, so you only have to learn a method once.

Different Methods of Using the Same Data Twice

Let's say you're creating a budget report in Word 97 and you need to reference a few facts and figures stored in either Excel, PowerPoint, or Access. Here are your choices for getting the information from one program to another:

➤ **Copy and Paste it.** Still the most common method, this duplicates the information in two locations. Pasting has come a long way now, and you can paste in different ways, from a simple copy of static information, or maybe a link that can be updated, or perhaps an embed that carries the tools with it.

➤ **Drag and Drop it.** This typically moves information, deleting it from the first location, and adding it to the second (dropping the selection onto the program icon in the Windows 95 or Windows NT Taskbar does the same thing). You can also use this method to create hyperlinks now (see below).

➤ **Link to it.** Use this method when you want the most up-to-date information included in one or more documents. One location is considered the source of the "real" information, while the other locations have a link to this source and the information stays updated automatically.

➤ **Embed it inside.** Besides the information, when you want to include all of the tools necessary to edit that information, you embed the information. It's like carrying around multiple programs inside of your document.

➤ **Hyperlink to it.** Here's a new way to leave the information where it's at, and just jump directly to it when you feel the urge.

➤ **Store them all in a binder.** Here's an organizational method for sharing the information, by storing the individual files created by different programs in the same place, called a Binder. The different files are treated as a single unit, making it easier to view, edit, or print, all at the same time.

When to Copy into Your Document

The Copy command in Word is simple, almost always works, and should never give you any trouble. If you see something you like just the way it is, and you're happy that it will always stay the same, then use Copy to insert it into your document. It becomes a static addition to your document. You can think of it as a picture of the information you selected. You can't edit it anymore, except to get rid of it. No matter what information you choose, in any of the Office 97 programs, you can always select it, click the **Copy** button, and then change to Word and click the **Paste** button to insert it into your document.

You can also move something into your Word document, and it acts as if it has been copied into your document. One way to move text, graphics, or other objects is to select them and click the **Cut** button. Then move to Word, find the location you want, and click the **Paste** button.

Drag-and-drop editing is another way to move text, graphics, or other objects from one place to another, and the end result is as if you copied it there. You can drag and drop selected information from any of the Office 97 programs into your Word document.

When to Link into Your Document

For times that you want to add information that is likely to change in the near future, you might be better off linking to that information, instead of copying it into your Word document. The only requirement is that you'll always need to have access to the original source, in case it changes in the future. Linking is a good method to use when you want to share the same information between many documents and when you want to share information among documents in an Office Binder.

You can link virtually any information from an Office program into your Word document. For instance, to make sure budget figures from an Excel worksheet are up-to-date in a quarterly report written with Word, you would copy and link the information. Then if the figures change, they can be automatically updated in your Word document.

To link existing information in any Office 97 program, copy the information, and then switch to your current document in Word. Place the insertion point where you want the information placed. Open the **Edit** menu and click **Paste Special**, and then click to select the **Paste Link** option. Click **OK** and the object will be linked to your document.

Do you want to control *when* these links are updated? All you need to do in Word is open the **Edit** menu, click the **Links** command, and then click the name of the link you want. Choose the **Manual** button to set the link to update only when you specifically request an update, otherwise, the link will be updated each time you open this document.

Linking an Excel worksheet inside your Word document.

[Screenshot of Microsoft Word showing the Paste Special dialog box]

Microsoft Word - Real Professional Report

File Edit View Insert Format Tools Table Window Help

List Number | Arial | 10 | 50%

To create a Table of Contents for this report, position your cursor on the blank TOC page.

Paste Special

Source: Microsoft Excel Worksheet
Sheet1!R5C3:R6C4

As:

○ Paste:
● Paste link:

Microsoft Excel Worksheet Object
Formatted Text (RTF)
Unformatted Text
Picture
Bitmap

OK
Cancel

☑ Float over text
☐ Display as icon

Result
Inserts the contents of the Clipboard as a picture.
Paste Link creates a shortcut to the source file. Changes to the source file will be reflected in your document.

Page 2 | Sec 2 | 4/5 | At | Ln | Col | REC TRK EXT OVR WPH

When to Embed into Your Document

Sometimes you need to include information from another program, but you aren't sure if that program will be available in the future. If this is your concern, then you should Embed the information into your Word document. Embedding is the process of taking the selected information—and the program that created it—and merging it into your document. Once you've embedded an Excel worksheet for example, you'll always be able to edit the information. Just double-click it and you'll see full-functioning Excel toolbars ready to help you, right inside your Word document!

Remember, however, that there is no longer a link to the original source of your information, so if the source changes, the information in your Word document could be outdated.

To embed existing information in any Office 97 program, copy the information, and then switch to your current document in Word. Open the **Edit** menu and click **Paste Special**, and then click the **Paste** button. To create and embed any new information, such as an audio clip, a graphic object, or an Equation Editor object, position your pointer where you want it to appear in your Word document. Open the **Insert** menu and click **Object**. On the **Create**

Check This Out...

Need to Keep File Size to a Minimum? Link information instead of embedding it. Embedded objects increase file size because the object itself is stored in your document. A linked object, however, is stored in the source document. Only a representation of it is displayed within your current document.

New tab, choose the object you want. If you know the name and path of an existing object, click the **Create From File** tab, type the name of the file you want to embed (or click the **Browse** button to help you locate the file). The object will be embedded in your document.

Here's a New Way to Link to Information!

Now you can link directly to the application and the data source automatically by using the new **Paste As Hyperlink** command found on the **Edit** menu. By clicking on a hyperlink in your document, you quickly jump to the source of information, including the application that created it. These destinations can include other computers on your company network, or locations on the Internet and the World Wide Web. Find out more about hyperlinks in Chapter 23.

When to Use Hyperlinks

Sometimes you need to link to current information, have it presented in the application that created it, and keep the document size as small as possible. Word 97 introduces a new feature that fits the bill. It's called a *hyperlink*, and you probably have experience using them already, in either the Windows Help menus, or browsing a Web page.

A hyperlink is a method of linking information together by specifying the whereabouts of the information. By clicking on a hyperlink in your document, you quickly jump to the source of the information, presented in the application that created it. The advantage is that your document doesn't have to carry around the Excel baggage, as in embedding, so your document file size remains small. In fact, as long as you know the application and data is always available, a hyperlink is probably the best way to link information to your Word document.

Sharing Information Between Your Office 97 Programs

Each Office 97 application includes convenient ways to copy, link, embed, or hyperlink information quickly from one program to the next. For example, in Microsoft Access, click the **OfficeLinks** button to transfer database information to other Office applications. Here are specific examples that can help you share information between all of your Office 97 programs.

Create Hyperlinks to Any Office 97 Program

You'll learn more about hyperlinks in Chapter 23, but for now think of hyperlinks as jump commands. Hyperlinks appear as blue-colored and underlined text in your Word document. Click a hyperlink and you immediately jump to the destination specified by the hyperlink. A good example is the Windows 95 Help screens. When you click an underlined word (the hypertext), you jump to the detail of that subject. Sound interesting? Hyperlinks are a great way to jump around common groups of documents quickly, and they work the same way in Word as they do on the World Wide Web.

A hyperlink acts differently than a link or an embed, but you create them in almost the same way. Start at a destination, for instance, the budget summary figures in an Excel worksheet. Select the budget summary figures to which you want to create a hyperlink , then click the **Copy** button. Change to your Word document and place the cursor where you want to insert the hyperlink. Open the **Edit** menu and choose the **Paste As Hyperlink** command. The hypertext that appears will either be the name of the destination, a few words of identifying text or figures, or any name you choose. You can also create a hyperlink if you drag and drop a bit of the destination text or object wherever you want a hyperlink to appear. It's a fast method to use when all destination documents are currently opened on your screen. For example, you can create a hyperlink by using the right mouse button to drag selected text or graphics from a PowerPoint slide, a selected range of worksheet cells in Excel, or a selected database object in Access and drop it right into your Word 97 document (dropping it onto the Word icon in the Windows 95 or Windows NT Taskbar does the same thing). Word automatically recognizes the location of the information, so you don't have to worry about it.

Get Excel Worksheet Information into Your Word Document

If you have some data existing in an Excel worksheet that you'd like to make part of your Word document, you can copy and paste selected cells directly into your document. To try this yourself, start Excel and open the worksheet that contains the data you wish to copy. Select the cells with your mouse, click the **Copy** button in Excel, click in your document where you want it to appear, then click the **Paste** button in Word. The Excel data will appear in your document.

But that's not the only way to move information between Word and Excel. If you feel daring, you can get Excel and Word to share your screen at the same time, as either tiled or cascaded program views. Now try dragging and dropping a selected portion of text from your Word document directly into your Excel worksheet (if you prefer not to drag, you can also use the Copy and Paste buttons). The selected text will be pasted right where you drop it, and the formatting will be as crisp as it was in Word.

Excel Data Inside Your Word Document

Prefer a hyperlink in your Word document that jumps to that spot in your Excel worksheet? Try dragging and dropping the top left cell of your choicest region of worksheet, and use the right mouse button to drag it onto your Word document. In the shortcut menu that appears, click **Insert Hyperlink**. You'll now have a working hyperlink in your Word document. Click it and you jump to that chosen spot in Excel. If Excel isn't open at the time, your hyperlink will start it automatically and find the correct worksheet.

If you want to insert a new Excel worksheet into your Word document, just click the **Insert Microsoft Excel Worksheet** button on Word's Standard toolbar. A grid pops up that looks just like the one we used to create a table, and it works the same way. Click the size of worksheet you want to start with right on this grid (such as four rows, three columns, for example). Your document will come alive with what looks like a junior Excel worksheet sticking out at you. There's nothing junior about it, though, because all the Excel tools are now at your disposal while you work inside this object. Go ahead and fill it with data and use tools to sort, sum, or even graph this data. When you're finished, just click outside the worksheet (anywhere on your document) and you'll find the worksheet still there, but supporting tools hidden back into the woodwork. The worksheet is really part of your document. Double-click it and all the tools return.

Maybe a particular worksheet becomes more important to you than the document. In those cases, it might be better to go the opposite way, and insert your Word document into your Excel worksheet. To do this, start Excel and open your worksheet. Now open the **Insert** menu and click **Object**. In the Object dialog box find the object called **Microsoft Word Document**. Click the **Create From File** tab and click to check the **Link To File** box, to keep this document updated each time the original is changed in Word. If the document is large, you might want to also click the **Display As Icon** box, which leaves an icon on the worksheet representing your document. Your reader simply double-clicks this icon to read the Word document.

Slide a PowerPoint Slide into Your Document

If you see information in a PowerPoint slide presentation that you want to include in a Word document, go get it! An easy technique is copy and paste, so start PowerPoint, open the presentation, and find the slide that holds your interest. Select the information on the slide using your mouse, then click the **Copy** button. Now bring up the Word document and find the spot in which you'd like it to appear, then click the **Paste** button in Word. If you prefer to link this information, don't use the Paste button, but instead open the **Edit** menu and choose the **Paste Special** command. Now you have the opportunity for a **Paste Link**, which will keep this slide information in sync with the original presentation in PowerPoint. If someone updates that slide in the future, your document will be updated automatically.

You might have noticed another helpful command while you were inside the Edit menu. It's the **Paste As Hyperlink** command, which is another way to present PowerPoint information in your Word document. Using the same previous example, choose **Paste As Hyperlink** instead of Paste Special. Now, instead of seeing the actual slide data, you see a hyperlink that you can save in your Word document. All you do is click the hyperlink in your document and you will jump to this exact slide in the PowerPoint presentation. After viewing the slide, you close PowerPoint, and you are returned to this exact spot in your Word document.

Incidentally, the opposite direction works just as well. If you prefer to have Word document information inside a PowerPoint presentation, copy and paste the selected text the same way, but starting in Word and pasting in PowerPoint. Or if you prefer hyperlinks, open the Edit menu in PowerPoint and choose **Paste As Hyperlink**. Either way, you can have Word text in your slide presentation.

If you prefer to create your own new PowerPoint slide from scratch while inside your Word document, open Word's **Insert** menu and click **Object**. Find **Microsoft PowerPoint Slide** on the **Create New** tab and then click **OK**. You'll have a new slide in your document, surrounded by the PowerPoint collection of editing tools at your disposal.

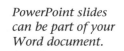

PowerPoint slides can be part of your Word document.

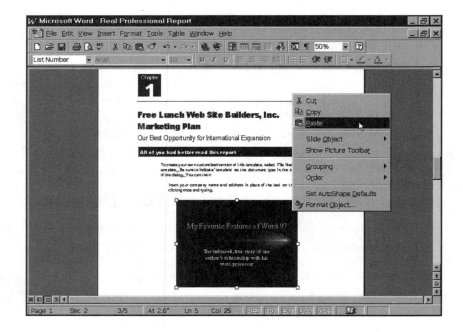

You can also grab a slide or two (or a whole presentation) that appeals to you from a PowerPoint presentation and plant them firmly into a new Word document. To do this, start PowerPoint and open the presentation containing the desired slides. Click to select the particular slide you want to copy. Open the **File** menu in PowerPoint, point to **Send To** and choose **Microsoft Word**. In the Write-Up dialog box you have your choice of page layout designs to be used with your slide. The default places the slide on the left, and presenter notes on the right. Next, choose either **Paste**, to copy this slide into your Word document, or **Paste Link**, which provides a link to this presentation file. If you expect the author of this slide to update it in PowerPoint and want the copy inside your Word document to be updated right along with it, choose Paste Link. Click **OK** and the slide will be pasted as requested inside a new Word document.

Link Your Document to an Access Database

Microsoft Access is a powerful relational database that can store almost anything you need. Once it's in there, you might decide that you want a copy of a portion of database inside your Word document. For instance, you're creating a budget report and you want to include the latest budget summaries from the database. It can be done, and Access provides an easy tool to use just for this purpose. It's called the **OfficeLinks** command, and it's available on the **Tools** menu in Access.

Even Access data can be presented in your Word document.

To give this a try, open Access and find the database table or report that contains the information you need. Select the region of data you want to include, open the **Tools** menu and click **OfficeLinks**. In the OfficeLinks dialog box, you must decide how you want the data to be copied into Word. The first option, **Merge It With MS Word**, is used to copy the selected data into your existing Word document. The second option, **Publish It With MS Word**, can be used to create a new Word document while inside Access. With either option, you'll have the data you need inside a Word document.

Copy and Pasting data is also supported with Access, following the same steps as in Excel and PowerPoint. Select the data in Access, click **Copy**, change to Word and click **Paste**, **Paste Special**, or even **Paste As Hyperlink** from the **Edit** menu.

Store and Organize Common Work in a Binder

Office 97 provides a whole new way to organize your electronic documents. It's similar to the way you might clean up your desk if it's cluttered with many documents, worksheets, and presentation materials. You wouldn't stack all the worksheets in one pile, and your documents in another. It makes more sense to group project files together, such as budget reports with budget worksheets and budget presentations. Then make another pile for all the types of sales information. Office 97 provides a way to organize related electronic documents in a single electronic *binder*. The documents always stay in the order you place them in, and they can be saved, moved, and printed as a single file.

Start a New Binder and Add Documents

Binders are ideal places to store finished documents. To create a new binder, start the Office 97 Binder program. Open the **File** menu and choose **New Binder**. You can create a new empty binder by clicking **Blank Binder** on the **General** tab, or choose a ready-built binder template by clicking the **Binders** tab. Here you'll find collections of common project documents that have a consistent style of appearance.

To add finished documents to your binder, right click in the binder margin on the left side of your screen and choose **Add** from the shortcut menu. Locate the document, whether it's Excel, PowerPoint, Word, or Access, and click **OK**. An icon representing this document will now appear in the Binder.

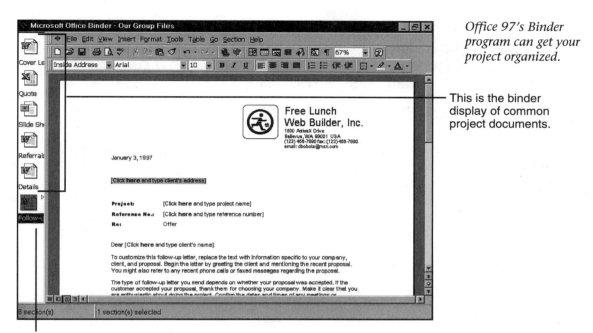

Office 97's Binder program can get your project organized.

This is the binder display of common project documents.

Right-click in this area to add new documents.

The Least You Need to Know

Word 97 is an integrated component of Office 97, which means you can benefit by using the absolute best tool for whatever your task. You can quickly move yourself, and your data, among these applications, in a variety of different ways.

How do I create a hyperlink to a PowerPoint slide in my document?

You can create quick hyperlinks to other Office 97 programs. It's easiest if you get both programs running at the same time. Use the right mouse button to drag the selected object in the destination over to the place you want the hyperlink to appear. The hyperlink will be created automatically.

Can I hyperlink if the other program isn't open at the moment?

You can still drag between programs when they are full-screen. Just drag the selection onto the application's icon on the taskbar and continue holding down the mouse button until the application opens. Then drag the selection where you want it. The hyperlink will be created automatically.

Can I get data from Excel, PowerPoint, and Access into my Word document?

Yes, and you have several choices. The easiest method is to simply copy and paste the information, and Word will maintain the appropriate format for the data. Other options include hyperlinks, file linking, and file embedding.

My project contains files created in all the Office 97 programs. How can I keep track of them all?

The best way to organize a group of similar project files is by using the Office 97 Binder program. All common files are at your fingertips, and they can be easily moved as a group or printed all at the same time.

Part 4
Taking Word 97 for a Spin on Your Intranet (and the Internet)

Creating your own Web pages and building your own Web site is no longer a big deal—you can do it today with your own computer, Word 97 Web authoring tools, and this part of the book!

Of course, it helps if you are connected to an intranet, or the really big one—the Internet—because then others can visit your site. Whether you use your Web personally to learn or manage your files, or publicly as part of your business, you can start building and connecting Web pages now. Give it a try, and see if you can make it to the Top 10 Web Sites today!

DUE TO A TYPO MR. OLSEN'S WEB PAGE "HOT SAX", WAS GETTING A LOT OF EMAIL.

Creating a Web Page in Word 97

The world changes quickly, and Word 97 has improved to help you change with it. The *World Wide Web* has become a standard method of sharing information, but until recently it's been difficult to create and support your own Web documents. Word 97 helps you meet that challenge by providing tools to help you create Web pages.

Introducing the Intranet

What makes the Internet so famous and popular is the availability of information—fast, free, and easy to find. Well, at least it used to be all of those. It's become so popular that the enormous increase in people using it has caused it to slow down, and the addition of zillions of pages of information makes it harder (and takes longer) to find what you're looking for.

Browsers and Search Engines The tools that made the Internet famous are browsers and searching tools. *Web browsers* provide a graphical interface to make it easier to navigate and understand. The two most popular browsers include the Netscape Navigator and the Microsoft Internet Explorer.

Search engines enable you to type in key words and then search and provide you with a listing of Internet information sources that match your key words. Your intranet can even include these search engines like Yahoo! and Lycos to help you find the proverbial needle in your company's haystack.

Recently, businesses have discovered that they can take advantage of the same tools that have been developed for the Internet and use them on their own private networks. These are called intranets (*intra* means *inside*), and are usually designed to be available only within a company for sharing company information toward the goal of becoming more productive and efficient. By keeping them private and cut off from the Internet mainstream, a business can maintain high intranet performance and be able to provide easy access of company information for employees. An intranet includes most of the advantages of the Internet while avoiding all of the disadvantages.

Almost any computer network can be turned into an intranet by adding a single computer called the intranet server (larger intranets may have several servers). Then all computers on the network can use a Web browser to access information on the server. When you use your browser, you are actually viewing Web pages that are stored on the server, and these pages contain the information shared by your company. This chapter is all about creating these Web pages.

Create a Web Page Fast

Do you need a certifiably beautiful, interesting, and most important—*functioning*—Web page but have only 15 minutes to spare? No problem, as long as you own Word 97, because all the tools you need are provided. Pull up a chair and let's see how it's done.

World Wide Web The World Wide Web is a system for navigating the Internet by using hyperlinks. When you use a Web browser, the Web appears as a collection of text, pictures, sounds, and digital movies.

Brand new in Word 97 are two new features to help you construct Web pages—the Web Page Wizard and the Blank Web Page template, both used to create new Web pages. The Web Page Wizard is fully automated and gives you different layouts and color schemes that you can choose from, like a personal home page, a table of contents, a survey form, and so on. Once you're comfortable with how a page is constructed, you might prefer the speed of the Blank Web Page template (especially after you've used it to create your own template).

The Web Page Wizard, at Your Service

The Web Page Wizard consists of two questions that cover the type and visual style for your Web page. Open the **File** menu and click **New**. In the New dialog box, click the **Web Pages** tab, and then double-click **Web Page Wizard** to start it into action.

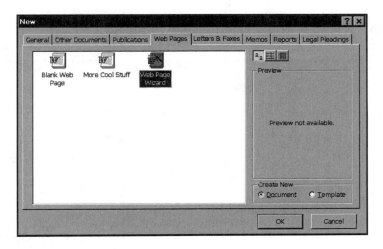

You have plenty of choices to create the page you need.

First you must choose a type of Web page. Think of Web pages you've seen. They might be surveys, table of contents or indexes, or plain information pages. Word 97 gives you all of these, plus a lot more. If this is your first Web page, then a good choice is *Personal Web Page*. Click to choose it, then press the **Next** button.

Now you can choose a visual style for your page. These are color-coordinated combinations of text and graphics that follow a general theme, like an *Elegant* page, or perhaps a *Festive* one, or even a *Professional* style if you want to look like everyone else. To match this example, click to select the *Harvest* style and then click the **Finish** button. That's right, the **Finish** button in record time, and a striking new Web page will appear on your Word 97 screen.

Speaking of Word 97, where did this view come from? It sure looks like the view from a Web browser, and that's what Microsoft intended. It's called the Online View, which you can prove by clicking the **View** menu, or peeking down at the View buttons on your horizontal scroll bar. It's a very helpful view while creating a Web page because you get to see exactly what it will look like (other Web tools often force you to switch back and forth from your Web browser as you edit).

So what's next? Just click on the **Insert Heading Here** and type the title for your Web page. Click the next line **Insert Subheading Here** and give credit to yourself, or perhaps a description, address, or warning label.

This is a good time to save this Web-page work of art. Click the **Save** button and provide a name and folder location. Notice the file type is something called an HTML document, which is the native language of Web pages. You don't have to worry about the type for now; just understand that Word 97 easily opens documents of this type, and opens them in the Online Layout view.

Before going further in Web page customization, let's take a look at the other creation choice, the **Blank Web Page** template, and see what's different.

Visual styles provide themes for your Web pages.

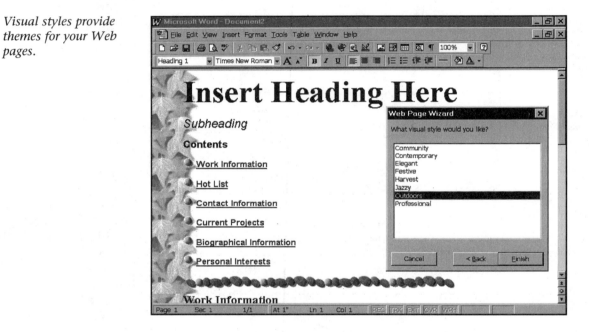

Build Pages from Scratch with the Blank Web Page Template

The **Blank Web Page** template is the no-frills version of the Web Page Wizard. No questions asked, just an ordinary Web page ready for you to customize and save. As you become more experienced, you'll want to try creating a page from scratch, and this template provides the canvas for your artistic abilities.

Open the **File** menu and click **New**. In the New dialog box, click the Web Pages tab, and then double-click **Blank Web Page** template. A new Web page appears on your screen, which is changed automatically to Online Layout view.

The remainder of this chapter describes how you can customize your new Web page. When you finish with the customization, be sure to save your work as a new Web page. Click the **Save** button, be sure that the document type is HTML Document, and provide a name and folder for your Web page.

More Free Pages, Please

Several additional Web templates are available for you to download from Microsoft's World Wide Web site. Find out how to download them in Chapter 24.

Saving Any Word 97 Document as HTML

Trivia question: What's the *third* way to create a Web page fast in Word 97? Answer: Just convert something you've already got! You can do a **Save As** on any current document and save it as the type HTML, and it will be converted to a Web page. This is the real kicker in creating complete Web sites fast—you probably have most of the content already! Maybe you've already got a phone list document, job notices, employee profiles, and so on, in Word format. That's perfect, because you simply open the existing document, click **Save As** on the **File** menu, and save the document as an HTML document.

It's not always simple and perfect, however, and you need to look at the conversion to see what formatting may have changed. Follow the examples in this Chapter (and the next) to clean things up. You should find that the format fixes are a heck of a lot easier than re-keying all the information in your document.

Save Your Own Custom Web Page Template

Don't forget, both the Web Page Wizard and the Blank Web Page template can be used to create your own custom template. After you browse the remainder of this Chapter, create your own customized Web page and plan to use it as a template. A custom template will help you keep all your pages looking consistent, besides saving you lots of time if you have many pages to create. You'll also reduce errors, since the common page parts will already be tested and placed into the page.

To save a Web page as a template, open the File menu and click the **Save As** command. Choose **Document Template** in the **Save As Type** box, then provide a name you'll recognize in the future. Notice that the default storage folders for templates are displayed in the Save As dialog box; it's good practice to stay organized, so store this template in the Web Pages folder. The next time you start a new document by opening the **File** menu and clicking **New**, you'll see the new template listed in the Web Pages tab.

Glorify Your Web Page with Formatting Features

Now that you've got a great start to your Web page, it's time to customize it. You can take advantage of many Word 97 editing and formatting features, automatic text correction, spelling and grammar checking, tables, and the list goes on and on. But not all formatting options provide results that can be viewed with a Web browser, and those forbidden options are hidden while you're creating Web pages. You'll learn ways around these shortcomings in the next Chapter.

Basic Text Formatting on a Web Page

Once you begin to create a Web page, Word 97 adjusts the toolbars to match the task. Notice the slightly different buttons on the Formatting toolbar? Use the standard tools in Word 97 to apply bold, italic, underline, strikethrough, superscript, and subscript formats to selected text. You can align text with the **Align Left**, **Center**, or **Align Right** buttons. You can also change the font size of selected text, but it must be in supported Web page increments. The easiest way to change font size is to click **Increase Font Size** or **Decrease Font Size** buttons that appear on the Formatting toolbar while you're in Online Layout view. Likewise, use the **Increase Indent** or **Decrease Indent** buttons on the Formatting toolbar to adjust indenting in standard Web increments.

Increase that font
to the next size. ⌐Alignment buttons.

*Toolbars change to
match the task at
hand.*

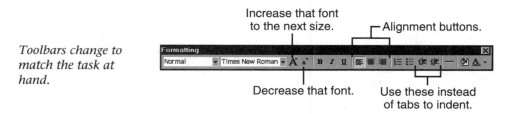

Decrease that font. Use these instead
of tabs to indent.

Give That Web Page a Title

The Web page *title* is different than the heading text that appears at the top of a Web page. The title appears in the title bar of the Web browser when it's viewing your page, and it also appears in history lists and favorites lists, if someone stores a link to your Web page. So give your page a good title. Open the **File** menu and click **Properties**. Type the title you want in the Title box.

If you choose to ignore this step, your page will still have a title. Word 97 will choose a title based on the first few words or characters of your Web page.

Adding Bullets and Numbered Lists to a Web Page

Web pages are usually full of lists, and yours will be easy to create. Just use the standard features of Word 97, by clicking the **Numbering** or **Bullets** button on the Formatting toolbar. Or, if you don't want to bother clicking, just make sure the AutoFormat feature is turned on (found on the Format menu) to automatically create bullet or numbered lists following your lead. You start the list, and AutoFormat continues it as you press the Enter key.

If the standard bullets are too boring for your page, change them. To add a new bullet for selected text, click **Bullets and Numbering** on the **Format** menu, and then select the bullet you want.

Pardon Me, but Where's the Numbered Outline?

Outline numbering works differently in Web pages, because HTML doesn't support automatic numbering in outlines. You can, however, simulate the look of an outline by indenting numbers in different levels and applying different numbering formats. Pick your top level text and open the Format menu, click Bullets and Numbering, and then click the Numbering tab. Choose the number format that you want. Use the Tab key to indent the text that belongs to the next level in the list. While tabs aren't used in HTML, the format for Web pages, Word 97 can convert tabs in a numbered list to an indented level.

Break Things Up with Horizontal Lines

They're not as common as they used to be, but horizontal lines are still used quite often in Web pages to separate logical sections of text. First click where you want to insert the line in your Web page. Then be pleasantly surprised to see how fancy Word 97 lines are by opening the **Insert** menu and clicking **Horizontal Line**.

Don't shy away from that first boring line. In fact, that line is the only one that's created in HTML, which means it's the fastest line that can be drawn on your Web page. That gets to be pretty important as your Web page grows. Those other beautiful lines? They're actually images—pictures—of lines pretending to be horizontal lines. One or two can spice up your page nicely, but stay away from too many of them, for performance reasons.

Only the first horizontal line is true HTML; the others are actually graphics.

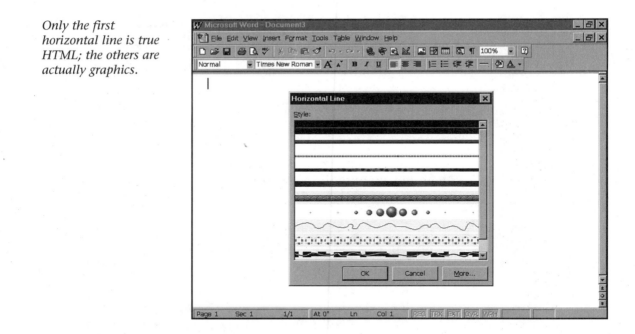

Doing the Background Work on Your Web Page

What makes a Web page interesting, even if the words don't mean a thing to you? Background color and texture, of course! You can add or change the background color on any Web page by clicking it from a palette of colors. And adding texture is just as simple. Texture is the make-believe bumps and shading you can add to your flat background to make it appear three-dimensional.

Open the **Format** menu and point to **Background** (it's only visible while you're in Online Layout view). Review the palette of colors and click the color you want. It's always best to choose a background that contrasts with your text color (no yellow on white, or brown on gray, please). Although you can also click **More Colors** to see additional color choices, be forewarned that not all browsers can "see" these additional colors, and might substitute another color without asking your permission.

To add a texture to your background, open the **Format** menu, point to **Background**, and click **Fill Effects**. Click to select the special effects you prefer for your background. You can only choose one texture per Web page.

Create Your Own Fancy Background Texture

You can use any graphic or image as a background texture, beyond the ones displayed on the Texture tab. Don't worry about the size; small graphics are tiled, or repeated, to fill the entire Web page.

Find a good graphic, then click **Other Texture** on the Texture tab and change to the folder that contains the graphic file you want to use. Once your file is selected, click **OK**. Now use it in your Web page. Each time it's used, Word 97 will save this new texture as a separate graphics file (with a name like GRAPHIC1.JPG) in the same folder that you create and store your Web page.

You'll only see these backgrounds and textures while you're in Online Layout view. And don't forget, these backgrounds aren't designed for printed documents. They'll chew up printer memory faster than that newspaper we did in Chapter 19. Limit background colors and textures to your Web pages, or documents that you'll use online only.

If you change your mind and want to get rid of the background color, open the **Format** menu and point to **Background**. Click the **No Fill** command.

Coloring Your Words

All text on your Web page can be colored instantly using the **Font Color** button on the **Formatting** toolbar. Select the text, click the **Font Color** button, and choose a color from the palette. It's best to change the text color to contrast with the background color. Use lighter colors on darker backgrounds, and vice versa. Avoid using the color white for text, since white text won't print on many printers. Also avoid choosing a text color so light that it's hard to read without the background, since readers can adjust their browsers to ignore backgrounds.

Add Scrolling Text to Your Web Page

Ready for a little more action? How about a cute little marquee that flies across your Web page, like an invisible airplane pulling a banner across the sky? You even have control over the speed and scrolling behavior of your text.

First click the line in your Web page where you want the scrolling text to appear. Open the **Format** menu, click **Scrolling Text**, and click the **Options** tab. Here's where you pilot the text. Type the text that you want to scroll under **Type the Marquee Text Here** (marquee is another word for *scrolling text*). On the **Size and Speed** tab, enter the height, width, and distance from text in pixels. Also select the scrolling speed that you want.

Scrolling Text is one of those newer formatting options that might not appear to scroll in all Web browsers. The good news is that the text will still be displayed (stationary), even if it doesn't scroll. Another tip—don't use more than one or two scrolling texts per page, or you'll be slowing down the page-loading needlessly, and the novelty wears off quickly for a visitor.

Inserting and Aligning a Graphic into Your Web Page

Inserting a favorite graphic, clip art, or scanned picture can be as easy as clicking a button, as long as you can locate the graphic file. Click the **Insert Picture** button that appears on the Standard toolbar while you're in Online Layout view. Find your graphic with the **Browse** button and click **Insert** to plant in into your Web page.

Once the graphic lands on the page, you can move it anywhere you like. Get the hang of clicking the graphic, then pointing near the edge of it until you see the pointer change to the positioning symbol. Then click and drag it to a new spot. You can also stretch or scrunch it by clicking and dragging the picture handles. Be sure to save your Web page after you've added a graphic.

To align your images, make it easy on yourself and use the alignment buttons on the Picture toolbar that appears when you click on a picture. You can align images in Web pages to the left of text, to the right of text, or with no alignment so that they don't flow around the image.

Your Web Page Can Warble

Time to move into the multimedia arena. Let's start with sound. Ever notice that some Web pages make sounds when you open them? That's called a background sound, and you can add one to any Web page. A background sound plays automatically as the reader views your Web page with a Web browser. The sound can be long or short, but short is preferred, to keep your Web page fast. You can still have a longer sound—if you play the shorter sound over and over again. You can determine the number of times the sound repeats or have it play an unlimited number of times.

Hardware Requirements for Sound

Don't forget, in order to hear sound files in a Web page, your computer must have the necessary equipment as described in Chapter 13. This includes a sound card and external speakers or headphones. If you want to record sounds, you'll also need a microphone that plugs into your sound card.

Where can you find sounds to use in your Web page? Several good samples are included in the Word 97 (or Office 97) CD-ROM. As we learned in Chapter 13, the best way to access this collection is to place the CD in your computer, open the Insert menu, choose the Object command, and choose Microsoft Clip Gallery. Click the Sounds tab and you'll find the available sounds labeled with descriptive names and their time duration.

You can also use sounds from other sources, including the Internet (**www.midifarm.com** is one example of a Web site offering sounds to download). Any sound file with the extension of WAV, MID, AU, AIF, RMI, SND, and MP2 (MPEG audio) formats can be inserted into your Web page. Your best bet is to use the MID or WAV files, because they provide the best sound quality while keeping the file size reasonably small. Once again, not all Web browsers support all sound formats, and the reader's computer must have sound support to hear them, so don't make the sound critical to understanding your Web page.

Once you've decided on which sound file to use in your Web page, open the **Insert** menu and click **Background Sound**. Click Browse to locate the sound file and select it. In the Loop box, click the number of times you want the sound to repeat. Each time your reader opens this Web page, they will hear your sound played the number of loops you've chosen.

Your Web Page Can Do Video, Too

You can also add short video clips to your Web pages to make them more interesting. They can be fun and informative for your reader, but you should remember that they aren't supported by all Web browsers and they might take a long time to download. It's always good to provide text-based alternatives to videos you place in your Web page.

To insert a video clip, open the **Insert** menu, point to **Video**, and then click **Properties**. In the **Video Source** box, click Browse to search for and select the video file you want. Now see the **Alternate Image** box? That's where you can place a plain graphic in place of your video for browsers that can't do video. It's much better than a blank area. Find a tiny clip art and include it here. "Wait a minute," you say, "what if my reader has turned off graphics on his browser?" Good point, and that's why the Alternate Text box exists. Type the text (something like *"Boy, you missed the movie!"*) that you want to appear in place of your video or your alternate image, which will be displayed if the Web browser doesn't support videos or if images aren't being displayed.

In the **Start** box, click an option to specify how the video will play in a Web page. The easiest option isn't the smartest (unless your video is extremely short—less than a second or two). **File Open** will cause the video to play when the user opens your Web page. That means your reader must wait until the entire video is downloaded to completely open your Web page. **Mouse Over** is better, as it causes the video to play when the mouse pointer is placed over the video. Just like you could repeat a short sound many times to make it seem longer, you can also repeat short videos. In the **Loop** box you can enter the number of times you want the video to repeat.

Probably the best way to let your reader decide whether or not to play the video is to include video controls, like as **Start** and **Stop**, along with your video. Click the **Display Video Controls** check box and select the options and placement of your controls.

> *Check This Out...*
>
> ### Hear and See Them Now
>
> You probably want to preview a sound or video after you've added to your Web page. Click the Refresh Current Page button on your Web toolbar and you'll experience the events programmed for your Web page opening.

Create Hyperlinks in Your Documents

Ready to learn one of the most important new features of Word 97? It's called a *hyperlink*, and you can use them to jump back and forth quickly to different places. These destinations can be inside the same document or Web page, inside different documents stored in your computer or out on your network, in other Office 97 program files, or even remote locations out on the World Wide Web. You can even use hyperlinks to jump to multimedia files, like recorded sounds and videos.

> ### Hyperlink
>
> A *hyperlink* is a jump to a location in the same file or another file represented by colored (usually blue) and underlined text, called hypertext. Hyperlinks can also be represented by a graphic. You click a hyperlink to jump to a file, a location in a file, an HTML page on the World Wide Web, or an HTML page on an intranet.

A hyperlink is usually represented by a word or phrase that's typically colored blue and underlined. A hyperlink can also be a graphic that the reader clicks to jump to a different location. After using a hyperlink, its display is changed slightly—now typically colored purple and still underlined. This change helps you remember where you've been as you jump around the links.

There are basically three ways to insert hyperlinks. All have the same result: You choose the method that's easiest for your current situation.

➤ Use the Hyperlink button to insert a hyperlink when you aren't using the automatic formatting features or when you want to browse for the destination address.

➤ Use a drag-and-drop operation when you want to use the mouse to quickly create a hyperlink inside the same document.

➤ Use the automatic formatting features in Word 97 when you happen to know the path and filename, or URL syntax that you want to format as hyperlinks.

Use the Insert Hyperlink Button

Here's a quick way to insert a hyperlink if you're using *bookmarks* or know the name of the destination document or *URL*.

In your Word document, click where you want the link, then click the **Insert Hyperlink** button on the Standard toolbar. If the destination is inside the same document, you must first create a bookmark to identify it (I'll tell you how to do this in just a minute). Then, in the **Link to File or URL:** drop-down list, choose the bookmark as the destination for your hyperlink. If the destination is outside of the current document, type in the full filename and path of the file to which you want to link, or if it's out on the Internet, type the complete URL. You can also click the **Browse** button to help you find the destination document.

What are bookmarks, you ask? They're things inside a document that identify a particular spot. It's easy to create a bookmark; try it now. Click at the beginning of a good destination, like a new chapter heading, index, chart, graphic, or anything. Now open the **Insert** menu and choose **Bookmark**. In the Bookmark dialog box provide a name for this location. This name must not contain any spaces. Then click the **Add** button and this bookmark will be saved. It's easy to hyperlink anything to this bookmark now, because you'll now find this bookmark name as a destination choice in the Insert Hyperlink dialog box.

Can't Get Hyperlink to Work? Here's something important to remember: Your document must first be *saved* before you can create hyperlinks!

Where Are You, URL?
URL stands for Uniform Resource Locator, which is an address for an Internet site. The Web uses URLs to specify the addresses of the various servers (and the various documents on each server) on the Internet. For example, the URL for Macmillan Publishing is **http://www.mcp.com**. The "http" means this is a Web site containing Web documents, "www" stands for the World Wide Web, "mcp" is the identifying name chosen by Macmillan, and "com" designates this as a commercial site. Other types of sites include gov (government), edu (education), and org (organization).

What's HTTP:// and Why Should I Care?

When you type a string beginning with http:// into a Web browser, you're entering what's called a Universal Resource Locator (URL), also known as Universal Resource Indicator (URI). The protocol specifier (the part before the colon) indicates the protocol your computer will use to request and retrieve the document. Besides HTTP (HyperText Transfer Protocol), you might also see ftp:// (File Transfer Protocol), gopher:// (Gopher protocol), or even c:\file// (your own computer's file system).

Most browsers try to guess your intentions if a protocol specifier is omitted. But because mix-ups are possible, it's best to specify the one you want.

The Hyperlink Button asks for a destination.

Insert Hyperlink

Link to file or URL:

C:\webfiles\Page2.html   Browse...

Enter or locate the path to the document you want to link to. This can be an Internet address (URL), a document on your hard drive, or a document on your company's network.

Path: .\..\..\..\webfiles\Page2.html

Named location in file (optional):

Browse...

If you want to jump to a specific location within the document, such as a bookmark, a named range, a database object, or a slide number, enter or locate that information above.

☑ Use relative path for hyperlink

OK   Cancel

Add bookmarks for easier hyperlinks.

Bookmark

Bookmark name:

Summary ———————— These names must not contain spaces.

Bottom
CompanyLogo
Contents
ReportDetails
Top

Sort by: ⦿ Name ○ Location
☐ Hidden bookmarks

Add   Delete   Go To

Cancel

Create a Hyperlink with a Drag and a Drop

Another way to create a hyperlink is to drag and drop a bit of the destination wherever you want the hyperlink to appear. It's a fast method to use when all destination documents are currently opened on your screen. It's also the easiest way to hyperlink between different Office 97 products. You can create a hyperlink in your Word document by dragging selected text or graphics from a PowerPoint slide, a selected range of worksheet cells in Excel, or a selected database object in Access right into your Word 97 document, at the location you want the hyperlink to appear. From now on, when you click this hyperlink, Word automatically recognizes the location of the information, opens the appropriate program, and displays the information.

To try your hand at a drag-and-drop operation to create a hyperlink. Go to the destination text (the information you want to link to) in a PowerPoint presentation and select a word or two of the beginning text. Drag this text using the right mouse button (hey, wake up! I said the *right* mouse button), and drop it where you want to create the hyperlink. Choose the command **Create Hyperlink Here** from the shortcut menu that appears. If it's not working for you, remember that both target and destination files must be saved first before a hyperlink can be created.

Drag and drop a hyperlink with the right mouse button.

Use the AutoFormat Feature to Create Hyperlinks as You Type

If you have a good memory, this option might be the best method of creating hyperlinks for you. Use the automatic formatting features of Word 97 to turn filenames into hyperlinks—just by typing the address of the document.

If you can remember the exact name of the destination file, whether it's a local file, network file, or Internet URL, you can simply type that location into your document and AutoFormat will convert it to a hyperlink automatically. For instance, if I want to create a hyperlink on my Web page that takes you to Microsoft's home page on the Web (even if I've never been there before), I just type **www.microsoft.com** and those words automatically turn into a hyperlink! If I have a file on my hard drive, I can type **c:\webfiles\default.htm** and it will also convert to a hyperlink automatically after a few moments, as long as I know it exists and have the proper URL for it.

AutoFormat is also handy when using Internet e-mail addresses in your document. AutoFormat can automatically format the addresses into hyperlinks as you type. For instance, let's say you run the Web page for the cafeteria menu. You want to find out if the chili special has been the cause of recent employee turnover. On the Web page you ask for feedback, then type your e-mail address. AutoFormat converts it to a hyperlink immediately. Then, when the reader of your page clicks on your hyperlink, an e-mail message with your correct address already in the To: line is created, making it fast and easy to get feedback from your reader. They just type a comment and send it.

To make all this magic happen, open the **Tools** menu and click **AutoCorrect**, to open the AutoCorrect dialog box. Click the **AutoFormat As You Type** tab. Under **Replace As You Type**, click to place a check in the **Internet And Network Paths With Hyperlinks** check box, and click **OK**.

Web page assistance from the AutoCorrect dialog box.

Changing Your Hypertext Words Once They're Created

Does it bother you that all three hyperlink creation options automatically provide the *hypertext* for you? It's either the selected text you dragged, the name of the bookmark, or the ugly file and path name. These words don't always fit grammatically or contextually. It really bugged me, until I learned how to change the hypertext words after they're created.

It sounds easy, but there's a trick to it. You must first *select* the hypertext, and then type the new words over it. I almost blew a gasket trying to select the text at first, because any left click and you're launched into the hyperlink. No, the trick is to select the hypertext by *right-clicking* it. Find the hypertext you want to change, click it with the right mouse button, point to **Hyperlink** on the shortcut menu, then choose the **Select Hyperlink** command. The hypertext will be selected and you can change it by retyping or backspacing. Click outside the hyperlink when finished, and it will be saved.

> **Refresh Your Display to Keep It Current**
> When you work in a document that contains hyperlinks to other documents on your intranet, those documents might be modified by the author while you have it open. You can click the **Refresh Current Page** button on the Web toolbar at any time. When you update a document, the document is refreshed from the original file that is located on the network server, the Internet, or your computer hard disk.

Removing Hyperlinks

To remove an outdated or obnoxious hyperlink, right-click on the hyperlink, point to Hyperlink on the shortcut menu, and choose the **Edit Hyperlink** command. In the Edit Hyperlink dialog box, click the **Remove Link** button and the hyperlink will disappear. The hypertext will return to its previous formatting.

Buggy Hyperlinks?

If you're having problems with a hyperlink that once worked, consider these tips:

➤ The destination of the hyperlink may have been removed or renamed.

➤ The path to the destination may have moved to another location.

➤ If the destination is located on your intranet, check your network connections to make sure the network server you use is running.

➤ The destination on the Internet may be too busy. Try to open the document later.

The Least You Need to Know

Creating a real Web page is easy in Word 97. And browsing this chapter provided lots of helpful hints.

I know nothing about the Internet but my boss needs a Web page. Can Word 97 help me?

Yes. Use either the Web Page Wizard or the Web Template to create perfect Web pages fast. Open the **File** menu, click **New**, and click the **Web Pages** tab to select a wizard or template. Follow the steps to create the Web page in simple stages until completion.

Do I need any other fancy tools to create a Web page?

Word 97 comes with the Web Page toolbar, and it provides all the tools you'll need to customize your Web page like the pros. If it's a feature supported in a Web page, you'll find a helpful tool to create it on the Web Page toolbar.

How can I include video and sound in my Web page?

Adding sound, video, and special effects to a Web page is done quickly by opening the **Insert** menu, clicking **Object**, and locating the particular object type in the list. Add the location of your audio clip, video clip, or other file, and it will appear on your Web page.

How do I add a hyperlink to my Web page?

Hyperlinks are used to provide additional or reference information in your documents or Web pages. When you click on a hyperlink, you immediately jump to the destination of the hyperlink. You can create hyperlinks by clicking the **Insert Hyperlink** button on the Standard toolbar, then providing the destination for the jump.

Chapter 24

Working with Web Tools

In This Chapter

➤ Creating tables for your Web page

➤ Consider these alternative format tools

➤ Converting Word 97 documents to HTML format

➤ Proofing tools for your Web page

➤ Keeping your tools up-to-date from Microsoft's Web page

Word 97 is loaded with tools to help you build and maintain your Web pages. You already know how to use some of them—the table creation and alignment tools, and the automatic proofing tools, for example—because the Web tools work the same way as their normal document counterparts. That frees up lots of time to learn the new tools that make Web pages a breeze to create.

Do I Need to Understand HTML?

Heavens no! You don't even have to recognize the acronym. Word 97 Web authoring tools allow you to create Web pages in their final form, without understanding the language that's holding it together. By the way, HTML is that language, and it stands for HyperText Markup Language. HTML is used to define the location and description of elements on a Web page. An HTML document includes the text you want to display, information on how that text should be formatted (such as the size of the text, whether or not it's centered, and so on), the names and pictures that will appear (but not the pictures themselves), and other important information. When you connect to a Web page, your Web browser creates the page you see by following the HTML instructions.

Word 97 creates your Web page using HTML behind-the-scenes. You never have to mess with it. That's the benefit of Word 97—you always work with the final product displayed; other programs require you to understand and create the HTML first, and then view the finished product. With Word 97, you adjust something on your Web page, and Word writes the corresponding commands in HTML for you. When you save the Web page, it is saved with the extension .HTM, so a browser can recognize it as a Web page.

This chapter describes special formatting you can include in your Web pages, such as tables, headers or footers, and other special effects. Before Word 97, you were required to understand and write the HTML commands yourself (or purchase special programs to do so), which was no picnic. An ordinary table appearing on your Web page could require hundreds of lines of HTML code. Here in this chapter, you can create beautiful tables in ignorant bliss.

Set Your Table on a Web Page

If you lived through Chapter 14, you'll have no problem creating a table for your Web page. You use the very same Word 97 table tools as you would in a normal document. Quick tables can appear with the click of a button, or you can decide to put your drawing talent to good use and sketch a completely custom table. Either way, you'll find tables to be an indispensable addition to your Web pages.

Create a Simple Table Instantly

To quickly insert a table, click the **Insert Table** button on the Standard toolbar. The size grid will stay open while you decide the number of rows and columns you need (and you can always change them later). Click the table size you want and a perfect table will appear in your Web page.

Once the table exists, you can modify it with the standard table tools you know and love in Word 97. Use your mouse to click and drag any table border or line to move it where you want. Start adding your data, and then use the formatting tools to improve the appearance of your data. All the rules for text formatting on Web pages apply to tables, too, which means you've got more choices than you'll need. Choose your colors, font types, font sizes, and special text effects to give your table the appearance it deserves. Then save it. Saving often is always a good idea when working with tables, especially large tables.

Draw Your Own Custom Table on a Web Page

Click the **Tables and Borders** button on the Standard toolbar and its toolbar will appear on your screen. Remember drawing your own table in Chapter 14? You can do it here and now the same way for your Web page. Click the **Draw Table** button and sketch out the table exactly as you want it. Erase lines here and there with the **Eraser** button to customize the headings or columns. If you want to straighten things out, make good use of the table alignment tools, with the **Distribute Rows Evenly** and **Distribute Columns Evenly** buttons.

Drawing a custom table for the Web is fast and easy.

Now start filling your table. Use the cell alignment buttons **Align Top**, **Center Vertically**, and **Align Bottom** to place the data in the cell just the way you like. You can use the full power of new Word 97 table tools like Merge Cells or Split Cells if you need to adjust your tables after you've added the data. Don't forget you can also sort the entire table, based on any column, using the **Sort Ascending** or **Sort Descending** buttons.

What? You Want Gridlines?

Don't get thrown off by that button **Hide/Show Gridlines** that appears on your Tables and Borders toolbar in Online Layout view. Sure, you see gridlines, and then you don't, by clicking this button, but these lines are imaginary! Don't believe me? Click the **Web Page Preview** button to start your browser and reveal the truth. Your table information will be present and accounted for, but the lines have gone AWOL.

If you want your table to be constructed with real lines, you need to give it a border. You'd think a **Border** button would be pretty handy if it was in the Tables and Borders toolbar, and you'd be right, but it's not there so don't waste your time looking for it. You can either read Chapter 21 and add the button yourself by customizing that darned toolbar, or you can open the **Tables** menu and click the **Borders** command. If you're handy with the mouse, you'll find the fastest way to the **Borders** command is to right-click anywhere in your table and it's right there on your shortcut menu.

Choose a border for your Web table.

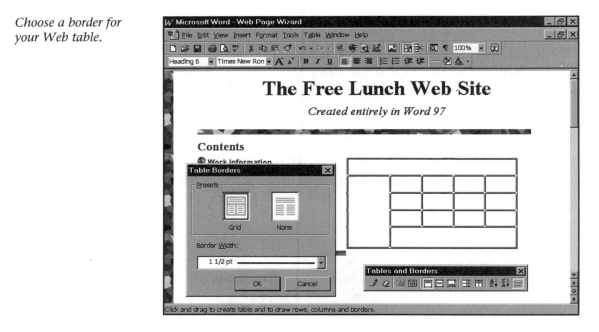

Your options may appear limited in the Table Borders dialog box, but at least you've got choices in line size. Click the **Grid** in Presets, and then choose a **Border Width**. Click **OK** and you'll see a nice 3-D style of border surrounding your table. This border appears in Online Layout view the same as it will using your browser.

Use Tables to Organize Your Web Page

If you're having trouble aligning your graphics and text on a Web page, try using a table as a layout tool. It works, and it's fast to create. Suppose you want your Web page to have a graphic on the left and a column of text on the right. Create a one-row, two-column table by clicking the **Insert Table** button. Insert the graphic in the left cell, and type the text in the cell on the right. What could be easier?

Not All Browsers Do Tables!

Some early versions of Web browsers don't support tables, so you may want to provide a version of your Web page that has the same information, but doesn't include tables. For instance, you could insert a hyperlink guiding readers who aren't seeing your table to a different page containing the same data in plain columns.

Flowing Text Around Your Web Page Table

If your table doesn't take up the whole width of the Web page, you can flow text around it. Right click anywhere inside your table and choose **Table Properties** from the shortcut menu. In the Table Properties dialog box, choose the Text Wrapping example you prefer by clicking on it. You can also define how close text gets to your table by changing the values of Horizontal and Vertical Distance boxes.

Flowing text might look terrific to you, because you're using Word 97 and the Microsoft Internet Explorer, but if you plan to post your page where others might browse, see how it looks in their browser. Flowing text might not appear to flow at all using an older browser, and you might not see the text or graphic at all.

Using Word 97 Styles with Your Web Page

As we learned in Chapter 20, styles can make it easier to quickly format paragraphs in a document. You can also apply the existing Word 97 styles that correspond to formatting that's supported by HTML to help you build Web pages. And you can apply styles to your Web page the same way you apply styles to Word documents, although there are some differences in how styles work.

To make styles easier to use with Web pages, only those styles that correspond to HTML have been added to the Styles box on the Formatting toolbar. To use a style, just click the Styles box on the Formatting toolbar and choose a style. The style will continue as you type, until you choose a different style, or click to a different location where another style is in effect.

A New Style for a Rainy Day

One special new style is called HTML Markup, and it's designed for HTML source codes that you want to enter manually.

Styles are not automatically defined as you type inside your Web pages. You might think you've set this feature up correctly, but Word 97 silently turns it off while you're editing an HTML document. To see for yourself, open the **Tools** menu, click **AutoCorrect**, and click the tab called **AutoFormat As You Type**. The **Define Styles Based On Your Formatting** check box has been cleared while you work with a Web page.

It's not advised to try defining new styles while creating Web pages, since the actual styles will not be converted to HTML. Only formatting associated with the supported HTML styles will be saved. Formatting that's not supported by HTML won't be converted.

Convert Existing Word 97 Documents to Web Page [HTML] Format

You can take any of your existing documents and convert them to the format of Web pages. This will be a great revelation when you start building your own Web site in the next chapter. You don't have to worry about the formatting of the document—the conversion process will keep what it can, then delete the formatting it can't convert.

You won't hurt yourself or your friends trying this. Just open the existing Word 97 document, open the **File** menu, and click the **Save As** command. In the Save As dialog box, click to open the **Save As Type** box and choose HTML Document. An HTML document is a Web page.

When you save a Word 97 document as a Web page, your original document is closed and then it reopens in HTML format. Word displays the Web page similar to the way it will appear in a Web browser. Formatting and other items that aren't supported by HTML have now been removed from the file. Here's an idea of what kind of formatting gets lost during this conversion:

➤ Drawing objects

➤ Custom styles
  ➤ Fields from forms
  ➤ Indexes
  ➤ OLE Objects
  ➤ Paragraph formatting
  ➤ Revision Comments
  ➤ Table of authorities
  ➤ Table of contents
  ➤ Tabs

How Can You See the HTML Stuff?

Word 97 writes all the HTML code for your Web pages, so you won't have to. Each time you save your Web page, Word 97 conversion tools work hard behind the scenes to create HTML tags—the stuff a Web browser interprets to display your text, tables, horizontal lines, graphics, sounds, and videos. For instance, when you press the **Enter** key to create a new line on a Web page, it is converted to the characters <P>, called the paragraph tag, in the HTML source. Even a simple table can be made up of hundreds of these tags.

You should never find it necessary to view the HTML source as you create your Web pages, but you can view it if you like. Before viewing the HTML source, you should always save any changes to your file.

To view the HTML source, open your Web page, then open the View menu and click the **View HTML Source** command. You can also edit in this view, but only do so if you speak fluent HTML. When the excitement wears off, you can return to the normal view of your Web page by opening the View menu once again and clicking the same **View HTML Source** command to toggle off the view.

Ick! The infamous Web language called HTML.

Creative Substitutes for Tools Unavailable During Web Work

You're familiar with the many tools that are available in Word 97 while you create Web pages, including spelling and grammar checking, AutoCorrect, AutoText, tables, and so on. Some other features are customized to make Web work easier, like graphical bullets and lines. But some features just aren't there, like headers and footers for example. Web pages don't allow them. It's not a bug in Word 97, it's just that the language of the Web doesn't support these formatting capabilities.

Here's a list of some forbidden formatting tools in Web pages:

➤ Line spacing
  ➤ Margins
  ➤ Tabs
  ➤ Justified Text
  ➤ Character Spacing
  ➤ Embossed, Shadow, and Engraved Formats
  ➤ Kerning
  ➤ Text Flow Settings
  ➤ Spacing before and after paragraphs

So what do you do when you *really* need a particular formatting option? You compromise, get a little creative, and take a look at this cheat list. Here's a list of common features that aren't available when you are create Web pages, and ideas on another way to perform the task.

➤ **Columns** The standard newspaper columns aren't supported during Web creation, but you can use a table to create a two-column effect. Create a table in your Web page with two columns and only a single row. Start typing and continue to type in that row and your text will grow into a column.

➤ **Paragraph Borders** Borders around paragraphs aren't supported during Web creation, but you can place borders around graphical objects or tables. Try creating a large one-column, one-row table and type your paragraph inside. The table itself becomes the paragraph border.

➤ **Special Text Effects** Some special effects like shadows, embossed text, and engraved text aren't supported in Web pages. You could always take a picture of the text and insert it as a graphic, but that's probably too much work. Try substituting text effects that are supported on Web pages, like strikethrough, bold, italic, colored text contrasting with background coloring, and scrolling text.

➤ **Headers and Footers**   Web pages don't have headers and footers. If you're converting a Word document to HTML, the information will be preserved, but it will no longer be in a header or footer. You'll have to maintain it as normal text near the edges of your Web page. Common text near the top or bottom of your Web page, simulating headers or footers, can be included in your Web page templates to save you the time of entering it on each page.

➤ **Footnotes**   Footnotes aren't supported in Web pages, but you could substitute the formatting with horizontal lines and superscript numbering. A better solution is to convert all your footnotes to hyperlinks and use them like endnotes—click a number and you hyperlink to the reference elsewhere in the document. Click Backward to return to where you were.

➤ **Styles**   You can use styles in Web pages, but they aren't defined automatically as you type. The styles in Web pages are customized so they match the styles supported by HTML, the format for Web pages.

➤ **Cross-references**   Cross-references aren't supported in HTML, but you can manually create them using hyperlinks.

➤ **Comments and Track Changes**   Word 97's comments and track changes features aren't supported in Web pages. Instead, use strikethrough formatting to represent text that might be deleted. For comments, you can format text with the Comments style. When the document is saved as a Web page, the text will not display.

➤ **Updatable OLE Objects**   If you save a graph, chart, equation, or some other OLE object in your Web page in hopes that it stays automatically updated, forget it. Inserted objects become simple static graphics. You could use a hyperlink to go to a page you try to keep current manually, or you can simply include a reminder in the Web page that the information is current as of such-and-such a date.

Build a one-row, two-column table.

Tricky ways to create text columns in a Web page.

What a great idea for creating columns of text in a web page!

To do this, just create a simple table consisting of one row and two columns.

I suppose you could make it three columns and use the middle for spacing between these two text columns.

You might see a slight table border, but that's because I'm typing in the text right now. When I preview this page in my web browser, all table lines will be hidden. The text will appear in columns.

Type in the cells to create text columns.

Using the Web Toolbar

If you haven't noticed already, I'll tell you. Whenever you work with Web pages, there's a great new toolbar that appears. It's called the Web toolbar and you can use it anytime, including when working on normal documents. This is the toolbar that makes Word 97 look like a Web browser, with the colorful buttons and peeks at strange addresses in the long box. Here's a quick review of the new gadget.

 Back   Press to jump to the previous page.

 Forward   Press to jump to the next page.

 Stop Current Jump   Cancel a jump that is taking too long.

 Refresh Current Page   This updates the current page by reloading it.

Start Page   Press this and open the start page or home page. You can specify the start page using the Web toolbar.

 Search The Web   This button opens a search page so you can search for words or phrases.

 Favorites   You create this list of URLs—just click to go to the page. The Favorites folder contains shortcuts to files, folders, and hyperlinks you use often. Add your favorite shortcuts to the selected file, folder, or link here.

Go   This gives menu choices for setting Start and Search pages and more.

Show Only Web Toolbar   Press this to hide all toolbars except Web.

C:\webfiles\default.html   **Address**   Display complete location information by pressing this button.

The New Web Toolbar

The Web toolbar is available in all Office 97 programs to make it easy to browse through documents that contain hyperlinks. Use the Web toolbar to open a start page or a search page in your Web browser. You can also add interesting documents you find on the Web to the Favorites folder so they'll be easier to find next time. The Web toolbar keeps a list of the last 10 documents you jumped to by using either the Web toolbar or a hyperlink, so you can easily return to these documents again.

Proofing Your Web Page for Errors

Before releasing your page to the world, take care to remove any misspellings, grammatical errors, and other typos. Word 97 makes this real easy with the automated proofing tools. And see for yourself that the final product meets your approval by browsing it yourself.

Spelling and Grammar Checker

You can run the new Spelling and Grammar Checker on your Web page just like any ordinary document. Click the **Spelling and Grammar** button on the Standard toolbar. It will pick up errors in all parts of your Web page, including hyperlinks, scrolling text, and labels. And be sure to turn on the AutoText and AutoCorrect features to automatically correct common typographical errors while you type.

Preview Your Web Page

To preview your Web page, click the **Web Page Preview** button that appears on the Standard toolbar while you are in Online Layout view. This button actually tells your computer to start running whatever Web browser program you have installed, and tells it to browse this page. You'll get to see exactly what your page will look like on the Web, and there shouldn't be any surprises. For most people, the biggest corrections to be made are usually small alignments of text or graphics.

Quick Tips Before You Let It Out the Door

Who am I to call a Web page good or bad? Well, my browser and I have seen a few in our day, and we'd like to tell you about them. You'll find lots of books describing the best way to structure and design Web pages, so I'll just mention some basics. Don't forget, some of the best material—including tips, examples, and style guides—can be found on the World Wide Web. Use a Web searching tool and you'll find hundreds of hits on the words "Web style guide."

Here are a few guidelines that can be applied to most Web pages:

➤ **Get your page organized** Your home Web page should be simple and clean, not scary and wordy. The content should be organized well, moving most detail off of the home page and into subject pages. You should have clear and accurate hyperlinks taking the reader directly to sources of information they want, without wasted page stops along the way.

➤ **Use fonts and colors that are easy to read** All text in your Web pages should be easy to read. Think like Goldilocks as you add the text—not too large, not too small; not too bright, not too dark, and so on. If you add a background to your Web page, it should contrast pleasantly with the text color.

➤ **Keep your graphic size small** Large images and background textures increase the time it takes to open your Web page. Sure, you might think good graphics (and lots of them) make your Web pages more interesting, but your reader might not wait to see them if it takes minutes to load your page. Find or convert your graphic files so they take up less room, like simple line drawings, smaller-sized graphics, fewer colors, and so on. A good graphic photo editor comes with Word 97 and does this kind of conversion.

➤ **Provide alternative text for graphics and tables**   Some users turn off the display of images in their browsers, and some Web browsers don't even support viewing tables. You should always include some alternate text for graphics, videos, and tables if they contain essential information, so your poor reader can still read the information you wish to convey.

Keep Your Tools Up-to-Date Using Microsoft's Web Page

Microsoft suggests that all of the Web authoring tools included in Word 97 may be updated periodically to keep up with changing Web technology. Microsoft Word 97 can automatically check to see if a new version of any tool is available. All you need is access to the Internet. The first time you connect to this free service, Word 97 will automatically check for the latest version of all tools. You'll be provided a listing of the latest versions of current tools, and you can decide which to download. You don't have to download all of them now; you can go back for the latest versions at any time. After you accept the offer, Word 97 downloads and installs the latest files on your computer.

Download Current Web Authoring Tools

Check for new versions of your Web tools today! Open the **Tools** menu, point to **AutoUpdate**, and choose **Web Tools**. The Internet connection will be made and a list of updates are provided. To download the latest version, click the **Yes** button.

Download More Web Templates and Forms

Sometimes you get the most current Web page template without realizing it. Several of the forms and templates you see in the New dialog box (Web Pages) are actually hyperlinks to the actual template on the Microsoft Web site. That way you're guaranteed to have the latest and greatest templates and forms when you need them.

Open the **File** menu, click **New**, and then click the **Web Pages** tab. Click to select and activate the hyperlinks for forms and templates. Be sure to check for updates to the Web Page Wizard. Double-click to select it, the click the **Browse Online** button to access the Microsoft Web Site. Click the right mouse button, point to **Hyperlink**, and then click **Save As**. Provide a name and store in a folder that you'll remember.

The Least You Need to Know

Maintaining your Web page is easier if you use Word 97 Web authoring tools. This chapter reviewed how to use these tools.

Can Word 97 create a table in my Web page?

Yes, you can create tables fast, even on a Web page, using the **Insert Table** button on the Standard toolbar. Use it the same way you create a table in a Word document. And if you feel artistic, you can even draw a custom table by hand using the new drawing tools of Word 97.

Why can't I place a graphic and text side-by-side on my Web page?

You can; it just takes some creativity. Create a one-row, two-column table, then type inside of one cell and paste a graphic in another.

Can I convert my existing Word 97 documents to HTML format?

Easily. You can convert any existing document into a Web page by opening the **File** menu, clicking **Save As**, and changing the document type to **HTML Document**.

Do I need to convert my Web page back to a Word document to check the spelling and grammar?

No, just click the **Spelling and Grammar** button on the Standard toolbar. It works just as you expect on your new Web pages.

How can I keep my Word 97 Web authoring tools current?

The World Wide Web standards are being continuously updated. Microsoft helps you stay current by providing the latest updated version of Word 97 Web authoring tools on its Web site, and you can download them at **www.microsoft.com**.

Chapter 25

Testing and Publishing Your Web Page on Your Intranet

In This Chapter

➤ Organizing all your Web files

➤ Managing hyperlinks

➤ Providing graphic and video alternatives

➤ Testing your Web page with a browser

➤ Saving your pages to a Web server

Creating your own Web site is no longer a big deal—you can do it today with your own computer, and this chapter will show you how. Of course, it helps if you are connected to an intranet, or the really big one—the Internet—because then others can visit your site. Whether you use your Web personally to learn or manage your files, or publicly as part of your business, you can start building and connecting Web pages now. Give it a try, and see if you can make it to the Top 10 Web Sites today!

Growing Beyond Your Home Page

First, congratulate yourself for getting this far. Creating a Web page is no small feat, and by using Word 97 Web authoring tools, even your first page can look as good as professional Web sites.

But now you want to expand and grow. A one-page Web site gets a little boring after you've seen it once. You can create lots of pages containing a wealth of information for your readers. Once you grow beyond a few pages you should take steps to organize your work. That way your Web site can continue to grow without putting a strain on your time to manage and maintain the growth.

Plan and Organize Your Web Pages

If your Web site will contain several pages, it's a good idea to plan ahead how readers will navigate among your pages by sketching out how users will jump from one page to another. For example, your first page might have headings called Our Catalog or My Phone Directory, which could be your second and third Web page. The Catalog page might reference a few different Departments, which also have their own page. By sketching your whole plan first, you can organize your Web site in your head before getting tangled in the Web creation process.

Using similar graphics and layout, tie your pages together and create a professional look. Using common elements helps people who visit your site know they haven't followed a hyperlink to someone else's site. The themes provided in the Web Page Wizard can help you create a consistent look.

Storing Your Web Parts in Folders

A Web page is made up of all sorts of things. If you created your Web page file in a new folder, take a peek and see how many files are there. Besides the actual page file, you'll find picture files, sound and video files, background color files, texture files, and more. You even find little bullet files, containing nothing more than the bullet graphic that appears on your page. Hey, this is Web language.

I don't have to tell you all of this starts taking up lots of space and gets difficult to manage. One way to manage the amount of files is to limit the number of pages in a given folder, and create as many subfolders in your Web folder as you need.

Check This Out...

Organize Your Web Folders

Your Web folder should contain subfolders to hold and organize all your Web pages by the subject matter they contain. You might have a Status Reports folder that holds all status documents, or a Catalog subfolder that holds many Department subfolders, which in turn hold your department catalog documents.

Tuning Your Web Page for High Performance

Even on a good day, the Internet isn't fast enough for us. The biggest bottleneck is usually your connection to the Internet, and that's what all of your Web pages files have to fit through. If you're mathematically inclined, your could add up the file sizes of all components on your Web page, and if it's a big number, Web browser viewing will be slow. The best thing you can do to improve performance of your Web page is to keep the file size down. Here are some tips to show you how:

➤ To decrease the file size of graphics, use fewer colors, shrink the size down, or convert it to a format that uses less space (JPEGs are much smaller than BMP or PCX, and the picture looks the same). You can use a graphics program (such as Photo Editor that's included with Microsoft Office 97) to edit any of your graphic or image files, or save them in a different format.

➤ You can also repeat the same graphic or image whenever possible on your page. For example, when you use the same graphic for a bullet inside all your Web pages, the image is downloaded only once, even if it appears on several pages. This can save lots of little bits of time.

➤ A video that's a few seconds long can take several minutes (or longer) to download on a slow computer, slow link, or slow Internet day. To decrease the file size of videos, you can consider black-and-white instead of color, reduce the height or width of the video, edit unneeded material, use fewer panels, and use file compression. And of course, instead of putting a video on your home page, choose a single frame and use it as a thumbnail hyperlink to the actual file. Your readers will thank you.

Your Home Page (A.K.A. default.htm)

Once you have more than a few Web pages, names become very important. Use good names for your pages, so you don't have to open them to know what they are. This makes creating hyperlinks much faster.

Word 97 places no limits on what you can name your files. Instead of WEB1.HTM, WEB2.HTM, and so on, use meaningful names such as CATALOG.HTM or POLICY1.HTM. If you plan to use your own computer as the final storage area of your Web site, feel free to use extended names such as Catalog of Women's Fall Fashion.HTM. It makes it easier on you and works just fine. If, however, you plan on submitting your files to another computer, Web server, or Internet service provider, it's best to stick to the old eight-dot-three naming convention. That's names limited to eight characters, to guarantee another computer won't have problems connecting all your links. It's a little more work on your part, since shorter names like FALLCATW.HTM are tougher to remember.

You're free to name your pages anything you want, and a common name for the home page (you should only have one) is DEFAULT.HTM (or INDEX.HTM, or possibly something else conforming to your Web server's default requirement). If you point a browser at a folder containing a file of this name, it will automatically display a file called DEFAULT.HTM. If your Web home page isn't named that now, you can rename it. Take extra care when you rename any Web files—you don't want to accidentally change the extension (those letters after the dot), or a browser may get confused.

Start Your Web Page

You can click the **Start Page** button on the Web toolbar to choose this page as the first one that appears when you start your Web browser.

You can also change your start page in your browser. To change your start page, go to the page you want to appear when you first start Microsoft Internet Explorer. Open the **View** menu and click **Options**. Cslick the Navigation tab, and then click **Use Current**. If you change your mind and want to restore your original start page, click **Use Default**.

If you use Netscape Navigator as your browser, this start page is called the Home Page. To change your home page in Navigator, open the **Options** menu and select **General Preferences**. Click the **Appearance** tab to see the options. In the Browser Starts With text box, enter the address of the Web page you want to use as your home page, and then click **OK**.

Creating Lots of Important Web Pages Fast

You know what's important to your little area of the world, whether it's your address book, finances, business reports, running a whole company, or even running a government. You should know—you've been doing it long enough. You've probably amassed zillions of tons of paperwork, and wouldn't it be great if you could harness that information that's already created? You can! And I'll tell you how!

Convert It, Don't Retype It!

Creating massive amounts of Web pages shouldn't come as that much of a surprise to you, especially if you've seen government Web pages. They're very good, containing literally thousands of pages, and did you think that someone created each Web page from scratch? It's more than likely that they converted existing documents into Web pages.

So gather up all the important paperwork that constitutes what you would like to add to your Web page. Prioritize it so you can start with only the most important. Now determine if you've got these documents in soft copy (*hard copy* equals paper, *soft copy* equals computer file). If not, you'll need to use a scanner to convert them to computer files, and then into Word documents. You can import them following the directions in Chapter 15.

Once you've got your computer full of Word documents, you can quickly open them and save each as an HTML document (open the **File** menu, click **Save As**, and save as type **HTML Document**). The first few words in your document will be used as the name of the document, unless you change it. Giving it a good name is extremely important, because you want to identify your pages without having to open them. It also makes for faster hyperlinking, because you'll know instantly what a file is, instead of wasting time opening it. Don't forget to store each new HTML document in the appropriate folder you created to keep yourself organized.

It's easy to convert existing Word documents to Web pages.

Managing Your Hyperlinks

Now that you have your documents converted into HTML format, and they are named and stored in an organized fashion, you can link them all together with hyperlinks. You learned this process in Chapter 23; now we put it to good use.

An Anchor in Each Web Page Harbor

In each subfolder of your Web site, it helps to create a single document that points to all the other documents stored in this particular subfolder. Maybe an existing document can already serve this purpose, like an Overview document in your Policies folder, or a Summary statement in your budget folder. You can get creative in creating these anchor documents, such as creating a Calendar document in your Status Reports folder.

Once you've got your anchor documents in each subfolder, open them up and create hyperlinks to all the documents in that subfolder. For example, open the Calendar document in your Status Reports folder, and click to choose the particular day a status report was created. Then click the Hyperlink button on the Standard toolbar and choose the appropriate document as the destination in your subfolder. Be sure to save your pages often during Web work.

Once you finish pointing to all documents in that subfolder, visit each document by clicking the hyperlink. In addition to testing your link for accuracy, you also need to add the return hyperlink. Click the Hyperlink button and add a link back to your anchor document for this subfolder.

Then Link Them All to the Home Page

After you've created working anchor pages in all the subfolders of your Web folder, it's time to tie them all together. In your Web folder, find the document that represents your home page. It should be saved as DEFAULT.HTM (or INDEX.HTM, depending on your Web server requirements) to be consistent with Web standards. Open this home page and locate where you want to place each hyperlink to your subfolder pages. Create a single link to each subfolder by choosing the anchor page as the destination. Save your work and then test it. As you connect to each page, create a hyperlink back to your home page, so it's easy for your reader to navigate your Web site.

To test your pages, click the **Web Page Preview** button that's available during the creation of any HTML document. You can also open your Web browser directly (be sure to type your home page address in the Address box). Try clicking all of your hyperlinks to be certain they take the reader where you expect. If not, edit your hyperlinks with a right-click, point to Hyperlink, and choose Edit Hyperlink. Sometimes it's easier just to delete a wayward hyperlink and try again.

Now sit back and enjoy your masterpiece! Your Web site is now ready for the real world.

Relative Versus Absolute Hyperlink Addresses

When building Web pages, you should plan the hyperlinks so they'll continue to work no matter where your Web page folder is stored, especially if you plan to publish on an intranet or the World Wide Web. In many cases, the location where you create your Web pages (your computer) will be different than the location in which they will be published (a Web server).

When all the materials you create hyperlinks to (like bullets, graphics, buttons, background textures, and other Web pages) will be published on the same Web server, you should probably use relative hyperlinks. This means the destination is relative to your home page. For example, the *absolute* address for files you are creating might be C:\WEBFILES\REPORTS\, while the same *relative* address is simply \REPORTS, which means you can store the home page on any drive, in any folder, and the hyperlinks will continue to find the files. Using relative hyperlinks makes it easier to move materials to another location, for instance, when it's time to move your Web Web development folders to the Web server. If you move the files or send them on disk to someone, you should maintain the same file structure, including all subfolders.

Hyperlinks in your pages connecting to other Web sites, like when you want to provide a list of your favorite Web sites for others to try, should typically use Absolute Hyperlinks that include the full path name, or URL. To indicate an absolute, or fixed location, when creating your hyperlinks, remove the check from the **Use Relative Path For Hyperlink** check box in the Insert Hyperlink dialog box.

Publishing Your Web Pages

Publish is the term used when you make your Web pages available to others. This might mean connecting your computer to a network and sharing your Web folder, submitting them to your site coordinator for posting onto a Web server, or sending them to an outside service provider that specializes in maintaining your site on the Web. Word 97 helps you get ready for the big event.

But It Doesn't Look the Same

Your Web page may not appear the same way to all people who view it, because some visitors may be viewing your pages with different Web browsers, possibly using different operating systems. While browsers support the same language, HTML, there are some differences among browsers. You should design a layout that will be readable by the majority of visitors expected to visit your site.

Sharing Your Web Folder

You can begin to publish your Web page now, if you happen to be connected to a local area network (LAN) or an intranet. You can set your Web folder to be shared on the network, and then users can connect to it.

Since we are going to be working with files and folders on your computer, we will use the Windows Explorer that can be found by clicking the Start button in either Windows 95 or Windows NT, pointing to Programs, and choosing the Explorer command. With Explorer open, locate your Web files folder. Right click the folder and choose the Sharing command that appears on the shortcut menu. Give your shared folder a name, then make sure the Access Type is set to **Read-Only**, so others can't make changes to your Web pages. Click **OK** and announce to your friends that your Web site is open for business!

Now other users on your network can use their Network Neighborhood icon to first connect a drive to your shared folder (for instance, the drive letter G), then use their Web browser to view your home page. Instead of worrying about what URL to type, they can reach your page by using their Windows Explorer. They start Explorer, open up the drive they just connected with Network Neighborhood (drive G, for example), click on the shared folder that will now be visible to them, then double-click on the name of your home page. Their Web browser will start automatically (if it's not already open) and your Web page will appear in all its splendor.

Sharing is another way to access Web pages on a network.

A quick way to protect all your Web files is Read-Only.

Click this button to manage a shared folder like a Web server.

Be sure to protect your Web files before making them public.

Or you can protect only specific Web file types.

Use this section to allow others to send Web updates to you.

Placing Your Pages on a Web Server

You'll soon experience the disadvantages of having your Web site stored on your own computer. It disappears when you shut your computer off! To publish your pages so that other people on the World Wide Web can see them all the time, you need to place them on a Web server. Perhaps you're creating pages for your company, which might already have Web servers established. In this case, you just need to find out from the Webmaster, or the person who manages the servers, where to place your pages. Your Webmaster will copy your entire Web files folder to a Web server, and then tell you how to reach it. Start your Web browser and point to that location. If you want to update your Web files, you'll probably involve your Webmaster.

Sending Your Web Files to a Service Provider on the Web

To publish your Web pages on the Internet, you either need to locate an Internet Service Provider (ISP) that hosts (provides storage space for) Web pages, or you need to create your own Web server. The easiest way is to locate a service that hosts personal Web pages. It's a good idea to ask about limitations, such as the total amount of disk space allowed for your files. If you plan to use graphics, forms, and multimedia, you may want to ensure your Web page service permits these features, since they involve additional maintenance.

Once you've negotiated your own Web site, you'll need to deliver all the Web pages you've created. Be sure to keep the folder and subfolder hierarchy intact, and be sure to copy all the required files. You can save them to disk, or copy them electronically to your Provider using the instructions they provide.

351

Saving Your Pages Directly to a Web Server

Here's a method to deliver your pages directly to a Web server. It's also a great way to update your pages as needed. To do this, your company must have an intranet or you must have access to an Internet site that supports saving files, and you must have access rights to save files to that site.

Open the updated Web page file and be sure to save all changes. Open the **File** menu and click **Save As**. In the **Save In** box, click **Internet Locations (FTP)**. In the list of FTP sites, double-click the site you want, and then double-click the location at the site where you want to save the document. You'll probably want to keep the filename the same to maintain any hyperlinks in the document. Click the **Save** button and the file will be sent.

If your list of FTP locations is empty, you can add to it now. Open the **File** menu, click **Save As**, and in the Save In box, choose **Add/Modify FTP Location**. In this dialog box you can enter the FTP destination, including a password if it's required. You can add as many as you need, and if your company has an intranet Web server, check to see if it also has an FTP address, then include it here.

Check This Out...

Set the Language for Your Web Page

When you are authoring a Web page, you can encode it so that it will display the proper fonts from a specific language. To do this, open the **Tools** menu, point to **Document Encoding**, and click the **Language** you want. When you save HTML documents, be sure to click **Set Save Encoding**, and then specify the language you want. If the **Preserve Original Document Encoding** box is checked, the default setting won't apply to documents that have no prior language coding.

Browse Your Web Page!

Time to have some fun and view your Web pages! Open your Web browser to find your home page. When you start a World Wide Web browser, the *start page* is the first page you see. You can set this location to any Web site you want or to a document on your computer hard disk. To set your start page, you must have Microsoft Internet Explorer installed, or you must have Microsoft Word 97 installed with Web page authoring tools.

To set your start page to your Web site's home page, you first must find it manually by typing the URL in the Address box. Once your page appears, you can save it as the start page. To save the current Web page as your start page, click the **Go** button and choose the **Set Start Page** command. Save the current page location. From now on, you can open your start page from the Web toolbar by clicking the **Start Page** button.

One method of sending Web page updates to your Web server.

Click here to send the Web page to an FTP site.

Post Web page updates to your intranet Web server.

You can include your own company's Web server here.

When you change the start page by using the Web toolbar in an Office program, the new start page used in your Office programs is also used in your World Wide Web browser as long as the browser is compatible with Office.

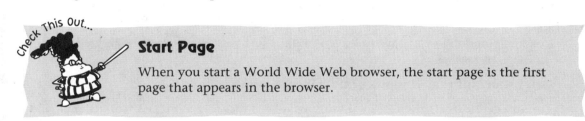

Check This Out...

Start Page

When you start a World Wide Web browser, the start page is the first page that appears in the browser.

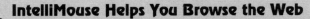

Check This Out...

IntelliMouse Helps You Browse the Web

The IntelliMouse can make it easier to perform these functions with the Microsoft Internet Explorer:

➤ **Hyperlink jumps** You can jump to any hyperlink by pointing to it, and then "datazooming" forward. To datazoom, you press and hold down the Shift key while rotating the wheel button. To return to the previous topic, datazoom back by rotating in the opposite direction.

➤ **Scrolling** You can scroll through a Web page by rotating the wheel button forward or back.

➤ **Panning** You can continuously scroll through the current Web page by holding down the wheel button while moving the mouse.

The Least You Need to Know

After you've created your Web site, it's time to publish it for the world to see! This chapter helped you get ready for the big day with additional productivity tips.

Is there a method of organizing Web page documents?

If you plan to have many Web pages, it's important to stay organized to control the many pages. Start with a single folder for your home page, then add folders underneath. Use folders to store similar pages.

How can I ensure that my hyperlinks work correctly?

Be sure to test them. Get the hyperlinks right the first time—always provide hyperlinks back from where you came, use relative addressing when you can, save often, and test them again before your friends see it.

How can I speed up my Web page?

You can speed up Web pages by providing text alternatives to graphics, videos, and sound.

Is there an easy way to see how my Web page will look with a browser?

Yes, and you don't even have to leave Word 97. Just click the **Web Page Preview** button on the Web toolbar.

Can I really turn my computer into a Web server?

You can get nearly that effect by sharing your Web files folder on a LAN or intranet, and having your coworkers point their Web browsers (or Word 97) to your folder. Or, you can send them to a real Web server and have everyone in the world look at them.

Speak Like a Geek: The Complete Archive

The word processing world is like an exclusive club, complete with its own language. If you want to be accepted, you need to learn some of the lingo. This glossary will help you get started.

accelerator keys   Keys which activate a command without opening the menu. Usually a function key or a key combination (such as Alt+F10) is displayed next to the menu command. To use an accelerator key, hold down the first key while you press the second key.

active document   The document you are currently working in. The active document contains the insertion point, and if more than one document window is being displayed onscreen, the active document's title bar appears darker than the other title bars.

add-ins   Document templates that automate the creation process. You can use existing templates as an add-in, design your own add-ins, or purchase add-ins created by other companies for use in Word 97.

alignment   How text in a paragraph is placed between left and right margins. For example, you may select left-aligned or centered text.

ASCII file   A file containing characters that can be used by any program on any computer. Sometimes called a text file or an ASCII text file. (ASCII is pronounced "ASK-EEE.")

border   A line placed on any (or all) four sides of a block of text, a graphic, a chart, or a table.

bulleted list   A list similar to a numbered list made up of a series of paragraphs with hanging indents, where the bullet (usually a symbol such as a dot or check mark) is placed to the left of all the other lines in the paragraph. A bulleted list is often used to display a list of items or to summarize important points.

cell   The box formed by the intersection of a row and a column in a Word table. The same term is used when describing the intersection of a row and a column in a spreadsheet. A cell may contain text, a numeric value, or a formula.

click   The single press or the release of the mouse button after you have moved the mouse pointer over an object or an icon.

clip art   A collection of prepackaged artwork whose individual pieces can be placed in a document.

Clipboard   A temporary storage area that holds text and graphics. The Cut and Copy commands put text or graphics on the Clipboard, erasing the Clipboard's previous contents. The Paste command copies Clipboard data to a document.

columns   Vertical sections of tables. See also *newspaper-style columns*.

command   An order that tells the computer what to do. In command-driven programs, you have to press a specific key or type the command to execute it. With menu-driven programs, you select the command from a menu.

cropping   The process of cutting away part of an imported graphic.

cursor   The vertical line that appears to the right of characters as you type. A cursor acts like the tip of your pencil; anything you type appears at the cursor. See also *insertion point*.

data source   A special document file that contains information (such as names and addresses) that is later merged with another document to produce form letters or mailing labels.

desktop publishing   A program that allows you to combine text and graphics on the same page, and manipulate text and graphics onscreen. Desktop publishing programs are commonly used to create newsletters, brochures, flyers, résumés, and business cards.

dialog box   A special window or box that appears when the program requires additional information prior to executing a command.

disk drive   A device that writes and reads data on a magnetic disk. Think of a disk drive as a cassette recorder/player. Just as the cassette player can record sounds on a magnetic cassette tape and play back those sounds, a disk drive can record data on a magnetic disk and play back that data.

document   Any work you create using an application program and save in a file on disk. Although the term document usually refers to work created in a word processing program (such as a letter or a chapter of a book), a document is now used to refer to any work, including spreadsheets and databases.

Document map   A new view in Word 97 that displays a column of document headings on the left, allowing you to quickly browse the structure of a document.

document window   A window which frames the controls and information for the document file you are working on. You may have multiple document windows open at one time.

double-click   Pressing and releasing the mouse button twice in quick succession after you move the mouse pointer over an object or icon.

drag   Pressing and holding the mouse button when moving the mouse pointer from a starting to an ending position.

drop cap   An option used to set off the first letter in a paragraph. The letter is enlarged and set into the text of the paragraph, at its upper-left corner. Word calls this letter a dropped capital.

edit   To make changes to existing information within a document. Editing in a word processor usually involves spellchecking, grammar checking, and making formatting changes until the document is judged to be complete.

embedded object   An object that maintains a connection to the application that created it, so that if changes are needed, you can access that application by double-clicking on the object. An embedded object is stored within your Word document.

end mark   Mark designating the end of the document. As you enter text, this mark will move down.

field   Part of a file record containing a single piece of information (for example, a telephone number, ZIP code, or a person's name). A field is also a code inserted into a document which is updated when the document is opened, such as the Date field.

file   The computer term for your document. Anything can be placed in a file: a memo, budget report, graphics images. Each document you create in Word 97 is stored in its own file. Files have file names to identify them.

floppy disk drive   A disk drive that uses floppy disks.

floppy disks   Small, portable, plastic squares that magnetically store data (the facts, figures, and documents you enter and save). You insert the floppy disk into the floppy disk drive. See also *disk drive*.

folder   A place to store documents. Folders can exist on disks or hard drives, and folders can be stored inside other folders. Before Windows 95, folders were known as *subdirectories*.

font   Any set of characters which share the same typeface (style or design). Fonts convey the mood and style of a document. Technically, font describes the combination of the typeface and point size of a character (as in Times Roman 12-point), but in common use, it describes a character's style or typeface.

footer   Text that can be reprinted at the bottom of every page within a document. Footers appear in the lower margins of a document.

footnote A place to store extended detailed information referenced in the main body of a document. Footnotes usually appear above the lower margin and reference the location by using matching superscript numbers.

formatting Changing the look of a character (by making it bold, underlined, and slightly larger, for example), a paragraph (by centering it on a page, indenting it, or numbering it), or a page (changing margins, page numbers, or paper orientation).

Formatting toolbar A set of buttons and commands arranged in a single bar that provide an easy method for changing the appearance of text within Word 97.

FTP Short for *File Transfer Protocol*, a set of rules that governs the transfer of files between computers. You can download files from the Internet with an FTP program.

function keys The 10 or 12 F keys on the left side of the keyboard or the 12 F keys on the top of the keyboard. F keys are numbered F1, F2, F3, and so on. These keys are used to enter various commands in the Word 97 program.

Gopher An indexing system that allows you to access various Internet services by selecting menu options. Menu options can take you to submenus of additional options, other Gopher sites, FTP sites, newsgroup sites, or other servers, until you find the information you want.

Grammar Checker A special program within Word 97 that reviews your grammar and offers suggestions on improving it. This feature is now combined with the Spelling Checker, and can be set to automatically check grammar as you type your document. See also *Spelling and Grammar Checker*.

graphic A picture which can be imported into Word in order to illustrate a particular point.

gutter An unused region of space that runs down the inside edges of facing pages of a document; it's the part of each page that is used when the pages of a book or a magazine are bound together.

handles Small black squares that surround a graphic or text box after it is selected. Handles can be dragged to change the size or shape of a graphic.

hanging indent A special kind of indent in which the first line of a paragraph hangs closer to the left margin than the rest of the lines in the paragraph. It is typically used for bulleted or numbered lists.

hard drive A nonremovable disk drive that stores many megabytes or gigabytes of information. Because it is fixed in place inside the computer (see *disk drive*), it performs more quickly and efficiently than a floppy disk.

header Text that can be reprinted at the top of every page within a document.

home page The first Web page providing the entrance to a Web site.

HTML   Short for *HyperText Markup Language*, the programming language used for creating Web pages.

HTTP   Short for *HyperText Transfer Protocol*, a set of rules that govern the exchange of information between a Web host and a client (a Web browser on your computer). The address for every Web server starts with **http**.

Hyperlink   A jump to a location in the same document or another file represented by colored and underlined text, or by a graphic. You click a hyperlink to jump to a file, a location in a file, an HTML page on the World Wide Web, or an HTML page on an intranet.

icon   A small graphic image that represents another object, such as a program or a tool.

indent   The amount of distance from the page margins to the edges of your paragraph (or the first line of a paragraph).

Insert mode   The default typing mode for most word processors and text editors. Insert mode means that when you position your cursor and start to type, what you type is inserted at that point, and existing text is pushed to the right.

insertion point   A blinking vertical line used in Word 97 to indicate the place where any characters you type will be inserted.

intelligent field   Text within a Word document that is updated automatically as changes are made. Some intelligent fields, such as the date and time fields, are updated when the document is opened or printed.

IntelliMouse   A mouse that includes a wheel between the buttons that you can spin with your finger. Using this wheel in Word 97 allows you to scroll, zoom, and pan documents easily.

Internet   The world's largest system of interconnected computer networks. Originally developed for university and military communication, the current Internet is used mostly by private individuals for exchanging electronic mail, finding information, education, and entertainment.

intranet   A small version of the Internet, usually private and designed for the business needs of a single company, using the popular tools of the Internet (like Web browsers and search engines) for employee access to company information. Intranets are typically *not* directly connected to the Internet in order to maintain higher performance, controlled access to information, and security of information.

kilobyte   A unit for measuring the amount of data. A kilobyte (K) is equivalent to 1,024 bytes.

landscape orientation   Your document is oriented so that it is wider than it is long, as in 11-by-8^1/$_2$ inches. The opposite of landscape orientation is portrait.

leader   Dots or dashes that fill the spaces between tab positions in a list.

linked object   An imported object (such as a graphic) that maintains a connection to the program that created it, so that if changes are made to that object, those changes can be updated (either automatically or through a command) into your document. A linked object is stored separately from your Word document.

links   Also known as hyperlinks, these are icons, pictures, or highlighted text that connect one source of information to another, including locations of information in other documents, other programs, graphic, sound or video files, and Internet sites.

macro   A recorded set of instructions for a frequently used task which can be activated by pressing a specified key combination. Macros resemble small programs.

margin   An area on the left, right, top, and bottom sides of a page that is usually left blank. Text flows between the margins of a page.

megabyte   A standard unit used to measure the storage capacity of a disk and the amount of computer memory. A megabyte is 1,048,576 bytes (1,000 kilobytes). This is roughly equivalent to 500 pages of double-spaced text. Megabyte is commonly abbreviated as M, MB, or Mbyte.

memory   Electronic storage area inside the computer, used to store data or program instructions temporarily when the computer is using them. The computer's memory is erased when the power to the computer is turned off.

menu   A list of commands or instructions displayed on the screen. Menus organize commands and make a program easier to use.

menu bar   A bar located at the top of the program window. This displays a list of the names of menus which contain the commands you'll use to edit documents.

merging   The process of combining information stored in a data source (such as names and addresses) with a main document (such as a form letter) in order to produce a series of form letters or mailing labels.

Mirror margins   An option you can use when creating magazine-like reports. When open, the pages of your report would face each other.

mouse   A device that moves an arrow (or other pointing symbols) around the screen. When you move the mouse, the pointer on the screen moves in the same direction. Used instead of the keyboard to select and move items (such as text and graphics), execute commands, and perform other tasks. A mouse gets its name because it connects to your computer through a long "tail," or cord.

mouse pointer   An arrow or other symbol that moves when the mouse is moved. When the mouse pointer is over text, it changes to a large I-shaped symbol. When the mouse pointer is over an element on the screen, it usually takes the shape of an arrow.

mouse wheel   The wheel located between the buttons on the Microsoft IntelliMouse. You can spin this wheel with your finger to scroll, zoom, and pan Word 97 documents easily.

multimedia   The general term used to describe information that we observe using more than one of our five senses, particularly sound and motion. Documents containing multimedia might include animated graphics, sound effects, and motion picture video.

newspaper-style columns   Similar to the column style found in newspapers. Text in these columns flows between invisible boundaries down one part of the page. At the end of the page, the text continues at the top of the first column on the next page. Columns can be "interrupted" by graphics (pictures or charts) that illustrate the story being told.

numbered list   Similar to a bulleted list. A numbered list is a series of paragraphs with hanging indents, where the number is placed to the left of all other lines in the paragraph. A numbered list is often used to list the steps of a procedure in the proper order.

Online Layout   A new view in Word 97 that displays the formatting of a Web page.

Overtype mode   The opposite of Insert mode that is used in word processors and text editors. Overtype mode means that when you position your cursor and start to type, what you type replaces existing characters at that point.

page break   A dotted line which marks the end of a page. A page break can be forced within a document by pressing Ctrl+Enter.

pane   What Word 97 calls the special boxes that you use when adding headers, footers, and comments. In Normal view, a pane appears in the bottom half of the document window. (Since it's part of a window—rather than being a separate box like a dialog box—it's called a pane.)

paragraph   Any grouping of words that should be treated as a unit. This includes normal paragraphs as well as single-line paragraphs (such as chapter titles, section headings, and captions for charts or other figures). When you press the Enter key in Word 97, you are marking the end of a paragraph. (Note: Some computers call the Enter key Return.)

passive voice   A type of sentence that states what is done by (or to) the subject, rather than what the subject does (active voice). For example, compare "The race was won by our team" (passive voice) to the same phrase in active voice: "Our team won the race."

point, point to   To move the mouse pointer so that it is on top of a specific object on the screen.

point size   The type size of a particular character. There are 72 points in an inch. Font families usually have only certain point sizes available; if you need larger or smaller letters than your font offers, switch to a different font.

portrait orientation   Your document is oriented so that it is longer than it is wide, as in $8^1/_2$-by-11 inches. This is the normal orientation of most documents. The opposite of portrait orientation is landscape.

pull-down menu   A type of menu containing selections for a Main menu command. Pull-down menus are activated by clicking them, and the menu appears similar to the way a window shade can be pulled down from the top of a window frame.

readability index   A measure of the educational level a reader would need to understand easily the text in a given document. It is determined by counting the average number of words per sentence, and the average number of characters per word. A good average is about 17 words per sentence. The capability to assess the readability of your document is a feature built into Word 97.

record   In a data file, a record is a collection of related information contained in one or more fields, such as an individual's name, address, and phone number.

Restore button   The middle button found in the Title bar located in the top-right corner of all windows in Windows 95 or NT. The picture on the button (called the icon) is two small cascaded windows. When you press the Restore button, a window is restored to its previous size, and the Restore button changes into the Maximize button.

ruler   The thin bar in Word 97 that makes it easy to set tabs, stops, indentations, and margins.

scaling   The process of resizing a graphic so it does not lose its proportions.

scroll   To change the portion of a document you are viewing on the screen. Scrolling moves text up or down, or to the right or left on the screen.

scroll bars   Bars located along the bottom and right sides of the document window. Use scroll bars to display other areas of the document. To scroll around a document, you can either click the arrow boxes on either end of the scroll bar, click on either side of the scroll box, or drag the scroll box within the scroll bar.

scroll box   The moving square in the scroll bar that tells you roughly where you are within your document. If you click on the scroll box with the left mouse button, the current page number will be displayed.

section   A part of a document that has different settings from the main document (for such things as margins, paper size, headers, footers, columns, and page numbering). A section can be any length: several pages, several paragraphs, or even a single line (such as a heading).

Selection bar   This invisible area runs along the left side of the document window. It provides a quick way for you to select a section of the text that you want to edit.

selection letters   A single letter of a menu command, such as the *x* in Exit, which activates the command when the menu is open and you press the key for that letter.

shading   The box of gray that is placed behind text or behind a cell in a table in order to emphasize it.

shared document   A document set up to allow a group of users to access and modify it.

shortcut menu   A small pop-up menu that appears when you point at an object and click the right mouse button. Shortcut menus contain commands that are specific to the object you're pointing at. For example, if you point to a block of text and click the right mouse button, you'll see a shortcut menu for copying, moving, and formatting text. Shortcut menus are also referred to as context-sensitive menus because they sometimes change based on what you are doing.

Shrink to Fit   If only a small amount of text appears on the last page of a short document, you may be able to reduce the number of pages with this feature. In order to shrink the document, Word decreases the font size of each font used in the document.

software   Programs that tell your computer (the hardware) what to do. There are two types of software: operating system software and application software. Operating system software (such as Windows 95 or Windows NT) gets your computer up and running. Application software (like Word 97) allows you to do something useful, such as type a letter.

Spelling and Grammar Checker   A special program within Word 97 that assists you in correcting spelling and grammar errors within a document. In Word 97, misspelled words are underlined with a red wavy line; grammar errors are underlined with a green wavy line.

split bar   Located on the right side of a document window; when you double-click on this bar, the window splits vertically into two smaller windows called panes.

Standard toolbar   One of the most often used toolbars because it contains the most commonly used commands (such as opening, saving, and printing a document) in button form.

status bar   Located at the bottom of the program window, the status bar displays miscellaneous information about your document, such as the page and section number, the current line and column number location of the insertion point, and the new spell checker status icon.

style   A collection of specifications for formatting text. A style may include information for the font, size, margins, and spacing to a section of text. When you apply a style to a block of text, you format it automatically (according to the style's specifications).

Style Area   An area that can be made to appear at the far-left side of the Word 97 screen, and that displays the name for the style of every paragraph in a document.

tab   A keystroke that moves the cursor to a specified point. Tabs are used to indent paragraphs or align columns of text.

table   Used to organize large amounts of data in rows and columns. Tables consist of rows (horizontal) and columns (vertical). The intersection of a row and column is called a cell.

template   Defines the Word environment, such as margin settings, page orientation, and so on. The template also controls which menu commands are available and which buttons are located on the various toolbars. Word 97 comes with over 30 additional templates (and hundreds more from the Microsoft Web page) you can use to create specialized documents. If you are using one of these templates, your screen may look different from the ones shown in this book. Also, you may have additional commands available on the menus.

text area   The main part of the document window. This is where the text you type will appear.

text box   A drawing object that takes advantage of the Word 97 Art features, such as 3-D effects, fills, backgrounds, text rotation, sizing, and cropping. Used as an invisible container to position text or graphics at a specific location in a document, or to make text flow around other text and drawing objects.

text file   A type of file that contains no special formatting (such as bold), but simply letters, numbers, and such. See also *ASCII file*.

toolbar   A bar across the screen that presents the most common Word commands in an easy-to-access form. For example, clicking on one of the buttons on the Standard toolbar saves your document.

URL   Short for Uniform Resource Locator, an address for an Internet site. An example of a URL is **http://www.whitehouse.gov**. The "http" stands for HyperText Transfer Protocol, which means this is a Web document. The "www" stands for World Wide Web, and the remainder of the URL identifies the name of the company or organization.

View mode   A way of looking at a document. Word 97 comes with several view modes: Normal, Online Layout, Outline, Page Layout, Print Preview, Document Map, and Master Document.

Web browser   Any of several programs you can use to navigate the World Wide Web. The Web browser controls the look of the Web documents and provides additional tools for jumping from one Web document to another. Examples of Web browsers include the Microsoft Internet Explorer and the Netscape Navigator.

Web page   A document on a server that is viewed with a Web browser.

Web server   A computer on the Internet that's dedicated to storing and serving up Web documents for clients requesting them from computers with Web browsers.

Web site   A location consisting of one or more Web servers that provides storage of Web documents.

word processor   A program that lets you enter, edit, format, and print text. A word processor can be used to type letters, reports, and envelopes, and to complete other tasks you would normally use a typewriter for.

word wrapping   Causes text to remain within the margins of a document. As the text you're typing touches the right margin, it's automatically placed at the beginning of the next line. When you insert text into the middle of a paragraph, the remaining text moves down. If you delete text, the remaining text in the paragraph moves up.

World Wide Web   A collection of interconnected documents stored on Web servers all over the world. These documents can contain text, pictures, video clips, sounds, and links to other documents. You navigate through the Web by clicking hyperlinks or typing URLs inside your Web browser.

Wrapping   A feature of Word 97 allowing text to flow smoothly around a graphic, with different levels available to control the distance between the text and graphic.

Windows 95/98/NT Primer

Windows 95/98 and Windows NT are graphical operating systems that make your computer easy to use by providing menus and pictures. Before you can take advantage of either operating system, however, you need to learn some basics that apply to both of them.

Fortunately, Windows 95/98 and Windows NT operate very much alike (in fact, they're so similar I'll refer to them both just as Windows throughout the remainder of this appendix). If the figures you see in this primer don't look exactly like what's on your screen, don't sweat it. Some slight variation might occur depending on your setup, the applications you use, or whether you're on a network. Rest assured, however, that the basic information presented here applies, no matter what your setup might be.

A First Look at Windows

You don't really have to start Windows because it starts automatically when you turn on your PC. After the initial startup screens, you arrive at a screen something like the one shown in the following figure.

The Windows screen.

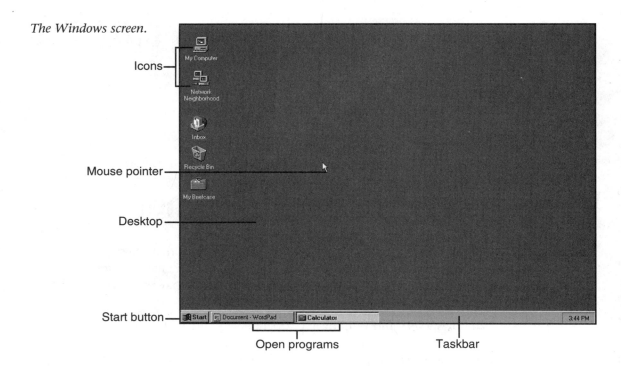

Icons

Mouse pointer

Desktop

Start button

Open programs

Taskbar

Parts of the Screen

As you can see, the Windows screen contains lots of special elements and controls. Here's a brief summary:

➤ The Desktop consists of the background and icons that represent programs, tools, and other elements.

➤ The Taskbar shows a button for each open window and program. You can switch between open windows and programs by clicking on the taskbar button representing the program you want. (The program you are currently working on is highlighted in the taskbar.)

➤ The Start button opens a menu from which you can start programs, get Help, and find files. To use it, you click on the **Start** button, then click on a selection from the list that appears. When you move your pointer over a command that has a right-facing arrow beside it, a secondary—or cascading—menu appears.

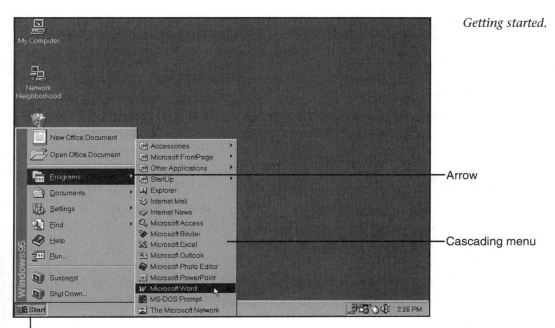

Getting started.

Arrow

Cascading menu

Start button

➤ The icons that appear on your desktop give you access to certain programs and computer components. You open an icon by double-clicking on it. (An open icon displays a window containing programs, files, or other items.)

➤ The mouse pointer moves around the screen in relation to your movement of the mouse. You use the mouse pointer to select what you want to work with.

You'll learn more about these elements as you work through the rest of this Windows primer.

Also Appearing: Microsoft Office

If your computer has Microsoft Office installed on it, the Office Shortcuts toolbar also appears onscreen. It's a series of little pictures (strung together horizontally) that represent Office programs. Hold the mouse over a picture (icon) to see what it does; click on it to launch the program. See your Microsoft Office documentation to learn more.

You might have some other icons on your desktop (representing networks, folders, printers, files, and so on), depending upon what options you chose during initial setup. Double-click an icon to view the items it contains.

369

Using a Mouse

To work most efficiently in Windows, you need a mouse. You will perform the following mouse actions as you work:

➤ **Point**   To move the mouse so that the onscreen pointer is touching an item.

➤ **Click**   To press and release the left mouse button once. Pointing and clicking on an item usually selects it. You click with the right button (called *right-clicking*) to produce a shortcut menu. (You can reverse these mouse button actions if you want to use the mouse left-handed. To do so, click **Start**, **Settings**, **Control Panel**, **Mouse**, then choose **Left-handed** in the Button tab of the Control Panel dialog box.)

➤ **Double-click**   To press and release the left mouse button twice quickly. Pointing and double-clicking usually activates an item or opens a window, folder, or program.

Double-clicking might take some practice—the speed needs to be just right. To change the speed so it better matches your "clicking style," choose **Start**, **Settings**, **Control Panel**, **Mouse**. In the Buttons tab of the Mouse Properties dialog box, you can adjust the double-clicking speed until it's just right for you.

➤ **Drag**   To move a window, dialog box, or file from one location to another, place the mouse pointer over the element you want to move, press and hold down the left mouse button, and move the mouse to a new location. Unless you're told to do otherwise (for example, to right-drag), you drag with the left mouse button.

Controlling a Window with the Mouse

Ever wonder why it's called "Windows?" Well, Windows' operating system sections off rectangular areas of the desktop into work areas called *windows*. These windows are used for particular purposes, such as running a program, displaying options or lists, and so on. Each window will have common features, as described in the following list:

Click to access a menu with commands for controlling size and location.

Drag the title bar to move a window.

Click to close the window.

Use your mouse to control and manipulate windows.

Click to expand the window so it fills the entire screen.

Click to shrink the window and make it a button on the taskbar.

Drag the scroll bar to view the entire contents of the window (or click on the arrow buttons at either end).

Click these arrows to see the entire contents of the window.

Click on any button on the taskbar to reopen or reactivate the associated window.

Drag the border to resize the window.

Scrolling for Information

If your window contains more icons than it can display at once, scroll bars appear on the bottom or right edges of the window. To move through the window's contents, click on an arrow button at either end of a scroll bar to move in that direction, or drag the scroll bar in the direction you want to move.

If you're using the professional version of Office 97, you'll also have enhanced scrolling available to you via your *IntelliMouse*—a new mouse by Microsoft that includes a scrolling wheel. Using this mouse is described in all Que books that cover Microsoft Office 97 and its individual applications.

371

Getting Help

Windows comes with a great online Help system. To access it, click on the **Start** button then click on **Help**.

Windows offers several kinds of help—this figure illustrates the Contents tab.

Open book with contents displayed

Help documents

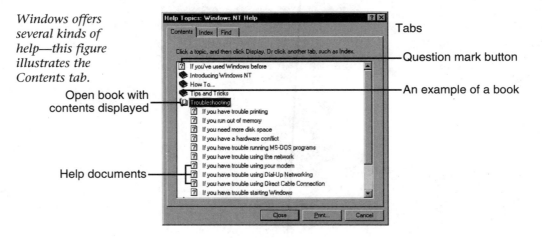

Tabs

Question mark button

An example of a book

The Help box contains three tabs (Contents, Index, and Find), each of which provides you with a different type of help. To move to a tab, just click on it.

Here's how to use each tab:

➤ **Contents**   Double-click on any book to open it and see its sub-books and documents. Double-click on a sub-book or document to open it and read the help topic.

➤ **Index**   When you click this tab, Windows will ask you for more information on what you're looking for. Type the word you want to look up, and the Index list scrolls to that part of the alphabetical listing. When you see the topic that you want to read in the list, double-click on it.

➤ **Find**   The first time you click on this tab, Windows tells you it needs to create a list. Click **Next** and then **Finish** to allow this. When Windows finishes, it will ask you to type the word you want to find in the top text box. Click on a word in the middle box to narrow the search, review the list of Help topics at the bottom then double-click the one you want to read.

When you finish reading about a document, click on **Help Topics** to return to the main Help screen, or click **Back** to return to the previous Help topic. When you finish with the Help system itself, click the window's **Close** (X) button to exit.

Another Way to Get Help

In the upper-right corner of the Help window, you should see (next to the Close button) a question mark. This is (surprise!) the Question-mark-button. Whenever you see this button (it appears in other windows besides the Help window), click on it to change your mouse pointer to a combined arrow and question mark. You can then point at any element in the window for a quick, "pop-up" description of that element.

Some applications or application suites (such as Microsoft Office 97) may also offer online help. The use of online help is discussed in the application documentation, or in any Alpha book that covers the application.

Starting a Program

Of the many possible ways to start a program, this is the simplest:

1. Click the **Start** button.

2. Move your mouse pointer over **Programs**.

3. Click on the group that contains the program you want to start (such as **Accessories**).

4. Click on the program you want to start (such as **Notepad**).

Here are a few more ways you can start a program in Windows:

➤ Open a document that you created in that program. The program automatically opens when the document opens. For example, double-click on the **My Computer** icon on the desktop, find the icon of the document you want to open, then double-click on a document file.

➤ (Optional) Open a document you created in that program by clicking the **Start** button, moving your pointer over **Programs**, and then clicking **Windows Explorer**. The Window Explorer window opens and looks very similar to the File Manager window you've worked with in Windows 3.1. Locate the directory (or Folder, in Windows 95/98/NT 4 terminology) and double-click the filename. The document is opened in the program in which it was created.

➤ Click the **Start** button and select a recently used document from the Documents menu. Windows immediately starts the program in which you created the file and opens the file.

> ➤ If you created a shortcut to the program, you can start the program by double-clicking its shortcut icon on the desktop.

Work through the Start menu and its successive submenus until you find the program you want to start.

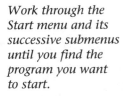

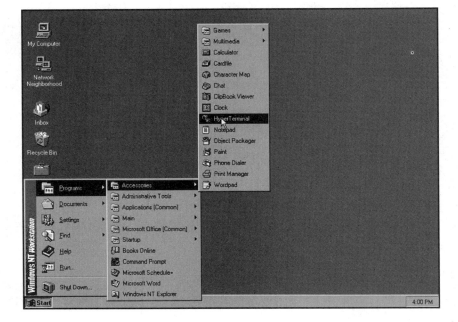

What's a Shortcut?

Shortcut icons are links to other files. When you use a shortcut, Windows simply follows the link back to the original file. If you find that you use any document or program frequently, you might consider creating a desktop shortcut for it. To do so, just use the right mouse button to drag an object out of Windows Explorer or My Computer and onto the desktop. In the shortcut menu that appears, select **Create Shortcut(s) Here**.

Using Menus

Almost every Windows program has a menu bar that contains menus. The menu names appear in a row across the top of the screen. To open a menu, click on its name (after you click anywhere in the menu bar, you need only point to a menu name to produce the drop-down menu). The menu drops down, displaying its commands, as shown in the next figure. To select a command, you simply click it.

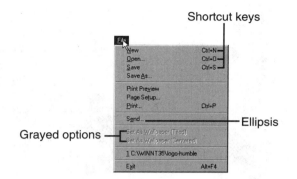

Shortcut keys

A menu lists various commands you can perform.

Ellipsis

Grayed options

Usually, when you select a command, Windows executes the command immediately. But you need to keep the following exceptions to that rule in mind:

➤ If the command name is gray (instead of black), the command is unavailable at the moment, and you cannot choose it.

➤ If the command name is followed by an arrow (as the selections on the Start menu are), selecting the command causes another menu to appear, from which you must make another selection.

➤ If the command is followed by an ellipsis (three dots), selecting it will cause a dialog box to appear. You'll learn about dialog boxes later in this primer.

Check This Out...

Shortcut Keys

Key names appear after some command names (for example, **Ctrl+O** appears to the right of the Open command, and **Ctrl+S** appears next to the Save command). These are shortcut keys and you can use them to perform the command without opening the menu. You should also note that some commands have their first letter underlined. By pressing Alt+the underlined letter, you can perform the command.

Using Shortcut Menus

A new feature in Windows is the shortcut menu (or *context-sensitive* menu). Right-click on any object (any icon, screen element, file, or folder), and a shortcut menu like the one shown in the next figure appears. The shortcut menu contains commands that apply only to the selected object. Click on any command to select it, or click outside the menu to cancel.

375

Shortcut menus are new in Windows 95/98 and Windows NT 4.

Navigating Dialog Boxes

A dialog box is Windows's way of requesting additional information or giving you information. For example, if you choose **Print** from the **File** menu of the WordPad application, you see a dialog box something like the one shown in the following figure. (The options it displays will vary from system to system.)

A dialog box often requests additional information.

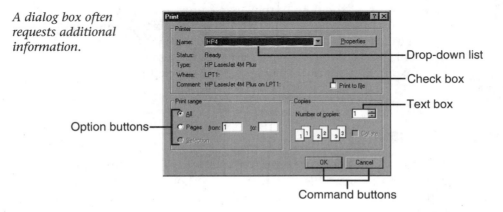

Each dialog box contains one or more of the following elements:

➤ List boxes display available choices. Click on any item on the list to select it. If the entire list is not visible, use the scroll bar to find additional choices.

➤ Drop-down lists are similar to list boxes, but only one item in the list is shown. To see the rest of the list, click the drop-down arrow (to the right of the list box), then click on an item to select it.

➤ Text boxes enable you to type an entry—just click inside the text box and type. Text boxes that are designed to hold numbers usually have up and down arrow buttons (called increment buttons) that let you bump the number up and down.

➤ Check boxes enable you to turn individual options on or off by clicking on them. (A check mark or "X" appears when an option is on.) Each check box is an independent unit that doesn't affect other check boxes.

➤ Option buttons are like check boxes, except that option buttons appear in groups and you can select only one. When you select an option button, the program automatically deselects whichever one was previously selected. Click on a button to activate it and a black bullet appears inside the white option circle.

➤ Command buttons perform an action, such as executing the options you set (OK), canceling the options (Cancel), closing the dialog box, or opening another dialog box. To select a command button, click on it.

➤ Tabs bring up additional "pages" of options you can choose. Click on a tab to activate it. (See the section on Help for more information on Tabs.)

From Here

If you need more help with Windows, you may want to pick up one of these books:

The Complete Idiot's Guide to Windows 95 by Paul McFedries

Easy Windows 95 by Sue Plumley

The Big Basics Book of Windows 95 by Shelley O'Hara, Jennifer Fulton, and Ed Guilford

Using Windows 95 by Ed Bott

The Complete Idiot's Guide to Windows NT 4.0 Workstation by Paul McFedries

Using Windows NT 4.0 Workstation by Ed Bott

Index

C

I

J-K

L

QUE'S MICROSOFT® OFFICE 97 RESOURCE CENTER

For the most up-to-date information about all the Microsoft Office 97 products, visit Que's Web Resource Center at

http://www.mcp.com/que/msoffice

The Web site extends the reach of this Que book by offering you a rich selection of supplementary content.

You'll find information about Que books as well as additional content about these new **Office 97 topics**:

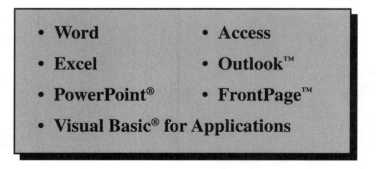

- **Word**
- **Excel**
- **PowerPoint**®
- **Visual Basic**® **for Applications**
- **Access**
- **Outlook**™
- **FrontPage**™

Visit Que's Web site regularly for a variety of new and updated Office 97 information.